# the series on school reform

**Patricia A. Wasley**
University
of Washington

**Ann Lieberman**
Senior Scholar,
Stanford University

**Joseph P. McDonald**
New York
University

**SERIES EDITORS**

*(Continued)*

**the series on school reform,** *continued*

# Peer Review and Teacher Leadership

## LINKING PROFESSIONALISM AND ACCOUNTABILITY

*Jennifer Goldstein*

Foreword by
Patricia A. Wasley

Afterword by
Susan Moore Johnson

Teachers College
Columbia University
New York and London

Published by Teachers College Press, 1234 Amsterdam Avenue, New York, NY 10027

The author wishes to express gratitude for permission to adapt from the following:

Goldstein, J. "Easy to Dance To: Solving the Problems of Teacher Evaluation with Peer Assistance and Review." *American Journal of Education, 113*(May), 479–508. Copyright © 2007 by the University of Chicago. (Used for Chapters 3–9)

Goldstein, J. "Designing Transparent Teacher Evaluation: The Role of Oversight Panels for Professional Accountability." *Teachers College Record, 114*(4), 893–933. Copyright © 2009 by Teachers College, Columbia University. (Used for Chapters 4 and 8)

Goldstein, J. "Debunking the Fear of Peer Review: Combining Supervision and Evaluation and Living to Tell About It." *Journal of Personnel Evaluation in Education, (18)*4, 235–252. Copyright © 2005 by Springer Science and Business Media. (Used for Chapter 6)

Goldstein, J. "Making Sense of Distributed Leadership: The Case of Peer Assistance and Review." *Educational Evaluation & Policy Analysis, 25*(4), 397–421. Copyright © 2003 by the American Educational Research Association. (Used for Chapter 7)

Goldstein, J. "Distributed Accountability: How District Leaders Create Structures to Ensure Teacher Quality." *Journal of School Leadership, 17*(4), 504–536. Copyright © 2007 by Rowman & Littlefield Education. (Used for Chapter 9)

*Library of Congress Cataloging-in-Publication Data*

Goldstein, Jennifer.
  Peer review and teacher leadership : linking professionalism and accountability / Jennifer Goldstein.
      p. cm. — (The series on school reform)
  Includes bibliographical references and index.
  ISBN 978-0-8077-5049-0 (pbk. : alk. paper) — ISBN 978-0-8077-5050-6 (hardcover : alk. paper)  1. Teachers—Professional relationships.   2. Peer review.   3. Educational accountabuility.   I. Title.
    LB1775.G64 2010
    371.14'4—dc22

                                                                                          2009052322

ISBN 978-0-8077-5049-0 (paperback)
ISBN 978-0-8077-5050-6 (hardcover)

Printed on acid-free paper
Manufactured in the United States of America

17   16   15   14   13   12   11   10      8   7   6   5   4   3   2   1

*To the one hundred 4th graders who touched my life from 1993 to 1996. You are still my compass.*

*One challenge [to teacher leadership] is to introduce capable people to a new role. . . . A second challenge is to introduce a new role to an institution and an occupation.*

—Judith Warren Little,

"Assessing the Prospects for Teacher Leadership"

# Contents

# Foreword

Jennifer Goldstein documents a school system's journey towards creating a peer review evaluation system that does three very important things: It creates opportunities for new teachers to grow; it works harder to locate teachers who are not able or willing to get better and to counsel them out; and it provides an excellent career opportunity for experienced teachers to develop their expertise in understanding and promoting high-quality teaching. I think the book is important in that it describes how an urban district created a system to promote teacher professionalism to create a system of more robust feedback that leads either to teacher growth or to counseling poor teachers out and that improves the accountability of the teachers in the district for the quality of teaching.

The book deals with several seemingly intractable problems in American education. First, despite years of work on standards and new assessments, the achievement gap persists. Policy makers and educators alike are turning their attention to teacher quality and are intent on finding stronger ways to retain the best teachers, support those who can get better, and remove those who are not productive at improving student achievement. The peer review system outlined in this book provides a powerful example of what districts can do to improve teacher quality using the teachers it employs.

Second, the PAR system Goldstein describes offers experienced teachers the opportunity to take responsibility for teacher quality in their district. As they learn to mentor newer and/or struggling teachers, the experienced group comes closer to a common—but not simplistic—view of what quality teaching looks like. This is an important dimension of reaching higher standards—that more of those involved agree on what it looks like.

Finally, the PAR system deals with what I believe is the single most detrimental dimension of teachers work lives: the isolation in which they work. All across the United States, teachers are hired to work with a group of children inside the four walls of their own classroom. They work alone almost every day, behind their own closed door, and they are expected to reach every child in their room, to unlock the learning mysteries that each child brings to school with them, without much— or in many cases any—guidance. Anyone who has had kids or who works with kids knows that they are tremendously complex at every age, and in order for them to learn well, they need teachers who are learning to teach well. To do that, teachers need all kinds of feedback on their teaching. They need feedback on their ability to teach subject matter, on their ability to understand individual differences between and among kids, and on their skill at generating multiple approaches to a given learning task that might appeal to a variety of children. Instead, teachers work alone, behind closed doors, and slowly grow wary of and defensive at even the mildest feedback. Their notions of what constitutes excellent teaching narrows to the scope of their own limited experience—hardly a picture of an interesting, challenging, growth and success oriented professional life.

Think about doctors and lawyers who apprentice for many years. Think about dental hygienists, filmmakers, plumbers, architects—all of whom learn to work in teams with regularized feedback—and then think about teachers. They get feedback twice a year from their principals, who are harried and have too much responsibility to attend to this critical dimension of improving learning in their buildings. For too many principals, teacher evaluations are dreaded, routinized, yearly tasks required by the personnel office, instead of their most significant opportunity to improve the quality of instruction students receive.

What happens to the professionals who get no real feedback? I know from my own experience as a teacher and as a researcher working with scores of teachers across this country that teachers grow *into* the imposter syndrome. Their working circumstances *create* the conditions that enable this syndrome to flourish. Most teachers work hard to be good, but without feedback, it is difficult to learn new approaches and techniques. The more teachers work alone, the more they fall into comfortable routines: lesson plans that seemed to work and subject matter material that seems to be productive. The more teachers work in isolation, the more they fear feedback *because* it might reveal that they do not know the full array of strategies for reaching second language learners or the highly capable children who are in their classes in a complex and every changing mix each year. Slowly, over the years, teachers *learn* to trot out their best and safest lessons for the principal when she or he comes in to do the yearly evaluation, and the rest of the time they work alone and hope that their efforts are enough to reach all the children they serve. Every teacher I have ever known knows they could reach more kids, but the system is organized to prevent their growth! It is, really, outrageous.

This existence proof—the system created by the California school district described in this book—suggests that teachers can create a more robust and effective teaching profession, that they are up to the task of accepting more significant responsibility for the quality of teaching. This is enormously important because it suggests that teachers themselves can improve the quality of teaching and learning in American schools—if only we would organize the system to let them.

—Patricia A. Wasley

# Acknowledgments

As with any long journey, support from many people contributed to bringing this book to fruition.

I am grateful to Michael Copland, James G. March, and Linda Darling-Hammond for serving as the always supportive dissertation committee for the original study. I am also grateful to the late Buddy Peshkin, under whose guidance I became excited about research, not just reform.

I am grateful to Julia Koppich and Charles Taylor Kerchner for being relatively lone voices regarding the role of teachers unions in education reform, and for the mentorship they have both generously provided to me over the years. Thank you also to Dal Lawrence and Adam Urbanski for supporting my early inquiries into peer review.

Thank you to Judith Warren Little and Linda Darling-Hammond for the significant conceptual contribution of their work to my own. Thank you also to Richard Ingersoll for, in 2003, publishing a book that brought me back to the heart of my research.

When one studies something deeply for a long time, it can inevitably grow stale. At those times, the enthusiasm of others for the work is priceless. I have been very fortunate to be gently guided and occasionally propped up by numerous knowledgeable, wise, and enthusiastic mentors and friends. Thank you to Pedro Noguera for giving the green light for me to teach in Compton all those years ago, and for his continued support. Thank you to James Spillane for taking me seriously when, as a doctoral student he had never met, I cold-called him at his hotel at AERA; thank you for meeting with me then, and for providing guidance along the way. Thank you to Mark Smylie for his perpetual willingness to share his deep understanding of teacher leadership. Thank you to Bruce Cooper for shepherding several chunks of this research to the light of day; his ever-present kindness and humor took some of the bumps out of being a new faculty member. I am grateful to Gary Anderson for his interest in engaging deeply with the questions I was asking. Our occasional "writing" group, together with Colleen Larson and Mike Johanek, forced me to look at the work periodically through a very different lens. Thank you to Susan Moore Johnson for reminding me of the value of studying one thing deeply. Thank you to Amy Hightower for always being there at the other end of the computer, and to Richard Halverson for his perpetual genuine interest in pushing the conversation forward. Thank you, ultimately, to Patricia Wasley for originally suggesting that my research on peer review should be published as a book.

I want to express gratitude to the American Educational Research Association, which provided the forum for me to meet for the first time many of the people mentioned here. May I repay the favor to others at annual meetings in years to come.

Two people deserve a special acknowledgment. Julie Slayton and Lisa Hansel stepped in, during the waning days of summer, and read the complete manuscript. As a result of their extensive feedback, the book is hopefully clearer and more thorough. Thank you, also, to my editors at Teachers College Press, who endured the learning curve of my first single-authored book project with patience.

I am, of course, forever indebted to my former fourth graders at Rosecrans Elementary School. You arrived ready and eager to learn, and made all the ways we shortchange you in the schooling process enormously evident. Your smiles stay with me, your good intentions still bring tears to my eyes, and your desire to learn provides the meaning for my work.

Finally, thank you to all of my study participants, in particular those who shared deeply not knowing what might happen to their words. Your voices have kept me in the best of company during this process. I hope I have done justice to your efforts.

# Introduction:
# Becoming a Teacher, 1993

I started teaching right out of college. I lacked a teaching credential or any preparation for the job, but was nonetheless given full responsibility for a class of fourth graders in Compton, California. As soon as I found out I would be working at Rosecrans Elementary, I jumped in my car and drove the 30 or so minutes to Compton from the Westside of Los Angeles; I had interviewed at the district office and had not yet seen the school itself. It was summer and the campus was deserted, but Major Thomas, the plant manager, humored my enthusiasm and walked me around. He opened an empty classroom and let me be. I stood there alone, taking in the room with tears in my eyes. Empty classrooms have an almost magical quality, a loud silence full of immense possibilities, and that one on that day even more so for its dilapidation, which I saw romantically: bare wood floors, old-fashioned wood and metal desks and chairs, sunlight streaming in through big metal-grated windows. I didn't yet know that elementary classrooms need rugs or carpets, that there would never be enough desks or chairs, or that the windows would be broken into anyway. I stood there at 23 years old the proudest I had ever been in my life: I was going to be a teacher.

I eventually took ownership of room 9, which became filled with an always fluctuating number of amazing children. Most were second-language learners, some spoke no English, and few could read fluently in any language let alone at grade level. All had fabulous stories to tell, and most were eager to learn. But I had absolutely no idea what to do with them. I mainly utilized the pedagogical tools of randomness and inconsistency, punctuated with frustrated yelling. Lacking coherent instructional skills, I did my very best day by day to get by, in no way satisfactory for kids who genuinely needed me to teach them something.

I was relatively fortunate that first year to teach across the hall from a quite competent veteran teacher, my assigned "buddy." Actually, Charlotte had only been teaching for three years, but that made her a veteran in Compton; more important, she was a bit older, had children of her own, and simply had experience and maturity that I lacked. Charlotte saved me from as much as she could that year, given her own teaching responsibilities. I don't recall actually ever meeting with Charlotte per se; it was more support on the run. She handed me lessons to

1

implement, took kids with whom I was struggling from my room on occasion, and declared sole responsibility for planning for the bilingual instructional assistant whom we shared. That instructional assistant spent 1 hour in my room three times a week that year working with a group of students, and I do not have the slightest idea what she did while there. It is just one example of the degree to which the whole year was a blur. In the end, Charlotte never actually saw me teach, nor I her. When the bell rang and the doors closed, I was on my own.

The other person who might have been expected to provide support or otherwise supervise the teaching that my students received, was, of course, the principal. She made one visit to my classroom that year, an occasion that stands out amid the blur. On April 15, the day teacher evaluations were due at the district office, she came in during a lesson, asked me to sign a form, and told me that she promised I would like what it said. I was thus initiated to the quality control mechanism of my profession.

You have likely heard some version of this story many times. Its need for attention, however, has become no less urgent.

Like so many marginalized school districts across the United States, Compton schools served low-income Latino and African American students. My students were attending the school ranked 24th out of 24 in the district ranked lowest in the state of California. Arguably, these were the students most in need of a high-quality teacher. Yet I was unprepared and uncertified to teach. I was in an organizational system designed neither to improve my performance nor assess it. In addition, after 3 years—or right around the time my teaching performance would be expected to improve significantly—I left the district.

Quite simply, I wrote this book to explore how the story might have been different. As a young teacher, I believed in my students' ability to learn and was committed to doing right by them. I worked extremely hard and put in ridiculously long hours (while earning roughly $25,000 a year, or $35,000 in 2009 dollars). I had extremely little knowledge, however, about how to actually teach my students well, and next to no support to acquire that knowledge and related skill set. As a researcher, therefore, I wanted to know more about how new teachers could be supported to develop as skilled professionals.

As a young teacher who was reasonably intelligent and well educated, as many are, I wanted to feel that I was entering into a partnership with an exciting cadre of more experienced and more skilled colleagues, what would today be called a professional learning community, although I certainly could not have articulated it that way at the time. However, while there were a few truly wonderful veteran teachers at the school, I was horrified that many of my more veteran colleagues seemed to be faring worse than I—or they successfully ran a tightly managed classroom while holding many of the students in disdain. In addition, as has been long documented, we all existed in isolation anyway. In fact, the more skillful I became over time, the more I isolated myself.

As a researcher, therefore, I wanted to know two things. First, I wanted to know how the work of teaching could be redesigned to be, for lack of a better word, adult. How could a career in teaching involve, as part of the fabric of the job, intellectual interaction with other skillful, curious, and reflective adults?

Second—and this is really most central to the focus of the book—I wanted to know how the system could be redesigned to generate professional standards and accountability. As a young teacher, I wanted to feel that the children were being honored, and that my efforts on their behalf were valued. I wanted—*needed*—some degree of quality control, rather than the mere prerequisite of a pulse that is so often joked about (but which is often a fair picture of the selection and assessment process in our most hard-to-staff schools). Ultimately, despite the passion I felt for the job, I was demoralized by the total lack of oversight and accountability, knowing that my work could be better, and angered to tears for the children who were ready, willing, and able if only we as a nation would take responsibility for them. My hunch as a 26-year-old coming out of a fourth-grade classroom in Compton, before academia taught me the proper terms for the concepts or that many far more agile minds had criss-crossed the terrain before I, was that the students needed professional teachers, which the system was simply not designed to deliver. Redesigning with that goal in mind would involve giving teachers more authority. As a researcher, I set out to discover whether this would help attract motivated people to the job, support them to develop their talents, provide them with a community of colleagues, and enforce quality standards.

I later made what can be described as an empirical leap. Studying the relationship between things usually requires a long time. As it turned out, I would engage in the studies that form the foundation of this book to varying degrees on and off for a decade, but that was not planned from the outset. At the outset, I was a doctoral student, and in order to design a study within the span of a doctoral project, I made an empirical leap. Rather than attempt to establish the relationship between increased authority for teachers (what I will refer to as "professionalization" throughout the book) and various teacher quality outcomes (who enters, how they teach, who stays, who gets fired, and so on), I would focus instead on one side of the equation. I focused on understanding one particular case of teacher professionalization well.

A serendipitous series of events, including a colorful teachers union president who crossed my path and a new governor's new education initiatives, led me to a policy that is alternately referred to as "peer review" or "peer assistance and review" (or the acronym "PAR"). It became the topic through which I would explore the questions I carried from Compton. At its most fundamental, peer review gives master teachers responsibility for the summative personnel evaluation of other teachers. It does many other things—provides new teachers with desperately needed support, provides master teachers with job variety, and generates professional community around questions of practice. Teachers evaluating teachers, however, is the policy's most novel component, and therefore its most controversial. I closely followed one urban school district's implementation of a peer review policy, conducting a year of full-time fieldwork but gathering data over approximately 6 years.

Peer review is a model of instructional leadership that may help redesign teaching by professionalizing teachers, giving them more responsibility and authority for the quality of practice. I study teacher professionalization because I believe it is our best hope for improving the quality of teaching in America's schools, and that systemically improving the quality of teaching is the best way to improve the quality of education that low-income students and students of color receive. Professionalization is not a popular topic for research these days. From the right, some might criticize this research for being too status quo and therefore irrelevant; the book explores how to transform our system of public education without blowing it up entirely, even including teachers unions as partners in reform. From the left, some might criticize this research for being too status quo and therefore hegemonic; the book explores how to transform our system of public education by giving some educators more, not less, authority. I take as my starting point the belief that educators across all levels of the system must be the ones responsible for improving education—not students, families, or community members, crucial as these stakeholders are to public education reform.

From the middle, perhaps most significantly, some might criticize this research for missing the point. For those who study educational organizations, leadership, and policy, a focus on questions of formal authority and control has given way almost entirely to questions of informal influence and professional networks. The role that a teacher's content-area expertise plays in the degree to which her colleagues seek her out for advice, for example, is considered a far juicier line of inquiry these days than the organizational decision-making ability the teacher holds as a result of that content-area expertise (or for that matter, how much the district pays her in exchange for it). Studying formal authority has become passé, almost crass, considered simply not what really matters.

The past decade, however, has demonstrated that such a position is dangerous to the quality of education. Teachers, schools, and public education itself have been under attack (and some of that attack is certainly warranted). The increased role of the federal government in education through the No Child Left Behind (NCLB) legislation has reduced teachers' abilities to make decisions for themselves and their students. And while an Obama presidency brings an administration that is friendlier to public education, teachers' lack of professional authority renders them vulnerable to the winds of political sentiment. Ultimately, as Elizabeth DeBray (2006) captured it, educators are people to whom things are done.

It is absolutely true that we do not want authority without substance, professionalization without professionalism. Indeed, the authority at the heart of professionalization should rest on the expertise at the heart of professionalism. We cannot afford, however, expertise without authority, professionalism without professionalization. To focus on the substance of the work without concern for who holds decision-making authority is to put our heads in the sand. Educators must bring to the table both the complexity of our best understanding of the substance of the work, and the courage to be the ones held responsible for the outcomes.

This book tells the story of one urban school district's effort to design organizational structures for complex professional development and courageous accountability (Wasley, 2001). The vehicle for the effort was peer review. Jonathan Supovitz (2006) elegantly captures my challenge in presenting the implementation of the program for analysis and discussion:

> Programs are the vehicles of reform but should not be confused with reform itself. Programs are the Trojan horses that allow new ideas to enter people's minds, while reforms are the ideas themselves. . . . Deep, lasting reform comes in the internalized understanding of the purpose and intent of the reform, not from implementation of programs. . . . The real purpose of education reform is to build habits of mind, not the adoption of particular initiatives. (p. 236)

If at the conclusion of this book you consider its primary purpose a discussion of peer review for teachers, I will have failed in my task. Peer review is indeed the topic at hand, but it is merely a policy vehicle, one programmatic initiative in the ongoing multidimensional efforts to reform American K–12 public education. Peer review is certainly not a panacea for all that ails teaching. True reform, however, would be a fundamental redesign of teaching that shifts authority relations, professionalizing both the occupation of teaching and the organization of public schools in the United States. True reform would be attracting, developing, and keeping young teachers in places like Compton—which would occur by a variety of means that would transcend any one particular program or policy.

The book, hopefully, offers a counternarrative to the forces of external authority and deprofessionalization that have taken hold of the job of teaching children and adolescents in the United States. I join those who believe that public education is still the best lever for a just and equitable society of citizens, and that public education's success is ultimately dependent on the knowledge, skills, and dispositions of those who do the work—teachers. To date, organizing our schools as hierarchical bureaucracies has not generated a nation of high-quality teaching. It is long past time to explore other options.

## ORGANIZATION OF THE BOOK

The book is organized into four parts. Part I establishes the central elements of the discussion. Chapter 1 explores the idea of professional accountability that sits at the heart of peer review. It identifies the main challenges to improving teaching quality as inadequate professional development and inadequate accountability, and situates these challenges as the rationales for the often opposing reform strategies of professionalism versus accountability. This chapter defines teacher professionalization, the core conceptual frame for the book, and introduces the way it may reconcile the reform strategies of professionalism and accountability through collective responsibility for quality control. Chapter 1 also introduces the ways that institutional theory helps us to understand the challenges of making sense of new, professionalized roles for teachers.

Chapter 2 provides an initial explanation of peer review, including the partnership between teachers union and school district necessary for PAR to come into existence. The chapter outlines the development of professional unionism, of which peer review is an example. Chapter 2 also introduces the case study district of Rosemont, an urban district in California that provides the central narrative of the book, and situates it in California's unusual story of statewide PAR implementation. The chapter provides an overview of the Rosemont study (with detailed methodological information provided in appendixes, described below).

Parts II and III then explore different aspects of Rosemont's implementation of peer review. This is partly a story of design, of how PAR differs by design from traditional teacher evaluation. That story is important, in particular, for anyone interested in implementing PAR or simply having a deep understanding of how the policy works.

This is also, however, a story about education's norms. Ultimately, PAR is not more widespread because it challenges a number of long-held beliefs and practices in education. Some of these beliefs are held proudly, such as the notion that formative and summative assessment should not be combined, or that teacher evaluation is the proper purview of administrators, not teachers. Other beliefs or norms lurk deeper below the surface, such as educators' tacit expectations to keep their work mostly free from scrutiny in the name of "autonomy," or the passive acceptance of the widespread absence of serious quality control. In Parts II and III of the book, I attempt to do justice to both of these stories, the policy's design as well as the ways it interrupts norms.

Part II provides descriptive detail about the two most significant program components of PAR, the teacher leader role of "coach" and the oversight panel. Chapter 3 details the core aspects of coaches' work with new and veteran classroom teachers in PAR. It highlights the factors that enabled coaches' work, such as the amount of time coaches could devote to the job on account of their full-time release from the classroom, the fact that coaches and teachers were matched by grade and subject area, the ongoing and individualized nature of the coaching, and the fact that the coaches' assessments were rooted in performance standards for teaching. The discussion includes some of the criticisms of the coaches' work by classroom teachers in PAR, and the challenges the coaches faced in being teachers of adult learners. Chapter 3 also discusses the ways that PAR may have supported teacher retention, issues of intervening with unsatisfactory veteran teachers, and the professional development that involvement with PAR provided to the coaches themselves.

Chapter 4 describes the work of the PAR panel, the body charged with oversight of the coaches and the program as a whole. The chapter describes the selection of the coaches by the panel, and the hearings that were the heart of the panel's work. At the hearings, the panel heard coaches' presentations about individual classroom teachers in PAR. Using transcripts from hearings, the chapter describes ways that the panel supported the coaches in their work of teacher assessment, and also held them accountable. The chapter draws a parallel between the traditional isolation of classroom teaching and the isolation that typically plagues the evaluation of teaching—which is altered by the panel's involvement with coaches.

Chapter 5 introduces the cases of two beginning teachers—Kim and Timothy—who participated in the program. One teacher was retained and the other was fired. These two teachers then provide a thread for analysis in Chapters 6 through 9.

Part III analyzes four norms, or habits of mind, that PAR interrupted in Rosemont in addition to adversarial labor relations—"being nice," hierarchy, isolation, and negligence—embedding design elements within the larger thematic treatment. Chapter 6 looks at one concern many educators have about linking professional development and evaluation, namely the question of whether mentees' trust in their support provider will be undermined by the specter of evaluation. I present data that suggest this concern is unfounded—or at least only an issue with a subset of underperforming teachers.

Chapter 7 dives deeply into the ways that PAR distributed responsibility for personnel evaluations for the teachers in PAR, in particular across coaches and principals. It describes an ambiguous policy context in which responsibility for teacher evaluation was left somewhat vague by the architects of Rosemont's program. The chapter demonstrates that, in that ambiguity, and given disparate beliefs about the wisdom of teachers evaluating teachers, Rosemont's educators held differing opinions about who was ultimately responsible for evaluation—although the data show the coaches holding that responsibility, whether named or not. In addition, however, the program changed over time. Despite widespread enthusiasm for the work of the coaches and the quality of their evaluations, almost everyone (except the classroom teachers) wanted a clearer and more formal role for principals, albeit one that still left coaches holding the bulk of responsibility. The chapter explains the codified and expanded role for principals created in the third year of the program.

Chapter 8 highlights PAR as a site for professional learning community, one that sheds light on the previously opaque practice of teacher evaluation. The chapter continues the examination of panel hearings begun in Chapter 4, looking closely at a small handful of cases in which coaches changed their employment recommendations as a result of the panel's questioning. I argue that the panel hearings served as a site for a particular type of professional learning community—one focused on accountability. A team of educators engaged in conversations about teaching practice, grounded in extensive documentation of that teaching practice, generated teacher evaluation decisions as a group that were probably better but certainly more confident than principal's typically isolated decisions.

Chapter 9 explains how the different aspects of PAR in Rosemont combined to create a higher level of accountability than typically seen. In short, Rosemont saw 10% to 12% of new teachers in PAR and almost all veterans in the program removed from classroom teaching in the district across the initial years of the program (the duration of the study). As summarized in Chapter 9, these relatively high dismissal rates were the result of the program elements described in the prior chapters: (1) coaches had more time for evaluation, (2) professional development was linked to evaluation, (3) more people were involved in evaluation, (4) the teacher union and school district collaborated on evaluation, and (5) those involved had more confidence in their decisions. The chapter discusses PAR as a system of distributed accountability, a rare empirical case of leadership distributed across a district (rather than a school). The chapter also examines the ways that Rosemont's district-wide focus on accountability for teacher quality opened up a conversation about equity across schools, as the panel pushed principals to think across the district and end the practice of considering a teacher "not good enough" for their school but okay to send elsewhere. Finally, the chapter shows the shortcomings of the PAR process in Rosemont, as some underperforming teachers still slipped through the cracks.

Part IV of the book explores implications. First, Chapter 10 presents key issues to be considered by those interested in implementing PAR: program quality, cost, state and local labor statutes, existing local programs that may house knowledge of good teaching and aversion to PAR, and current conceptions of instructional leadership.

Chapter 11 returns to the questions of teacher professionalism, professionalization, and accountability from Chapter 1. The chapter argues that Rosemont's educators were able to use PAR to advance teachers' professionalization, grounded in their professionalism, with benefits to accountability. Ultimately, however, despite the wide perception of program benefits, PAR was scaled back after a few years—like so many teacher leadership policies.

The book includes an afterword by Susan Moore Johnson, the Carl H. Pforzheimer, Jr. Professor of Teaching and Learning at Harvard University's Graduate School of Education. Johnson closes the discussion by putting the Rosemont case in the context of numerous PAR programs across the country. In doing so, she demonstrated that Rosemont was not an anomaly and that efforts to expand peer review, while challenging, are both important and possible.

## AVAILABLE ONLINE: METHODOLOGICAL APPENDIXES

The book ends with a brief summary of methodological appendixes that are available online. These appendixes provide extensive additional detail about the design and methods of the study, including interview protocols and survey instruments used. I refer to these appendixes where relevant throughout the book, but for parsimony the descriptions thereof and how to access them on the Web are gathered in the "Available Online" chapter at the end of the book. For the most part, I have chosen not to break up the flow of the narrative with the reporting of survey results, with the exception of Chapters 6 and 7, where it is crucial to the story.

# *Setting the Stage*

## CHAPTER 1

# Professional Accountability

> The principal and the superintendent emerged as persons of
> presumed greater expertise and standing [than teachers] during
> the latter decades of the nineteenth century. During the twenti-
> eth century, some professors of education became spokesmen
> for schooling and leaders in various pedagogical movements
> (Cremin, 1961). The specialist high school teacher emerged at
> the same time that colleges and universities expanded manyfold;
> those teaching particular subjects at the secondary level were
> placed in a less expert position than those teaching the same
> subjects in institutions of "higher" learning. Thus teachers never
> did gain control of any area of practice where they were clearly
> in charge and most expert; day-to-day operation, pedagogical
> theory, and substantive expertise have been dominated by
> persons in other roles.
>
> —Dan Lortie, *Schoolteacher*

Educator and civil rights leader Robert Moses has infamously called algebra the new
civil rights, the educational gatekeeper for low-income students of color around the
United States. Quite simply, though, who will teach that algebra? Will the teacher
know how to teach algebra well, or at all? Will the teacher find joy in teaching algebra to his or her particular students, thereby firing their imaginations? Will a full-
time teacher even exist to hire and assign to a class rather than a string of long-term
substitutes? This book begins with the premise that teacher workforce quality, specifically the radical inequity in the distribution of high-quality teaching among the
children of the United States, is the central civil rights issue in education in urgent
need of repair (Darling-Hammond, 1997a; Lankford, Loeb, & Wyckoff, 2002; Peske
& Haycock, 2006; Shields et al., 1999). Underlying assumptions about students' race
and class, and blaming low student achievement on home and community factors,
have often undermined commitments to improving schools (Peske & Haycock, 2006).
Policy interventions are needed to improve teacher and teaching quality, and to reduce their unequal distribution among students based on race and class factors.

One of the enduring dilemmas in education policy is how to improve the
quality of teachers and teaching. Although we know a fair amount about what sorts
of teachers and what type of teaching generate student learning (e.g., Newmann &
Associates, 1996; Wayne & Youngs, 2003), we know surprisingly little about how
to get those teachers and that teaching into the highest-needs schools systematically
(Lankford et al., 2002), and once there, how to retain them (Ingersoll, 2004).

This book takes a close look at one particular policy intervention, peer assistance and review, which is intended to address teaching quality by focusing on the assessment of teachers, both for support and evaluation purposes. In the process, the policy elevates master teachers into previously nonexistent leadership positions, and gives these teachers responsibility and authority for quality control. In the book, I address three sets of core questions:

1. *Program Design*: How does PAR work? How is it different as a quality control mechanism from traditional teacher evaluation by a principal? What are the design challenges to its implementation?
2. *Educational Norms*: What existing norms of behavior does PAR interrupt? How does it do so? In particular, how do teachers and administrators within a school district make sense of the new role of teacher as evaluator of other teachers that comes with PAR? How, if at all, are professional relations reconfigured? Ultimately, how do existing norms challenge PAR's implementation?
3. *Outcomes*: What are the outcomes for teacher assessment and quality control that result from the implementation of PAR, and what do teachers and administrators perceive as the outcomes of the new role for the quality of teaching practice?

This chapter presents the concepts and theories that run through the book. It begins by laying out the issues that make the improvement of teacher quality a challenge. It then identifies the central and enduring disagreement among reformers regarding the best way to address these problematic issues—namely, a focus on professionalism versus accountability. The chapter discusses the concepts of professionalism and professionalization, and proposes professional accountability as a way to bridge these disparate reform camps. The chapter ends with a discussion of the challenges to increasing teachers' responsibility for teaching quality.

## THE CHALLENGES TO TEACHING QUALITY

The most critical factor in a child's academic success is a high-quality teacher. The National Commission on Teaching and America's Future (NCTAF) has argued that what teachers know and can do is one of the most important influences on what students learn (1996), and the link from teacher expertise to student learning and achievement is well established by research.[1]

"Teacher quality" is a multifaceted construct. NCLB focuses on teacher licensure as proxy for teacher quality, but good teaching is certainly far more than the mere possession of a credential. Teacher quality begins with teacher qualifications (degrees, licenses, and so on), but also includes the dispositions or habits of mind that teachers bring to the work, the deepening quality of teaching practice, and the student learning outcomes that result from teachers' efforts (Goe, 2007). I am mainly concerned here with one of these four aspects of teacher quality: the quality of teaching practice. Peer assistance and review engages with the development and assessment of teaching. Teacher qualifications become an issue in the book in the differentiated support needed by the teachers in PAR who lack teaching credentials, as well as their increased dismissal rates, but I am not examining teacher qualifications per se. Similarly, teacher dispositions come into play only to the extent that they are captured in the conversations about teaching practice and the California Standards for the Teaching Profession, the document used for assessment purposes in the district studied.

Finally, I am also not looking at student learning outcomes, which are increasingly measured by test scores. This study was simply not set up in 2000 to do so, nor do I believe that students' test scores over a relatively narrow period of time would particularly enhance our understanding of the program's outcomes in a meaningful way. Standardized tests provide a partial picture of student learning (or lack of learning). Even the best value-added models, which are still rare and certainly were not in place in the case district at the time of the study, are only an improvement on the existing limitations of using student test scores to assess teaching quality (Koretz, 2008).[2] It is worth noting, in light of the current climate of focus on test scores, that recent research is beginning to establish a link between ratings of teachers' performance through comprehensive, standards-based evaluation systems, and the test scores of those teachers' students (see Toch & Rothman, 2008). Student learning outcomes, defined more broadly than test scores, appear in the book when they are a part of discussions of teacher assessment in the case district, but they are not analyzed in the research.

The focus, then, is on the quality of teaching practice—specifically, on a system to assess observed teaching practice. A collection of organizational factors contributes to low teaching quality, especially in high-poverty schools, which warrant summary in order to establish the rationale for PAR as a policy response.

## Inadequate Support and Professional Development

Teachers at all different career stages require professional support. To begin with, empirical research has established that mentoring and induction for new teachers improves their job satisfaction and reduces attrition (Johnson & The Project on the Next Generation of Teachers, 2004; Smith & Ingersoll, 2004; Strong, 2004). Yet support for new teachers has often been sporadic, informal, not institutionalized, or absent altogether, hindering new teachers' development and retention (Fideler & Haselkorn, 1999; Shields et al., 1999).

In particular, teacher turnover is often constant in high-poverty schools and districts, where 30 to 50% of new teachers leave the profession within the first 3 to

5 years, and those without support are 70% more likely to leave than those who receive a mentored entrance to teaching (National Commission on Teaching and America's Future, 2003). The persistent attrition of new teachers plays an enormous role in lowering teacher quality, in part because it requires the constant hiring of yet more new teachers, and beginning teachers often perform less well than more experienced colleagues. While the literature on teacher qualifications is vast, there is agreement that years of teaching experience matters to student achievement in the first few years on the job, with students of first-, second-, and third-year teachers performing worse on tests than those with teachers who have more experience (Boyd, Grossman, Lankford, Loeb, & Wykoff, 2006; Hanushek, Kain, & Rivkin, 2005).

Low-income students and students of color, however, are far more likely to be taught by a novice teacher than their wealthier and whiter peers (Esch et al., 2005; Peske & Haycock, 2006). For example, Hill (2006), citing a study by Neild, Useem, & Farley (2005), reports that in Philadelphia, "70 percent of open positions in high-poverty schools are filled by brand new teachers, compared to less than 50 percent for high-income schools in the same district" (p. 100).

Beginning teachers are not the only issue. More than two decades of research has established that meaningful professional development is ongoing and situated within a community of practitioners learning together—both for new teachers and their more experienced colleagues (see Cochran-Smith & Lytle, 1999; Darling-Hammond, 1997b; Johnson et al., 2004; Lieberman, 1988; Lieberman & Miller, 1991; Little, 1982, 1993; Wenger, 1998). Most professional development for teachers, however, continues to have little connection to teachers' own classrooms, little expectation that teachers work together on problems of practice, and little expectation that teachers be continual learners (e.g., Webster-Wright, 2009), as teachers are mostly isolated in their work (Lieberman & Miller, 1999). Professional development is still more likely conceived as a workshop presented to teachers (on, say, a newly adopted district curriculum) than as an ongoing, embedded aspect of teachers' collaborative work with one another to reflect on and improve their own practice (Gravani, 2007; Hawley & Valli, 1999). As a result, little differentiation between teachers (based on knowledge and experience) exists to meet their individual development needs across a career in teaching. The lack of authentic professional learning for all teachers, rather than packaged professional development programs, limits the degree to which experienced teachers develop the knowledge and skills needed to teach effectively.[3]

In addition, the career trajectory for teachers tends to be flat, with teachers performing essentially the same tasks after 25 years as they did in the first (Feiman-Nemser & Floden, 1986). Limited structural mechanisms exist for teachers to ease into the job with a lighter teaching load at the outset, or to move up in expertise, responsibility, and compensation over time. Consequently, teachers are left with the limited career options of moving into administration or out of education altogether.

## Inadequate Quality Control and Accountability

On the flip side of the support and development of teachers, teaching quality is also adversely affected by the profound absence of real accountability. Blaming teachers unions seems to have become a national pastime, and some of this ire, certainly, is deserved. School districts, however, are an equal contributor to the problem (Hess & Kelly, 2006). The reality is that many American school districts *and* their local teachers unions have formed a symbiotic partnership in mediocrity. To single out one side of that equation (teachers unions) as the cause of the problem is to fail to recognize the role that administrators have played in creating the mess.

In our woefully outdated and ineffective supervisory model for schools, administrators, not teachers unions, hire teachers, and administrators, not unions, hold responsibility for quality control. The flaws present in most teacher evaluation systems have been criticized strongly (Bridges, 1986; Koppich, 1998; Toch & Rothman, 2008; Weisberg, Sexton, Mulhern, & Keeling, 2009; Wise, Darling-Hammond, McLaughlin, & Bernstein, 1984). Principals notoriously cut corners on teacher evaluation, overwhelmed by other demands and short on time. As a result, their evaluations are typically based on minimal observation data. Even if principals had the time, they often lack specific subject-area or grade-level expertise matched to their evaluatee, which limits their ability to assess performance meaningfully. Principals are rarely well-trained to conduct evaluations, and they simply may not know what good teaching looks like. They typically apply the same teaching standards and criteria, which are often unclear or unstated, to all teachers regardless of years of experience. Notoriously, principals often opt to sidestep poor performance in order to avoid interpersonal conflict (Bridges, 1986). Because little time is actually spent by administrators observing teaching, teachers do not have confidence that their evaluations are sound (Dornbusch & Scott, 1975), and certainly do not rely upon them for professional growth. Many teacher evaluations simply go undone, and principals often lack the data needed to help teachers improve or to support a dismissal. At the end of the day, nearly all teachers across the country are deemed officially competent.

Adversarial labor relations then exacerbate the weaknesses in the system. Many teachers unions have indeed made it extraordinarily difficult for districts to remove teachers. Adam Urbanski, longtime president of the Rochester Teachers Association and a vice president of the American Federation of Teachers, has often said, tongue in cheek, that it takes heinous and egregious crimes in front of a large number of witnesses for a teacher to be fired. Dismissing poorly performing veteran teachers is prohibitively costly and time-consuming, running $50,000 to $200,000 per teacher and taking 3 to 6 years, depending on the state (Kaboolian & Sutherland, 2005). With teachers unions often locked in confrontation with district offices, principals come to understand that it is simply easier to move an underperforming teacher to another school than engage in the conflict and steps necessary to fire him or her—thereby making principals even less likely to complete their evaluations adequately (Bridges, 1986).

In fairness to principals, the supervision of teachers is only one of their increasingly myriad responsibilities, and it is definitely not my intent to blame overwhelmed principals for our failure to ensure a quality teacher for every child. At the same time, blaming teachers and their unions (usually by lambasting the practice of tenure) is to grossly oversimplify the matter. There are no doubt teachers union leaders and representatives around the country who paralyze change efforts, just as there are administrators who make it impossible for teachers to be successful. The bottom line is that the cumulative effect of this partnership in mediocrity is that teachers who wish to remain in teaching are able to do so, regardless of merit.

## COMPETING REFORM GOALS:
## PROFESSIONALISM VERSUS ACCOUNTABILITY

Education reformers disagree about how to improve teaching quality. In short, they disagree about which of the above impediments to teaching quality should be the focus of reform efforts. At the heart of the rift lie fundamentally different beliefs about the locus of change: whether we should focus our attention on building the capacity of teachers to teach better (teacher professionalism or professional development) or whether we should focus on measuring students' learning and enforcing consequences when it falls below standards (accountability).

Educators—including teachers unions—have largely advocated an emphasis on capacity building through policies such as mentoring and professional development, in order to create high-quality teaching. In this view, teaching is complex work and many teachers currently lack the ability to perform at high levels. Teachers must be supported, ideally through ongoing dialogue with skillful colleagues, to develop and transform their own work. The problem with this approach, however, is that change is voluntary. Little tends to be done about those who do not improve, in part due to lack of will, but also due to the organizational structure of schools. Administrators hold the formal authority to enforce standards—not those skillful teacher colleagues who may be working with teachers on professional growth and who may be intimately familiar with shortcomings. Administrators, meanwhile, tend not to enforce standards for all the reasons just outlined, while blaming teachers unions—often justifiably.

Meanwhile, attempts to increase accountability have come mainly from outside the teaching profession, down through layers of a hierarchical system, and have often been unconcerned with building teachers' abilities. In this view, certain basics of teaching work are fairly straightforward, and the problem is lackadaisical school personnel. Proper rewards for good teaching and consequences for bad teaching would motivate teachers to do a better job (and remove those who do not). This approach, however, problematically presumes that most educators either know how to improve the quality of teaching, and have the resources to do so—but have just been holding out on us—or that conversely, educators lack the ability to improve and should be fired. The tenor of these "get tough" policies has tended to alienate the very people they seek to affect.

The policy rift that I am characterizing with "professionalism" and "accountability" is long documented and goes by many names (Cuban, 1990). Charles Payne (2008) has aptly characterized the split between liberal and conservative theories of urban school change, although these familiar monikers have increasingly taken on *Animal Farm*–esque qualities and may no longer be useful. Richard Ingersoll (2003) quite usefully characterizes the distinction as between "disempowerment" and "disorganization" camps of reformers. One camp believes that teachers are disempowered and that education's problems can therefore be addressed by giving teachers more power; the other camp believes that schools are too disorganized and that the solution to education's problems lies in more organization. The bottom line is that, to some degree, both sides are right, and the road to improvement is not the sole province of either.

The mid-1980s brought a decade and a half of education reforms that sought to develop the talent of the teacher workforce, following the professionalism line of thinking.[4] Mentor teachers and resource specialists provided extra support to their peers (Fieman-Nemser, 1998; Feiman-Nemser & Parker, 1993; Little, 1990). Professional development schools established a whole-school environment in which novices learned together and from more experienced teachers (Darling-Hammond, Bullmaster, & Cobb, 1995). Peer coaching brought teachers together in partnership to observe one another teaching and to explore elements of good practice, validating the body of knowledge needed to be a skillful teacher as broad, complex, and self-reflective (Costa & Garmston, 1994; Feiman-Nemser, 1998). Action research provided teachers with the opportunity to critically examine their own practice (Cochran-Smith & Lytle, 1996). Networks allowed teachers to make connections not just across the boundaries of classrooms but also across schools and districts (Lieberman & McLaughlin, 1996). The National Board for Professional Teaching Standards (NBPTS) recognized master teachers for their demonstrated expertise with both a label and a monetary reward (National Board for Professional Teaching Standards, 1994). Collectively, these policies contributed to the growth of a shared knowledge base for teaching and a base of skillful practitioners.

These developments were short-circuited by the passage of NCLB in 2001, which generated an almost exclusive focus on standardized test scores. Gary Anderson (2009) aptly summarizes the reform transition:

> In the 1990s there was a movement to link testing to standards. . . . This ushered in a discourse of standards, accountability, and performance assessment. In theory, this approach to accountability made sense, and early on, standards were developed with considerable teacher input. . . . From being a major source of input into a standards movement early on, teachers later were framed as the problem. They were too "progressive" and their methods were not showing results on standardized tests. The "reading wars" was a major battlefield on which standards morphed into standardization. (pp. 161–162)

This national morphing into standardization meant a retreat from teacher professionalism, as teachers became largely shut out of the reform conversation. In the language of organizational theory, the shift from professionalism to accountability brought by NCLB was a shift in focus from inputs (teacher knowledge and skills) to outputs (student test results). Anderson (2009) argues that this accountability system relied on the hope that once poorly performing schools are identified, they will be shamed (through public exposure) or threatened (with reconstitution or state takeover) into improving. As Darling-Hammond (2004) has argued, however, this rests on the faulty assumption that schools currently have the capacity to improve. A system that devalues qualifications and allows almost anyone entry to teaching, coupled with little focus on building their capacity once on the job, while we focus national attention on high-stakes accountability at the tail end does little more than set our teachers up for failure—and, therefore, our children as well.

NCLB's crucial legacy is the imperative to disaggregate data. It has forced school personnel to focus on their responsibility for the learning of historically underserved students. In the process, a genuine contribution of NCLB has been a redefining of teacher quality from an exclusive focus on teacher qualifications and teaching practice to a focus on student learning outcomes—in other words, from an exclusive focus on inputs to a focus on outputs as well. This has been an important shift in our collective educational habit of mind. Yet this external-accountability-focused wave of reform has not yet helped, and many believe it has harmed, educators' ability to get better at what they do. The sad irony of NCLB is that while focusing attention on closing the achievement gap, it has shut down many of the alternate reform conversations that might have provided the map for how to get there. The move toward a reductionist approach to assessment succeeded in drowning out most other voices of reform. By narrowing the focus of attention to students' scores on standardized tests, NCLB merely identifies and measures a problem; it does not provide the tools for improving the system.

## WHY PAR?

The study of peer review at the heart of this book immediately preceded the NCLB juggernaut. My research spanned from 1998 to 2004, but the vast majority occurred during the 2000–2001 school year. It therefore provides an opportunity to view an alternate and possibly promising reform that was left unpursued once NCLB demanded attention.

Peer assistance and review potentially redesigns teaching in ways that affect both professionalism and accountability. PAR is a joint endeavor by a school district and its teachers union to focus resources on the comprehensive support, development, and assessment of teachers. With PAR, master teachers are released from classroom teaching duties full-time for 2 to 3 years, in order to provide mentoring to teachers who are new to the district or the profession and intervention for identified veteran teachers who are experiencing difficulty. Notably, they also conduct the formal personnel evaluations of the teachers in the program, instead of the principal. They report those evaluations to an oversight panel composed of teachers and administrators from across the district, which determines employment outcomes.

PAR's designers hope it will systematically target the current barriers to teaching quality in several ways: by providing extensive support to new teachers; by putting teachers in relationships with one another around questions of quality practice, providing extensive professional development for both mentors and mentees; by creating opportunities for career development by placing master teachers in positions of expertise; and by putting unions and districts in collaborative relationships focused on individual teachers' performance. Most unique, however, is that it provides summative assessment of teachers by a peer. Such assessment shifts authority relations between teachers and administrators, sometimes dramatically, while also appearing to be a far more rigorous means of accountability than traditional teacher evaluation by an administrator (Darling-Hammond, 1984; Gallagher, Lanier, & Kerchner, 1993; Goldstein, 2007a).

Teacher evaluation is rarely viewed as a sexy topic in the world of education reform. It conjures the worst of education's bureaucracy—principals' observation checklists, feedback to teachers about practice that is meaningless or entirely absent, and a system that rarely removes ineffective teachers from the classroom. As currently implemented, teacher evaluation provides little promise for altering the teacher quality landscape. Yet teacher evaluation in its broadest conception involves the formative and summative assessment of teachers, meaning both assessment for the purpose of diagnosing performance and improving it, as well as assessment for the purpose of determining fitness for employment or advancement.[5] If teacher evaluation were implemented deeply and systematically, in order to address meaningfully both professionalism and accountability, it would sit at the intersection of many of the challenges to teaching quality, bridging competing reform goals while providing a potent inroad for change.

## REDESIGNING TEACHING FOR PROFESSIONAL ACCOUNTABILITY

My examination of PAR took teacher professionalization as its organizing frame. I was primarily interested in learning about responsibility and authority for the quality control of teaching. I was, of course, also interested in learning about the substantive expertise of those holding this control, a matter of professionalism, but mainly insofar as it related to professionalization. This is a distinction I will explain further. My point here is that in order to support the particular questions I was interested in studying, I drew on literature that spans the sociology of professions and organizational theory, in particular the study of institutions. These theoretical underpinnings situate this particular study of PAR in a broader ongoing effort to understand teaching work in the United States.

### Professionalism and Professionalization

Increasing teachers' authority for teacher evaluation, as may occur with PAR, is a form of professionalization. It is important to start with a clear explanation of the distinction between professionalization and professionalism, as well as the way the two concepts are linked.

While professionalism is comprised of traits *possessed by* the individuals of the profession (such as one's knowledge and skills), professionalization, by contrast, is the authority *granted to* the individuals by society (such as one's control over the hiring and firing of other personnel). Tomas Englund (1996) distinguishes between professionalization and professionalism in the following way:

> I will characterize professionalization as . . . relating to the authority and status of the (teaching) profession, and professionalism as . . . concerned with the internal quality of teaching as a profession. . . . Professionalization is . . . a measure of the societal strength and authority of an occupational group. Professionalism, on the other hand, focuses on the question of what qualifications and acquired capacities, what competence, is required for the successful exercise of an occupation, in this case teaching. (pp. 75–76)[6]

Assessing teacher quality well requires both, internal professionalism and externally granted professionalization.

   The Process of Professionalization.  Professionalization can be defined as the process by which an occupation gains exclusive right to perform a particular type of work, control the training for and access to that work, control the standards for the work, and control the evaluation of the way the work is performed (Freidson, 1994). As Englund (1996) noted, this right is granted to the occupation by society. Professionalization, therefore, involves occupational self-regulation or self-governance[7]—the authority held by the profession itself for gatekeeping and quality control. Gatekeeping pertains to decisions about who will and will not be a member, and quality control involves decisions about how a member's work will be assessed (Van Maanen & Barley, 1984).

The link between a profession and its work is captured in the useful concept of "jurisdiction" put forth by sociologist Andrew Abbott (1988). Occupations hold jurisdiction over certain work tasks; over time, this link becomes cognitively ingrained and taken for granted. However, occupations exist within an ecology of interdependence in which jurisdictional boundaries shift and jurisdictions are seized by one occupation from another—which is to say, one occupation claims its right to the particular work of another occupation. Abbott (1988) notes: "Many occupations fight for turf, but only professions expand their cognitive domain by using abstract knowledge to annex new areas, to define them as their own proper work" (p. 102). By way of example, counseling was at one time the presumed domain of the clergy, until the field of psychology was born; as psychologists defined a new expert knowledge base, they staked their claim as the appropriately qualified counselors, and over time, their claim became so accepted as to be taken for granted.

As Abbott notes above, jurisdiction—or the process of professionalization— usually rests on claims by members of an occupation to possessing certain internal (Englund, 1996) markers of professionalism, like mastery of an abstract knowledge base. Although shifting slightly from author to author, definitions of professionalism generally include: 1) a shared knowledge base, 2) a concern for client welfare, and 3) collective responsibility for professional standards (Abbott, 1988; Darling-Hammond, 1990; Freidson, 1986).

Knowledge Base.  A shared knowledge base that is specialized, abstract, codified, and typically produced by university specialists contributes to defining and demarcating professions from other occupations (see Abbott, 1988; DiMaggio & Powell, 1983; Freidson, 1986, 1994). Education's formal and abstract knowledge base, however, remains weak. Richard Elmore (2006) identifies the lack of codified knowledge for practice as the biggest problem currently facing education, and one that leaves teachers without power as experts in the field.

The lack of a knowledge base fundamentally affects the organization of teaching work. Professionalism and bureaucracy are two approaches to organizing workers (Firestone & Bader, 1992), which emerge from the nature of the work being done within an organization. Within education, professional or bureaucratic schools emerge from different conceptions of the knowledge base for teaching (Firestone & Bader, 1991; Rowan, 1990; Weick & McDaniel, 1989). Bureaucratic structures are found where teaching is seen to involve routine information inputs, limited uncertainty, and finite solutions to the problems of practice (Firestone & Bader, 1991; Weick & McDaniel, 1989). Professional structures are more likely where teaching is viewed to involve non-routine information inputs, requiring both a complex knowledge base and judgment of situational considerations in order to overcome uncertainty (Firestone & Bader, 1991; Schön, 1983; Weick & McDaniel, 1989).

In Richard Ingersoll's (2003) meticulous study of control in schools, he addresses this perception of teaching as routine, finite work without specialized knowledge and its connection to the prevalent practice of assigning teachers to teach outside their licensed area:

> Few employers or organizations would, for example, require cardiologists to deliver babies, real estate lawyers to defend criminal cases, chemical engineers to design bridges, or sociology professors to teach English. Underlying the traditional professions is the assumption that a great deal of skill, training, and expertise are required, and so specialization is necessary. The prevalence of out-of-field teaching suggests that another set of assumptions underlies the work of precollegiate teaching—that school teaching is not especially complex work, that it does not require much skill, training, and expertise, and hence that specialization is less necessary. (p. 166)

Without this specialized, codified knowledge base, teaching has been historically considered a "semi-profession" (Etzioni, 1969).

The situation becomes even worse in the case of shortage. In school districts all over the country, there are simply not enough qualified teachers willing to staff classrooms. (Ingersoll [2004] has documented that there is not a teacher *shortage* per se, just a shortage of teachers who want to teach.) When there is more work to be done than there are professionals to do it, nonprofessionals are often allowed to fill the gap, regardless of academic knowledge (Abbott, 1988). In education, administrators hire unqualified teachers, meaning teachers who are uncredentialed or credentialed in a different field. Darling-Hammond, Wise, and Klein (1995) have pointed out that teaching is the only state-licensed occupation that continues to grant emergency certificates to untrained practitioners—although this practice has declined in the wake of NCLB. The phenomenon is typically worse, however, in districts serving low-income students and students of color, as the boundaries between professionals and nonprofessionals tend to disappear in overstressed worksites, especially in those serving "pariah" clients (Abbott, 1988). In California, for example, one in 15 teachers—approximately 20,000 total—were underprepared in 2004–2005, but *85% of these* were concentrated in schools serving predominantly "minority" students (Esch et al., 2005).

Concern for Client Welfare.  The second factor considered to demarcate professions is concern for the welfare of one's clients. Individual teachers are often understood to be devoted to their students—by the students themselves, by those students' families, and by the teachers' colleagues. In studies spanning the last 40 years, teachers have been found to be motivated by a public-service ethic (i.e., placing importance on the opportunity to contribute to the betterment of society) significantly more than those in other careers (Ingersoll, 2003). In addition, multiple studies in the 1990s showed teachers spending an average of $400–$500 of their own money annually for the purchase of materials and supplies, which would be a total collective donation to public education by 3 million teachers of over one billion dollars (Ingersoll, 2003).

Despite these patterns of commitment, however, teachers unions, and by extension teachers, have suffered greatly in public perception by the characterization of being more concerned with their members' benefits than students' education. The typical union weak point most relevant to the discussion at hand, of course, is the perception that underperforming tenured teachers cannot be fired due to union roadblocks. Also contributing to the perception that teachers unions do not have students' best interests at heart, however, are collectively bargained teacher placement policies. Paul Hill (2006) provides a lucid summary of the within-district inequity, and devastating impact on high-poverty schools, which results from the seniority placement policies in collective bargaining agreements as well as the district policies that support them (see Neild et al., 2005; Roza & Hill, 2004). Concern for client welfare provides a common source of derision for the concept of "professional" when it is perceived to be not present.

Collective Responsibility for Professional Standards. The third marker of professionalism is collective responsibility for professional standards. Collective responsibility, however, actually involves a trait possessed by the individuals of the profession (i.e., the courage to self-regulate) as well as an external granting of authority that results in the formal ability to act upon the possessed trait. Said another way, collective responsibility involves both professionalization and professionalism—both the authority to make decisions about standards, as well as the internal knowledge and commitments to make those decisions and make them well.

Expert teachers, admittedly, have not often been eager to engage in the quality control of their peers. They have also not held the authority to do so. In a national survey that asked principals how much control they have in regard to a number of the most important decisions in schools, the principals more often reported holding a high level of control over teacher evaluation decisions than any others (Ingersoll, 2003).[8]

Figure 1.1 displays the relationships between the concepts of professionalism and professionalization for the case of peer assistance and review.

## Leadership Responsibility for Quality Control

Although administrator control over teacher evaluation may now be taken for granted, the current hierarchical structure of the U.S. public education system was merely imported from the factory-model "efficiency" of the industrial era a century ago (e.g., Lortie, 1975; Tyack, 1974). Our ability to improve teaching quality is limited by an organizational structure imported from the industrial model at

Figure 1.1. Teachers' Professional Accountability

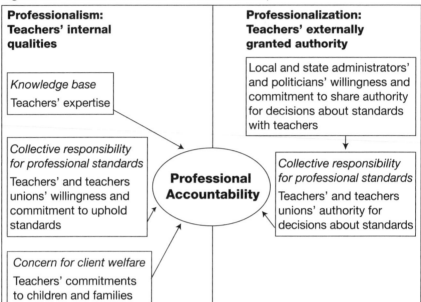

the turn of the 20th century (e.g., Callahan, 1962). The leaders of the efficiency movement took a hierarchical and bureaucratic[9] perspective on teaching work, the legacy of which mostly prevails 100 years later. The architects of our current public education system, in the early years of the 20th century, largely viewed teaching to be a routine activity involving only the knowledge needed to follow a textbook, rather than complex work involving judgment (Firestone & Bader, 1992)—precisely Elmore's (2006) point. Thus, they standardized and routinized education, compartmentalizing it into grades and subjects, and created layers of management to supervise teachers. Feminist scholars have argued that teachers' work became organized in this hierarchical way for primarily paternalistic reasons (Grant & Murray, 1999), as the process that divided educational administration from teaching at the turn of the 20th century has been considered a strategy that "upwardly mobile" male teachers used to set themselves above their mostly female peers (Abbott, 1988).

The problems of this hierarchical bureaucracy, however, lead directly to the problems with low teaching quality. Not only does this particular way of organizing teaching work grow out of a conception of teaching as low-skilled, but it reinforces it. In hierarchical bureaucracies, teachers often lack meaningful, professional opportunities to build their knowledge and skills. Under this structure, teachers have traditionally viewed professional obligations to one another as intrusive at worst and loosely invitational at best (along the lines of "ask me for assistance if you want it"). Feiman-Nemser and Floden (1986) call this a norm of noninterference. Instead, the responsibility for maintaining teaching quality and, hence, responsibility for evaluation has resided hierarchically above teachers in the chain of command, in administration (Little, 1988). As such, formal teacher evaluation falls under the purview of principals in all but the most progressive, alternative schools.

The automatic purview of administrators in matters of quality control has rarely been questioned by educational practitioners or researchers, in part because teachers and local teachers unions have rarely been willing to take responsibility for the evaluation of peers,[10] and in part because administrators have been reluctant to relinquish a task seen as central to their leadership. Administrator authority over teacher quality simply became the institutional norm (Lortie, 1975; Tyack, 1974), the taken for granted way of doing things in education (Scott, 1995).

A countervailing vision for education would alter this traditional hierarchy and vest teachers themselves with authority and responsibility for the quality of practice—it would professionalize them and vest them with collective responsibility for quality control. Rather than rely exclusively on administrators, in a more professional vision of teaching, "teachers would in fact expect to be their brothers' keepers" (Little, 1988, p. 94).

This is ultimately a study of one occupational group, teachers, increasing its self-regulation within a school district organization—which inherently requires some related reduction in the regulation of teachers by administrators. Charging teachers with formal responsibility for gatekeeping and quality control—in other words, for the evaluation of other teachers—creates the potential for a struggle between teachers and administrators over occupational boundaries.[11]

Let me be clear at the outset. Leadership by educational administrators is crucial (National Association of Secondary School Principals, 2004). Neither a professional vision of teaching broadly, nor peer review specifically, signals an end to the key role of principals in the enterprise of schooling. Research on collective models of leadership has demonstrated that as influence is distributed more broadly, principals remain highly influential (Leithwood & Mascall, 2008; Spillane & Diamond, 2007). In the case of PAR, it is not merely influence that is being distributed, but, in fact, formal leadership responsibility and authority. Ingersoll's (2003) findings of control in schools, however, were similar to Leithwood & Mascall's (2008): Schools with higher teacher control also had higher principal control, and vice versa. The professionalization of teaching that would assign jurisdiction for quality control to teachers need not remove principals from involvement in this task, and principals' leadership is comprised far more broadly than the quality control of teaching. Leithwood and Mascall (2008) write that organizations with "intelligent hierarchy . . . take advantage of the capabilities and strengths of most of their members while ensuring careful coordination of effort in a common direction" (p. 553). In short, in professionally organized districts, principals would remain active and important participants in conversations about teaching quality. Expert teachers have capabilities and strengths that render them well-suited to take a large piece of the responsibility for assessing the competence of other teachers, while principals would retain fundamental responsibility for coordination in a "common direction."

## Resistance to Expanding Leadership by Teachers

PAR, and the teacher jurisdiction for quality control that it can create, is a very specific and unusual case of teacher leadership. A host of policies over the past two decades have rested on expanded conceptions of the nature of leadership in schools. These policies have sought to expand teachers' responsibilities, both through formal career ladder roles (or what is increasingly called by the less hierarchical "career lattice") such as mentors, curriculum developers, instructional coaches, and researchers, and through informal networks of influence. The evidence on the efficacy of these reform efforts has been mixed (see Smylie, 1997; York-Barr & Duke, 2004; also Mangin & Stoelinga, 2008).[12] Particularly relevant for the study at hand, Ingersoll (2003) found educational benefits to increased teacher control over noninstructional matters such as teacher evaluation.[13]

Yet the norms against teachers in leadership roles have remained so strong that the policies are often undermined (Little, 1990; Sebring, Hallman, & Smylie, 2003; Smylie & Brownlee-Conyers, 1992)—even when those involved perceive positive outcomes, and even though some of these policies were designed specifically to challenge education's hierarchical norms (Grant & Murray, 1999; Tyack & Cuban, 1995). It may well be that part of the reason the evidence is mixed regarding the benefits to teacher leadership policies is that the norms against the policies seriously impede their chances for successful implementation. Indeed, York-Barr and Duke (2004) point out that it is extremely difficult to measure the effects of teacher leadership efforts, because these efforts sit on top of the existing design of teaching, which is not set up to support such efforts.

In her influential review of the literature on teacher mentorship, Little (1990) found a predictable pattern of conservative institutional responses to teacher leadership policies, where the new role was rendered "harmless—and thus useless" (Little, 1990, p. 15, citing Bird, 1986). Some of the recent research on teacher leadership, or the "distribution" of leadership to teachers, supports Little's (1990) findings. For example, in a study of three schools distributing leadership to teachers in various ways, Sebring and colleagues (2003) found that two of the three schools "emasculated" their programs after 2 to 3 years of good progress. Little (1990) notes that even when program goals are accepted, there is an inability to overcome long-established norms and patterns of behavior.

The vast majority of teacher leadership efforts, including the programs reviewed by Little and those in the Sebring study, do not specifically involve teacher evaluation (Smylie, 1997; York-Barr & Duke, 2004). The fact that the historic tendency has been to blunt the impact of even less controversial policies suggests that the same would likely occur with PAR.

## Making Sense of New Roles

PAR increases teachers' formal authority by altering district organizational structures for teacher evaluation (Darling-Hammond, 1984; Kelly, 1998; Kerchner, Koppich, & Weeres, 1997; Murray, 1998). As a result, PAR challenges education's norms for authority relations in novel and potent ways, as it challenges deeply held beliefs about teachers' and principals' appropriate roles. Most educators at the K–12 level, both teachers and administrators alike, have little prior experience with teachers as teacher evaluators; the shift is complex and challenging, and likely to generate tension and ambiguity (Smylie & Denny, 1990). Kerchner and Caufman (1995) argue that because PAR involves teachers making substantive judgments about teacher quality, it "places teachers in a social and intellectual position they have never before occupied" (p. 115). In particular, PAR requires changes in the beliefs and nature of authority relations, including redefining teachers' relationships with one another and redefining teachers' relationships with administrators (Costa & Garmston, 2000; Darling-Hammond, 1997b; Kelly, 1998; Murray, 1998).

Institutionalization is a social process by which certain behaviors are repeated, given similar meaning, and accepted as standard operating procedure (Scott, 1998), such as the tasks that are considered appropriate work for teachers to do as part of their job. The process of institutionalization rests on three pillars: regulations (legally sanctioned rules), norms (morally governed social appropriateness), and cognitive frames (culturally supported taken-for-grantedness) (Scott, 1995).[14]

No structure, norm, or cognitive category has existed for teachers as experts, as the meaning given to the task of teaching has not included authority or expertise. Scott (1995) writes that from a cognitive perspective, "compliance occurs in many circumstances because other types of behavior are inconceivable; routines are followed because they are taken for granted as 'the way we do these things'" (p. 44). The taken-for-granted way things are done in education, supported by staffing formulas, board policies, and public opinion, involves a conception of teachers and teaching in a classroom with a group of children (Little, 1988). Education has not established a cognitive frame through which to make sense of teachers in other roles, despite the growing proliferation of teacher leadership policies (Little, 1988; Scott, 1995; Weick, 1995). Feiman-Nemser (1998), for example, has identified how cognitive frames prevent most teachers in mentorship roles from viewing themselves as teacher educators. An adult providing assistance to a teacher, an adult managing a school, an adult developing policy—no cognitive link exists to connect these images of "experts" to the identity "teacher." Our formal structures, in turn, both reflect (Meyer and Rowan, 1977) and shape (Weick, 1995) our understandings of social reality.

This book focuses on the unlinked image of teachers as evaluators, exploring how teachers and those with whom they work come to make sense of this new role. The argument is that formal involvement in evaluation signals an expansion of teachers' roles, and, as I will show, that it was accompanied by new ways of defining the act of being a teacher. Peer review is appropriately understood as an attempt to push the envelope of legitimate roles for teachers; the book will explore whether or not it succeeded at doing so in the district studied. With PAR, new structures were created that placed teachers in roles as consultants, evaluators, leaders, experts, and colleagues to district-level administrators. Creating new institutionally legitimate roles, however, is not only about creating new positions and structures such as those established with PAR, but is also fundamentally about creating new norms and cognitive frames. With PAR, did it become legitimate for teachers to engage in quality control as part of their job description?

Quite simply, educators have little way of understanding and making sense of teachers in the types of leadership roles brought by PAR. Their prior experience has taught them that principals are responsible for quality control, and therefore conduct teachers' evaluations. As a result, they must make sense of and attach meaning to the new policy and the new role for teachers. Changed behavior required by new policy implementation involves complex cognitive processes in which those implementing the policy do not merely perform new roles but also frame and construct the new roles, "authoring" as well as "reading" the new policy (Spillane, Reiser, & Reimer, 2002; Weick, 1995). Sensemaking highlights this phenomenon by which people give structure to the unknown, and is most evident at times when expectations break down, when patterns of behavior are interrupted, and, hence, new cognitive frames are needed (Weick, 1995). As will be explored in Part III of the book, PAR generates multiple interruptions of patterns of behavior or social conventions. These interruptions have the potential to transform an occupation, because as action leads to cognition (Weick, 1995), the role innovation can create new ways of seeing and doing things (Van Maanen & Barley, 1984).

## CONCLUSION

Professional accountability through collective responsibility for professional standards is only one piece of teacher professionalization. Teaching cannot be a profession without a codified knowledge base for teachers that, in large part, we still do not have. PAR addresses one piece of the puzzle only. There is, of course, a much larger picture that is beyond the scope of this book—in terms of coming to some agreement about what students, and therefore teachers, need to know and be able to do. Nonetheless, PAR is the logical place for teachers themselves to start; it is a way for teachers to be a force for improving teaching at the local level.

Advocates of accountability may not trust teachers to engage in quality control, and advocates of professionalism may not feel comfortable engaging in behaviors considered the purview of administrators. Nonetheless, teachers' collective responsibility for teaching quality is the bridge between the two competing frames of professionalism and accountability, and PAR provides an interesting case.

Darling-Hammond (1990) notes that the bargain all professions make with society is the guarantee of competence of members in exchange for the privilege of control over work structure and standards of practice. She warns, however, that without expertise in a shared knowledge base—without professionalism—professional autonomy will lead to bureaucratization rather than professionalization (Darling-Hammond, 1997b). This is, in fact, a common criticism of policies like PAR, a form of career ladder. These policies communicate a view of a teaching career as progressing through stages of growing expertise, as master teachers are recognized for their skill and given increased authority and organizational responsibility. Critics argue that they merely create more formal authority and more rungs in the education hierarchy without creating more professionalism.

The degree to which PAR does not fall prey to this criticism depends on the policy's ability to be based in professionalism, or to simultaneously grow teachers' professionalism while promoting professionalization. In other words, if teachers are seen to hold authority for quality control with PAR, is the authority grounded in their expertise, in their commitments to children and families, and in their willingness to enforce collectively agreed upon standards? This will be the appropriate test of the policy.

Ultimately, developing both professionalism and professionalization will require not only building teachers' expertise, but also organizational structures, cultural norms, and ways of seeing the world that legitimate teachers' appropriate authority for standards and quality control. It is a radical notion when taken in the context of the last hundred years of public education in the United States—and, in particular, in the post–NCLB world.

## CHAPTER 2

# Peer Assistance and Review

## A Teachers Union-School District Partnership

> Among students of professionalism and sociologists of teaching,
> movement toward peer review is thought to be among the most
> powerful agents of occupational self-determination.
> —Charles Taylor Kerchner & Julia Koppich,
> *A Union of Professionals*

Peer review experienced a very specific birth in Toledo, Ohio, in 1981. Dal Lawrence served as president of the AFT-affiliated teachers union in Toledo from 1967 to 1997. In the early 1970s, he suggested to the school district as part of the bargaining agreement that they undertake an intern program for new teachers. Lawrence was frustrated with the caliber of beginning teachers, and when the state did not support his calls for a fifth-year teacher education program, he viewed master teachers supporting and evaluating new teachers as a plausible alternative. Each year between 1973 and 1981, the district rejected his suggestion, viewing it as a union grab for power. In 1981, however, a new negotiator for the district saw an opportunity. He came back to Lawrence and the union with a challenge: The district offered to support the new teacher intern program if the union would also take responsibility for intervention with seriously ineffective tenured teachers. The union accepted, and the "Toledo Plan" of peer review came into existence as an educational reform (Gallagher et al., 1993).

Over the next 2 decades, a handful of districts undertook the Toledo Plan, still the best-known blueprint of peer review policy, including Cincinnati and Columbus, Ohio; Poway and Mount Diablo, California; Rochester, New York; Dade County, Florida; and Salt Lake City, Utah (see Bloom & Goldstein, 2000).[1] The genesis of the program in Toledo was repeated in these districts; peer review was, in most cases, a union leader's passion, and in all cases it was the result of local union and district leadership willing to take risks with labor relations. The American Federation of Teachers (AFT) officially endorsed the idea of peer review in 1984, and the National Education Association (NEA) did so in 1997.

## PROFESSIONAL UNIONISM

Union reform is a unique case of teacher leadership, as unions are the only teacher organization with legal authority in the traditional school district structure. Although other teacher leadership policies have the ability to enact authority over the normative environment of teachers' roles as professionals, teachers union leadership has the additional ability to enact authority over the structural environment in which teachers' work takes place. For states with collective bargaining, it is simply not possible to reorganize schools or alter the duties of employees without changing the labor relations contracts (Kerchner & Koppich, 1993; Kerchner & Mitchell, 1988; Kerchner et al., 1997). As a result, while other teacher organizations (such as the councils of English or mathematics teachers) can set standards and provide services to their members, only unions can link standards of good practice to the allocation of time and other resources in classrooms (Kerchner & Caufman, 1995). In the case of PAR, unions gain the ability to link standards of good practice to the enforcement of those standards.

Teacher unionism, noted Kerchner and Mitchell (1988), "ranks alongside school desegregation and categorical funding as one of the three major structural changes in public education since World War II" (p. 2). The industrial model of labor relations emphasized rights and protections rather than responsibilities, and was, therefore, seen as quite distinct from the social contract of professionalism (Sykes, 1987). However, given the hierarchical structure of school organizations in the 20th century, as discussed in Chapter 1, unions became one of the few arenas in which teachers had opportunities for formal leadership and the shaping of policy (Bascia, 1998). The structural changes within education that came with teacher unionism were perceived by many to have a negative effect on the quality of schooling (e.g., Finn & Ravitch, 1995; M. Lieberman, 1994), although Johnson (1984) found that while collective bargaining changed schools, the effects were nowhere nearly as extreme as critics of unionism suggest. She found the professionalism of individual teachers to be a tempering agent against the effects of industrial unionism. She also found that although teachers were deeply ambivalent about industrial unionism, they nonetheless believed collective bargaining to be necessary, and its protections to be an appropriate and reasonable response to administrative excess. (Interestingly, principals interviewed by Johnson agreed.) Nonetheless, the time and expense needed to dismiss an underperforming teacher is perhaps the most notorious of the complaints against teachers unions.

In the 1980s, some union locals began to shift their labor relations practices, becoming increasingly involved in education policy and reform. This shift was motivated by a variety of forces, including the specter of vouchers and the apparent fragility of public education itself (rather than the regime of a particular superintendent) (Kerchner et al., 1997). In the late 1980s, Kerchner and Mitchell (1988) introduced the idea of "professional unionism," where unions do not cease to be concerned with teachers' material interests, but rather the scope of bargaining expands to legitimately include issues of educational policy.[2]

Kerchner and Mitchell (1988) employ a "generational theory" of union development. In the first generation, teachers meet with management to voice their issues and concerns. The interests of teachers and management are still considered to be the same—that of quality education—and where the two groups disagree, teachers are expected to defer to management. The second generation introduces collective bargaining and the model of industrial unionism. Here, teachers are no longer satisfied with airing their views, and instead want binding contractual agreements. Conflict is considered endemic to the workplace, protecting teachers' interests becomes legitimate, and labor relations are viewed as necessarily separate from organizational policy. The traditional bargaining of second-generation unionism assumes that labor and management have opposing interests (Hess & Kelly, 2006), and unions are considered "legally, functionally, and psychologically distanced" from responsibility for the institution of education (Kerchner & Mitchell, 1988, p. 14). Despite this, Kerchner and Mitchell argue that unions have had a significant impact on organizational policy, but that these effects are more "by-products" than intended results.

With the third generation of unionism, by contrast, both unions and districts begin to explicitly attempt to shape education policy through the contract, with "negotiated policy." Sometimes called "interest-based bargaining," this third generation of unionism is characterized by joint problem-solving and finding common ground (Hess & Kelly, 2006). Hence, in this more professional generation, district administrators take on a genuine interest in creating viable policy *with* teachers, while unions (and hence teachers) take on shared responsibility for the success of the organization.

Building on Kerchner and Mitchell's work, Kerchner and Koppich (1993) argued that professional unionism is about a departure from three of industrial unionism's "most cherished assumptions and central organizing concepts":

> First, unions are discarding beliefs about the inherent separateness of labor and management, teaching and administration. . . . Second, unions and management are questioning the necessity of adversarial relationships. . . . Third, ideas about teacher protection are being rethought. Unions are beginning to realize that *the quality and integrity of teaching*, as well as the due process rights of individual teachers, need protection (p. 9, emphasis added).

Kerchner and Koppich (1993) see professional unionism as a melding of the ideals of unionism (protecting teachers) with the ideals of professionalism (protecting teaching). This marked a critical shift from defining union work by rights and protections to including responsibilities. Kerchner and colleagues (1997) subsequently argue for fundamental change, where unions move beyond merely organizing teachers' economic rights to organizing teachers as educators. As part of this framework, they argue that peer review would support the definition and enforcement of teacher quality.

Ultimately, professional unionism is a case of teacher leadership writ large—leadership enacted by teachers as a group through their union, once the union has amassed sufficient power to be accepted as a partner in policymaking (Wise et al., 1984). This collective professionalism, more influential than individual profession-alism, "opens the way to collaborative control over teacher quality" (Wise et al., 1984, p. 79), which asserts that the most powerful form of accountability is account-ability to one's peers. In other professions, such as medicine or law, this collec-tively enacted quality control is mediated through institutions such as a board or bar. Such institutions have not historically existed in teaching.

If unions are to fill this role, they must respond, genuinely, to public criticisms of public education. Kelly (1998) notes that teachers unions are implicated as de-fenders of a seemingly failing system, and they must increase their professionalism by demonstrating their concern for client welfare. It is not my intent to turn a blind eye to or gloss over the very real issues involved in reforming labor relations for the improvement of educational equity and quality. Rather, I am focusing on peer re-view as one potent way in which the most progressive teachers unions have attempted to become more accountable for teacher quality and student learning.

## PEER ASSISTANCE AND REVIEW IN CALIFORNIA

In 1999, Gray Davis became governor of California and almost immediately spon-sored four keystone education bills, one of which was peer review for teachers. Spear-headed by State Assemblyman Antonio Villaraigosa, who would go on to become mayor of Los Angeles, the California legislature passed Assembly Bill 1X (AB 1X), which phased out the California Mentor Teacher Program and established peer re-view in its place. The legislation allocated approximately $100 million for PAR—$83.2 million in money previously attached to the mentor program, plus $16.8 million in new money. The bill, therefore, created a de facto mandate for peer review: The leg-islation required school districts to have a peer review program in place by 2000 for veteran teachers who had received an unsatisfactory evaluation by their principals, or *lose* the state mentor money that the districts were already receiving. Significantly, district leaders could decide for themselves whether new teachers would also par-ticipate in the program. With the California legislation, the term *peer review* was re-placed with *peer assistance and review*,[3] presumably to more accurately (and perhaps politically) represent the components of the program. The policy also became known by its acronym, PAR, pronounced like the word *par*.

The Toledo model of PAR involved both beginning teachers and veterans. Indeed, in most districts that implemented PAR prior to California's legislation, the program began with beginning teachers as the less controversial part of the policy, and later expanded to veterans once the idea of teachers conducting teacher evaluations was established in a district. California's Assembly Bill 1X, however, was borne out of politicians' desire to address the public's concern about ineffective veteran teachers; AB 1X's focus on veteran teachers reveals its intention as accountability policy rather than induction policy. However, while not requiring it, the law allowed for the inclusion of beginning teachers in the program. As a result of this policy flexibility and varying opinions about the wisdom of PAR among educators, school districts across the state created PAR programs that looked quite different from one another. Many California districts did not include new teachers in their PAR programs, since the state law only required the program for veteran teachers who had received an unsatisfactory evaluation from their administrator. In addition, many programs did not create full-time, out-of-classroom positions for master teachers, and many did not involve the master teachers in summative evaluation. The legislation required "maximum local flexibility" for program details. The legislation did, however, require that school districts negotiate the development and implementation of their programs with local teachers unions. Union locals, in effect, were given the unusual ability to approve or disapprove their districts' PAR programs.

Given the extremely small number of veteran teachers who typically receive unsatisfactory evaluations from principals, the relatively large amount of money attached to the policy, and the enormous need to provide support to large numbers of new and often unprepared teachers, some districts took the opportunity to design PAR programs with coaches providing support to and conducting evaluations of new teachers in addition to veterans. The district presented in this book is one such district.

California Assembly Bill 1X marked the first time PAR was instituted statewide, and the first time a major district had implemented the policy in over a decade. By 2002, a state budget crisis and competing state legislation had begun to chip away significantly at California's PAR programs. I undertook the bulk of the study presented here during that window of time, in one urban district in California that I call Rosemont. It is among the most in-depth studies of a PAR program to date.

## PAR in the Rosemont Unified School District

Rosemont (a pseudonym) is an ethnically and economically diverse urban district in California with approximately 100 schools and 3,000 teachers. Although many California districts and/or teachers unions shied away from the idea of PAR and focused merely on compliance with the new legislation, key leaders in Rosemont intended to implement the new policy as fully as possible, making the district a rich site in which to study PAR in California at the time.

I selected Rosemont after an extended pilot study in the district. The site was selected based on the degree of "interruption" (Weick, 1995) occurring, by which I mean there was the potential to witness the creation of new norms for teachers' roles in leadership and evaluation. In addition, the site was chosen because it had a prior experiment with PAR, perhaps increasing the potential for meaningful implementation in the first year of the program. In other words, although all districts needed to have a PAR program in place to continue to receive state mentor funding, many districts intended to limit the program to minimum compliance— namely, something available to those teachers who received unsatisfactory evaluations (typically a very small number). By contrast, I sought out a site that was planning a more comprehensive program than that required by the law. Because of Rosemont's prior experience with PAR, key figures in the district saw the state legislation and attached funding as an opportunity to do what they previously could not afford.

One condition of conducting this research was that the identity of the district would remain confidential, in particular because discussions surrounding employment decisions are sensitive. As a result, I have intentionally left out many contextual details about the district that might be useful to a reader, but that would simply be too identifying.

PAR Coaches. The first step to really understanding PAR is to understand the role of the master or expert teachers, what I will call *PAR coaches*, sometimes referred to as consulting teachers. (Different PAR locals use different terminology for the same or similar roles and program components.) In Rosemont, PAR coaches signed on for a 3-year position out of the classroom, with 10 coaches the first year and two more added the second year. They served on teacher lines, as "teachers on special assignment," and were based out of a PAR office housed at one school. The work of the PAR coaches, however, was not based at one school. Rather, they were matched by school level and/or subject area to teachers across multiple schools. This is a defining element of PAR. In this way, one master high school English teacher might be supporting and evaluating novice English teachers across four different high schools.

Coaching activities included things such as helping with short- and long-range planning, locating curricular resources, advocating for teachers with principals, jointly observing other teachers' classrooms, and providing general emotional support. The vast majority of coaches' time, however, was focused on observing teaching and providing feedback and suggestions on instructional strategies. Coaches observed teaching in both announced and unannounced visits, more or less once every 1 to 2 weeks, with three specified "formal" observations for summative purposes during the year. Formative and summative assessments were based on a locally modified version of the California Standards for the Teaching Profession. In addition to working directly with their mentees at school sites, coaches met together all day every Friday at their PAR office to discuss their coaching and support one another's work. They also met periodically with the PAR panel, discussed below.

Participating Teachers. The teachers the Rosemont coaches supported, whether they were beginning teachers, teachers new to the district, or veterans, were called "participating teachers" (PTs). Veterans were referred to the program after receiving an unsatisfactory evaluation from their principal. It was also possible for a veteran to be referred to the program by a union building representative (and the first such referral occurred in the fourth year of the program). Once referred, the panel examined the case to ensure that the teacher was appropriate for PAR participation. Across PAR programs nationally, only teachers with clear instructional issues can receive PAR support; veteran teachers with medical, mental health, or other personal issues get bounced from the PAR panel to other district services.

PAR was not implemented districtwide in Rosemont but only in some schools. As a result, beginning teachers' participation in PAR depended upon their school placement. In the first year of the program, 28 principals volunteered to participate after having PAR explained at a principals' meeting during the prior spring. New teachers at those 28 schools were then folded into the program. From the second year on, schools were selected based on state designation as a high-need (low-performing) school.

Each coach carried a caseload of 12 to 15 PTs by contract, but the load was closer to 10 in the first year of the program, with a lead coach carrying half a caseload. In total, there were 91 participating teachers in the first year of the program across the 28 schools (88 beginning teachers and three veterans), increasing to 143 total PTs in year 2 across 33 schools (139 beginning teachers and four veterans).

PAR Panel. Although teachers evaluating other teachers through the PAR coach role is novel to many educators and may be considered the defining aspect of PAR programs, one of the most important components of PAR is the oversight panel, or what is sometimes called a governing board. These panels have different names in different school districts while maintaining the same basic structure. The districtwide joint teacher/administrator panel is typically co-chaired by the teachers union president and the director of human resources (or some other high-ranking district office administrator), and often (though not always) consists of a majority of teacher members. In California the state legislation specified panels of five teachers and four administrators, with the teachers union president considered a teacher (Villaraigosa, Strom-Martin, & Alquist, 1999). Panels hold hearings several times a year, at which coaches provide reports about PT progress. At the spring hearing, and sometimes sooner, the coaches make recommendations about the continued employment of each PT, and when necessary, the panel challenges the coaches on the evidence that they have provided to support their recommendations. A PT must meet specified quality standards within a set period of time, usually 1 year, or face removal from the classroom. This is determined by the panel based on the recommendation of the PAR coach, sometimes together with the principal, at the panel hearing. The panel's employment recommendation is then passed to the superintendent, who makes a recommendation to the school board, the ultimate arbiter of personnel decisions. In most PAR programs, new teachers spend 1 year in PAR, and then shift to evaluation by the principal. For intervention cases, once a teacher has successfully exited the program, he or she returns to traditional evaluation by the principal.

In addition, some districts—though not Rosemont at the time of this study—also make PAR available to satisfactory veteran teachers as an optional alternative evaluation. In such cases, teachers typically work with one another on a professional improvement plan or some inquiry of their choosing. Although they do not work with a coach, they might report their work to the PAR panel.

The Study. I conducted an in-depth case study (Yin, 2003) of Rosemont's implementation of PAR. The data span a 6-year period of time, beginning in 1998 before PAR was implemented, through 2004 when Rosemont was in its fourth year of the program. The vast majority of data, however, was collected during the first year of PAR implementation in the 2000–2001 school year. In that year alone, I conducted almost 70 interviews and observed over 300 hours of meetings between educators. Follow-up data collection occurred in the second and fourth years of the program. (Readers interested in detailed information about the study's design and methods for data collection and analysis should see the online appendixes, outlined in the "Available Online" chapter.)

I collected preliminary data in Rosemont a couple of years before the implementation of AB 1X, when Rosemont was experimenting with a mentoring program that incorporated many of the features of peer review. Soon after AB 1X passed, district and teachers union leaders in Rosemont approached me to document their PAR implementation efforts. I served in this capacity for a year and a half, in exchange for using the site for a dissertation study. I was given wide access to program participants and events, but in no way acted as a participant in the process during that time. Relationships established during that period allowed me to also conduct follow-up interviews and focus groups at the end of the second and fourth years of implementation.

The primary actors in the study were the district's nine members of the PAR oversight panel (teachers and administrators) and 10 PAR coaches from year 1 of implementation. In addition, three of the 10 coaches were chosen for more in-depth data collection, influenced by their demography (years of experience, gender, and ethnicity) and degree of "sensemaking" (Spillane et al., 2002; Weick, 1995) about the reform as observed in ongoing meetings. I then included PTs and principals based on their connection to the three case study coaches, as well as additional principals and PTs who might represent divergent or unrepresented viewpoints

(Miles & Huberman, 1994). The sample of 19 core teachers and administrators included three African American women, three Latina women, one Chinese American woman, six White women, and six White men.

The study relied primarily on observations, interviews, and surveys. My observations AB 1X began with the inception of the panel in the spring prior to the first year of policy implementation, and therefore included the selection of the coaches by the panel as well as a 2-day summer professional development retreat for panel members and coaches that brought them together as a group for the first time. I then attended all panel meetings and hearings (approximately monthly) and almost every coach meeting (weekly) for 1 year, which provided rich opportunities to view the implementation of the policy and how Rosemont's educators made sense of it. Panel meetings were usually 2 hours in length, while panel hearings and coach meetings typically lasted a full day. See Table 2.1 for a breakdown of observation hours.

In addition to observing meetings, I repeatedly interviewed panel members and coaches, and also interviewed 11 principals, 15 PTs, and three key district-level administrators, including the superintendent, for a total of 67 interviews in year 1. I then conducted a handful of additional interviews with key stakeholders and focus groups in years 2 and 4. See Table 2.2 for a breakdown of interviews conducted. (For the interview protocols, see the online Appendix C.)

In year 1, all panel members and coaches completed a survey. Sixteen out of 28 principals returned surveys (57%); together with interview data, 20 principals were included in the study (77%). Fifty-seven out of 91 PTs returned surveys (63%); together with interview data, 61 mentees were included in the study (67%). I also collected a survey from PTs at the end of the second year of the program, with 112 of 143 surveys returned (78%). For a breakdown of survey data collection, see Table 2.3. (For the survey instruments used, see the online Appendix D.)

Table 2.1. Observations—Number of days (total hours)

| Data Source | Fall Year −2 | Spring Year −2 | Spring Year 0[a] | Summer-Fall Year 1 | Winter Year 1 | Spring Year 1 | Total |
|---|---|---|---|---|---|---|---|
| Panel meetings | 3 (9) | 3 (13) | 3 (8.5) | 3 (6) | 1 (2) | 2 (4) | 15 (42.5) |
| Panel hearings | | | | 3 (28.5) | 2 (19) | 3 (21) | 8 (68.5) |
| Coach meetings | | | | 17 (108) | 7 (42) | 8 (48) | 32 (198) |
| Coach professional development | | | | 3 (24) | | | 3 (24) |
| TOTAL | 3 (9) | 3 (13) | 3 (8.5) | 26 (166.5) | 10 (63) | 13 (73) | 58 (333) |

[a] Year 0 is defined as the year AB 1X passed, such that "Year 1" is the first year of state legislated PAR implementation (2000–2001). A pilot program involving elements of PAR occurred prior to AB 1X, in "Year −2."

Table 2.2. Interviews conducted ($N = 50$)

| Data Source | Fall Year 1 | Winter Year 1 | Spring Year 1 | Spring Year 2 | Spring Year 4 | Total |
|---|---|---|---|---|---|---|
| Panel members ($n = 10$)[a, b] | 9 | | 9 | 2 | 5[c] | 25 |
| Coaches ($n = 11$)[d] | 10 | 3 | 8 | 2 | 4[e] | 27 |
| Principals ($n = 11$) | | 6 | 5 | | | 11 |
| Participating teachers ($n = 15$) | | | 15 | | | 15 |
| Additional district office informants ($n = 3$) | 1 | 1 | 1 | | | 3 |
| TOTAL | 20 | 10 | 38 | 4 | 9 | 81[f] |

[a] The $n$'s in this column represent the total number of interviewees in the stakeholder category, not the universe of participants in the study.

[b] The 10 panel members interviewed were the original 9, plus the new union president in Year 4.

[c] 3 of the 5 panel members were interviewed together in Year 4.

[d] The 11 coaches interviewed were the original 10, plus the new lead coach in Year 4.

[e] 3 of the 4 coaches were interviewed together in Year 4.

[f] 80 interviews were actually conducted, because one principal was also a member of the panel and is counted twice in the Spring Year 1 tally.

The Players. I will often refer to characters in Rosemont's story simply by title, such as "one coach said . . . ," mainly because there are more voices involved in the telling of this story than I can reasonably expect the reader to keep straight. Ten coaches, nine panel members, 15 participating teachers, 11 principals, and three district office officials in the first year of the program alone, plus a handful of

Table 2.3. Surveys Returned

| | Year 1 | | Year 2 | |
|---|---|---|---|---|
| | Surveys Disseminated | Surveys Returned (Response Rate) | Surveys Disseminated | Surveys Returned (Response Rate) |
| Panel members | 9 | 9 (100%) | | |
| Consulting teachers | 10 | 10 (100%) | | |
| Principals | 28 | 16 (57%) | | |
| Participating teachers | 91 | 57 (63%) | 143 | 112 (78%) |
| TOTAL | 138 | 92 | 143 | 112 |

additions in subsequent years, makes for approximately 50 personalities. I will, however, give name and shape to some central and selected Rosemont educators along the way, as summarized in Table 2.4.

The Employment Outcomes.  Of 88 beginning teachers in PAR in Rosemont's first year of implementation, 11 beginning teachers were not offered the opportunity to renew their contract for teaching duties in the district, as well as the three veteran teachers in the program that year. In all, Rosemont removed 10 to 12.5% of the beginning teachers and almost all of the veterans in PAR from classroom teaching in each of the first 4 years of the program. [4] These are stark figures compared to education's norm. Regardless of one's reaction to fairly unprecedented rates of teacher firings, there was clearly something unusual at play. Quite simply: What accounts for the phenomenon?

## CONCLUSION

The teacher evaluation program presented in this book is remarkable because district leaders—both administrators and teachers union leaders—designed a new structure to alter the shape of teacher evaluation radically in the district. Rather than leave principals to conduct teacher evaluation alone in isolation and in opposition to the teachers union, they took a more coordinated and comprehensive

Table 2.4. Highlighted Educators in Rosemont's PAR Program[a]

| Panel Administrators | Panel Teachers | Coaches | PTs | Principals |
|---|---|---|---|---|
| | Doug (union president and panel co-chair with Brian) | | | |
| | | Bob (lead coach) | | |
| Brian (an associate superintendent and panel co-chair with Doug) | | Sarah | Regina | Emily |
| | Susanna | Eva | Kim | Betty |
| | (also Susanna) | Caroline | Timothy | Nancy |

[a] The educators are connected across rows. Brian worked with Sarah in quads (explained in Chapter 4), Regina was a PT in Sarah's caseload, and Emily was Regina's principal, and so on.

approach to the evaluation of teachers. Significant shifts in organizational structure occurred to support the PAR coaches in their role as evaluators.

On the one hand, an array of PAR's design elements coalesced to generate very different evaluation outcomes. These design elements fit together in a developmental chronology (as I will synthesize in Chapter 9). First, coaches were given full-time release from classrooms to focus on assessment. They were matched with PTs by grade level and subject matter, and they spent a year collecting data about a PT's performance and working with him or her to improve. They had to present those data to members of an oversight panel who reviewed their work and supported them in their jobs as evaluators. The evaluation team—including the coach, principal, and panel members—were reasonably confident in the coach's employment recommendation due to the amount of time spent with the PT and the data amassed. The teachers union president, as co-chair of that panel with the district, was part of the process for each PT from the beginning, not an adversary at the point of a negative recommendation, when one was made. Finally, the existence of the team meant that the weight of a negative evaluation did not fall solely on any one person.

On the other hand, despite the role that each of these design elements played, it is also true that without an initial agreement between the teachers union and school district to collaborate on teacher evaluation, PAR could not come into being. For that reason, a teachers union–school district partnership is more than a piece of the design puzzle; it is in fact prerequisite for PAR.

One of the striking things about studying PAR is the predictability of people's reactions when I explain the program. With rare exception, the first response is, "Wow, how does the teachers union feel about that?" Yet anywhere that PAR existed prior to California's state legislation, it existed because a reform-minded teachers union president fought to bring it into being.

Rather than take adversarial positions—the district against the union and vice versa—superintendents and teachers union presidents need to draw on collaborative models of labor relations by design. The teachers union presidents who have initiated PAR programs over the past 2 and a half decades sought postindustrial unionism, a unionism that would move teachers unions toward defending the profession of teaching rather than individual teachers.

Peer assistance and review is one method of doing so. It is not widespread, it is certainly not without flaws and shortcomings, and it is neither easy nor inexpensive. It is not always implemented well, and it does not always yield the results presented in this book. It is, however, worth understanding in order to more fully consider the options before us as we attempt to reform our education system in a way that will yield a caring, qualified, and competent teacher for every child.

# PART II

# *Understanding How PAR Works*

## CHAPTER 3

# The Work of the PAR Coaches

## *Supporting and Assessing Classroom Teaching*

Interesting how we survived all these years [with teacher
evaluation] by saying she is a cheerful, enthusiastic teacher.
Works well with colleagues. Easy to dance to. They give her a 3.
—Coach, Rosemont Peer Assistance and Review Program

Teaching has long been considered an isolating occupation, one where individual teachers work behind closed doors with their particular group of students, and where occupational norms typically prevent teachers from "intruding" on one another's practice. Judith Warren Little (1988) noted over 20 years ago that "traditional authority relations in schools and districts, as well as conventional teacher evaluation procedures, communicate a view of teaching as an individual enterprise" (p. 84)—and little has changed since. As a result, teachers often lack a means for discussing their practice with their peers, or an avenue for the critical reflection necessary for professional growth. In addition, teachers in high-poverty schools report even lower collegial interaction with their peers (Shields et al., 1999).

Limited collegial interaction about teaching practice limits the degree to which teachers can systematically get better at what they do. By contrast, as introduced in Chapter 1, scholars have documented the professional development benefits of models that view teacher learning as an ongoing reflective process intimately tied to their day-to-day practice, involving dialogue with their peers, centered on student work, and aligned to standards (e.g., Cochran-Smith & Lytle, 1999; Darling-Hammond & McLaughlin, 1995; Lieberman & Miller, 1991; Little, 1982; Rodgers, 2002).

PAR embeds professional development in the ongoing work of classroom teachers, putting them in dialogue with a more skillful peer around standards of teaching practice. By placing a mentor in PTs' classrooms on a frequent basis, PAR alters the historic isolation of teaching. Although certainly not unique to PAR, the ongoing nature of PT-coach interaction becomes a critical piece in the quality of participating teachers' evaluations, because increasing the publicness of practice is likely to increase the amount of information on which evaluations are based. After embedding professional development in the ongoing work of teachers, PAR then ties teachers' summative assessment to this work and the data it generated.

Most centrally, PAR rests on the work of the coaches as they support and evaluate the participating teachers. In this chapter, I look closely at the day-to-day work of the coaches with the PTs. Whether engaged in formative or summative assessment, the coaches' work is fundamentally about diagnosing teaching performance to help teachers improve and make tough decisions if they do not. The emphasis in this chapter is mainly on the formative aspects of teacher evaluation through PAR, the foundation that sets up the summative assessment at the heart of subsequent chapters.

## LOGISTICS

In Rosemont's first year of PAR, as introduced in Chapter 2, 10 coaches supported 91 PTs (88 beginning teachers and three veterans), with each coach carrying a caseload of about 10 PTs. The contract specified 12 to 15, but the panel reduced the amount in the first year in anticipation of the time that the coaches would need to spend on program development, discussed below. One of the 10 coaches (Bob) served as lead coach, and was responsible for program coordination and serving as liaison between the coaches and the panel. As such, he carried half a caseload.

The composition of the caseloads was complicated by Rosemont's partial implementation of the program—intended as temporary for program ramp-up, but which remained when funding for PAR from the state later dried up (discussed in Chapter 10). The coaches served 28 schools in year 1, but faced with far more new teachers than they could support, choices needed to be made about which teachers to include, and difficult issues arose. For starters, regardless of the partial implementation, they needed to define who qualified as a new teacher. As Bob said at one point in September to the rest of the coaches, "I made a strong case with the panel yesterday that defining a new teacher is not as easy as it sounds."[1]

Given agreement around who qualified for PAR at a school, the choice then had to be made about which of these teachers to select for participation, and at times it was not clear whether this choice was the coach's or the principal's to make. There were cases, for example, of principals wanting uncredentialed teachers who had been teaching in the district for many years to participate in order to get needed support, although there was agreement that such a teacher did not count as "new" regardless of credential status. At a time when coaches were trying to please principals and endear them to PAR, it was sometimes difficult for the coaches to know how to negotiate the situation.

Finally, the only partial inclusion of new teachers opened the door to complaints from PTs, when some teachers felt they would prefer not to have the on-going observation and assessment of PAR—perceived as pressure—and their friend down the hall was not in the program. Principals usually backed the coach and the PAR program, but there were cases of principals siding with a PT. All in all, the partial implementation served as an ongoing source of frustration to the coaches.

California employed a large number of uncredentialed teachers circa 2000 due to a myriad of factors, including the class-size reduction policy of the 1990s, increasing student enrollments, and retirements. In addition, Rosemont's human resources department was in a state of disarray at the time PAR was implemented. As a result of these issues, many of the 88 beginning teachers lacked a teaching credential. By the second year of the program onward, after a new director of human resources joined the district, many fewer uncredentialed teachers were hired. Looking back on the first year of the program from its fourth year, the teachers union president noted that it was never his intent for the program to be a filter for emergency credentialed teachers. Nonetheless, it ended up being that to some degree, because had they not been absorbed into the PAR program, he believed the chances were high that they would not have been looked at carefully by principals.

In year 2, Rosemont added two coaches, and the number of PTs increased to 143 (139 beginning teachers and four veterans). By year 3, the expansion continued to more than 200 PTs. The gradual expansion was intentional. Rather than hire a batch of coaches for 3 years and then have all of them leave simultaneously, the union president explained that they would expand the program in stages so that the coaches subsequently returned to the classroom in waves each year. In this way, the institutional knowledge about the program would not be lost.

Just prior to the start of the PAR program, the panel and coaches spent several days together on retreat away from the school district. In addition to a certain amount of getting-to-know-you for 19 people who had not necessarily worked together before, the focus of the retreat was professional development in coaching and assessment. A highly regarded independent coaching organization provided training in cognitive coaching, a reflective approach that relies on the coach asking questions of the person being coached. Later, the coaches themselves determined this method to be insufficient for their needs, given the large number of uncredentialed and otherwise brand-new teachers in their caseloads. In the middle of the year, they brought an additional trainer to a series of their ongoing "Friday meetings."

Coaches met as a group all day every Friday, and were largely able to decide for themselves how to use this time. Friday time was regularly scheduled to examine individual PT cases, which would allow the coaches to support one another in their coaching and assessment work. In reality, however, the coaches rarely spent as much time as they wanted or intended on cases. In the first year of the program in particular, much of the Friday meeting time was consumed by program development needs. They spent a lot of time at the outset of the year introducing PAR to principals, being public relations agents for the program, and gaining actual access to schools and classrooms (despite their supposed official access). Support for navigating the politics of this process, and their new roles, ate up a lot of time at Friday meetings. They spent a lot of Friday time at the outset figuring out their caseloads, which proved more complicated than anyone imagined given the partial implementation of the program and that not all new teachers at a school could be in PAR—so the coaches, together with principals, had to make decisions about whom to include. Once these most immediate issues were resolved, the coaches then spent a lot of Friday time developing the standards-based formative and summative assessment paperwork. All of this is to say, in short, that the Friday meetings provided the coaches with valuable time for professional development, but nowhere nearly as much time as some of them would have liked was actually spent on developing their skills as coaches, especially at the beginning. It is worth noting that the coaches also formed pairs of critical friends, and occasionally met with their partner to discuss their PT cases for extra support, or visited a PT's classroom together for a second pair of eyes.

The descriptive statistics for survey items addressing perceived effectiveness of PAR in Rosemont, as reported on the year 1 surveys, can be found in the online Appendix E. Panel members, coaches, and principals are presented together there and throughout the book, as there were no statistically significant differences between these groups in their responses to these items. Overall, panel members, coaches, and principals reported more of a strongly positive effect from PAR than did the 57 of 91 PTs returning surveys. PTs' responses were both less positive on surveys and of a wider range (larger standard deviation), although PTs interviewed tended to be quite positive about the program.

## THE CRITICAL ROLE OF TIME

If an award were given for the occupational group with the largest contrast between the size and importance of the task asked of them and the time in which they have to do it, school principals would have a very good shot of winning. All those who are intimately familiar with the workings of schools know that principals (even those with the best of intentions and maybe even the skills to be strong instructional leaders) invariably get bogged down in the bus schedule, the budget due last week to the district office, the parent justifiably upset over the way a teacher or student treated his or her child, the students caught fighting in the hall, the students who cannot be caught fighting in the hall because they are not even at school, and the fact that Johnny or Tariq or Miguel just managed to pull the water fountain off the wall. Larry Cuban (1988) documented the pull between leadership and the managerial imperative years ago. The situation has arguably only grown worse. Principals are phenomenally overwhelmed by the demands and expectations currently placed upon them (Copland, 2001; Grubb & Flessa, 2006), with little time for instructional leadership precisely at a time when the focus on accountability for instructional results is at its highest.

## Principals Are Overwhelmed

As I interviewed principals involved with the PAR program in Rosemont, they invariably drew contrasts between teacher evaluation as they typically conducted it and what they were seeing with PAR. Their responses make the issue of time our jumping-off point, because it is the precondition, the initial building block on which any effort to improve instructional quality rests. Principals are limited in the attention they can bring to teacher evaluation. They are often unable to find the time to thoroughly complete and document them, as evaluations are only one of an endless myriad of responsibilities (Darling-Hammond, 1984; Kelly, 1998; Painter, 2000). Noted one principal, "This is just the worst it's ever been in terms of my level of work. You feel so inadequate. You feel like, God, how come I can't do all this?! . . . I don't know of anybody that really [does it well]."

Principals admitted that they cut corners with their evaluations, by necessity, and described the "wiggle room" or need to be "creative"—typically doing fewer than desired or even required on teachers perceived to be performing acceptably. As one principal commented:

> We have a thing in our contract where, [for] a teacher who has outstanding
> or satisfactory evaluations, the principal can agree to just sign off, that
> that's going to be it for evaluation for this year. So that basically is saying
> you're fine the way you were two years ago when you were evaluated. Well,
> I do too many of those and it bothers me a lot. . . .

Another principal noted simply, "The current evaluation process really is a sham; it's a joke."

Many principals identified their need to be in classrooms and know what is going on across the school, but describe merely "popping" their heads in and out. Or, as one principal admitted, some see teachers based upon the whims of geography: "It probably depends how close they are to my office, too. Things as dumb as that even, whether they're on my trip. Like I'm going to go to the cafeteria in a few minutes and if they're on the way up, I'll probably see them more often than if they're over in the corner somewhere."

The lack of time for adequate (let alone high-quality) teacher evaluation has clear implications for teaching and learning. Noted one teacher on the panel:

> I was in a situation where I worked with a team member who was very
> unhealthy for the kids, and needed to be out of the classroom. [Other

teachers and I] got to a point where we went to the principal and we said, "You know this person is unsatisfactory. You know the kids aren't learning stuff. What's going on? Why didn't you give him an unsatisfactory [evaluation]?" He said, "I missed the deadline. I should have caught that. I'm just too busy." Those are the kinds of excuses we got.

Principals, coaches, and panel members agreed that with the traditional evaluation process in Rosemont, principals' lack of time allowed teachers who were not meeting standards to slip through the cracks. One principal explained, "[With traditional teacher evaluation], someone allowed me, not correctly, but allowed me to say you pick your battles and to be honest, you know, it's phenomenally hard to get rid of somebody. So I would say, 'Do I want to take the time to [get rid of them], knowing that I've also got this, I've got that, etc.' So you say, 'No.'"

## Coaches Are Given Time

In Rosemont's PAR program, because coaches were released full-time from teaching responsibilities to focus on their PT caseloads, there was a sharp contrast from existing teacher evaluation practices.

All coaches were expected to visit their PTs an average of one time per week, and to make some unannounced visits. In addition, they were to conduct three formal observation cycles during the year for summative assessment purposes, presenting one at each panel hearing (discussed in depth in Chapter 4). PTs did report meeting with their coaches on average once per week, especially at the start of the school year, but this ranged from "at least once a week" to once every 2 to 3 weeks, as coach visits to PTs' classrooms typically became less frequent for more effective PTs as the year progressed. Some coaches preferred to come by informally and unannounced, while others had a set time to visit every week. Noted one PT:

> On Tuesday, we had a pretty routine schedule, which made it a lot nicer. I knew she was coming during 2nd and 3rd period every Tuesday, so I could count on that, I could make questions ahead of time that I knew I was going to want to ask. I'd teach during 2nd. So, she would typically observe during that time, and almost every time, she would give me written feedback on things that looked good and ideas for improvement. And then, 3rd period's my prep, so we could talk then. That's two 50-minute periods, so she would probably spend close to an hour and a half in there.

A second PT echoed the sentiment:

> I think it's been a huge amount of support; it really helps having someone that can do that full-time. [My coach] would drop in unannounced at least

once a week for an hour to observe. And then we met formally once a week for an hour to talk. So [she was here] 2 to 3 hours a week at least. I think that's why I was so excited about the PAR program, because I really love the fact that you got weekly meetings with the coach and all that time that the principal doesn't have. It's really a great resource for a new teacher.

Coaches, too, described the freedom that their schedule allowed and their ability to spend large chunks of time with individual teachers.

PTs reported that coaches made their ongoing accessibility clear at the beginning of the year, provided email addresses and cell phone numbers, and could be reached as needed. The structure of coaches' full-time release allowed them to be on call to meet PT needs as they arose. Noted one coach, "There were a number of times where teachers called me on just specific little issues, whether it was a parent issue, a child abuse issue, an issue having to do with their principals, just little things, how-tos, that were very simple to solve, but having that relationship was important."

The regular and relatively large chunks of time that coaches were able to spend in PTs' classrooms gave them familiarity with students and the particulars of day-to-day operations. Coaches' full-time release from classroom duties allowed them to engage in support activities that were simply not possible to other support providers with their own classrooms—activities such as regular observations during class time, whole days spent together working on planning or observing other teachers, and going with PTs to educational conferences. Coaches' time allowed a high level of involvement in the details of PTs' day-to-day lives that principals could not match as they were busy running schools. A principal contrasted what she could provide to beginning teachers with what the coach provided:

> Before PAR started I had Friday meetings with my new teachers and they would go forever, because they'd have a million questions and I would answer them and I would write down things that they needed and I would try to support them. But I can't model a lesson in every one of their classrooms and I can't do the kinds of things that a PAR coach can do because I'm running the whole school. . . .

She then highlighted the level of coach involvement: "Here you have a colleague sitting across from you. . . . 'Let's do this. I'll help you set it up. Let's give you a release date. You and I can work together, set up these literacy centers. Here are the materials you can use and I'll even model for you the first time.' Who could beat that? That's really awesome. That [new teacher] isn't in the lion's den all by themselves, you know?"

The PTs recognized the difference between what their coach versus their principal could give them. Two of the 15 PTs interviewed had had negative experiences with their principals, and were therefore especially grateful to be involved with PAR.

The majority of PTs, however, regarded their principals with respect for their seemingly insurmountable jobs, and simply viewed the PAR program as a logical way for them to get desperately needed support. One PT made this compassionate contrast:

> My coach is a really good listener. I think more than my principal, my coach is a deeper more thoughtful listener. She is doing something very specific for me, where my principal is doing a million things for everybody. And he always says, "Whenever you want to come in, the door is always open, come in and talk to me." But you do get the feeling like "Hey, I'm really busy here, can we get this over with?" If my coach were principal it might be the same story. My principal wants to give me his attention, he's trying, I'm not going to say he's a total jerk who just sits there and says I don't have any time for you. I think he really wants to give his time. He's trying to do everything, but no one can do everything.

Everyone involved agreed that the structure of the PAR program, giving coaches full-time release from the classroom, allowed for a level of support to teachers that other support providers, including principals, simply could not give. In addition, all principals interviewed agreed that PAR eased the immense pressure they faced in some way.[2] Principals reported being able to relax a bit about their new teachers with the implementation of PAR, knowing the teachers were getting the consistent support and assessment they needed.

Adequately supporting teachers to teach well is intimately dependent upon the investment of sufficient time. A greater investment of time does not necessarily guarantee high-quality guidance, effective assessment, or a trusting mentor-mentee relationship, but it may well be a necessary precursor.

## FORMATIVE AND SUMMATIVE ASSESSMENT WITH PAR

Teacher evaluation has generally been defined as a mechanism for appraisal in order to determine fitness for employment rather than a means for improving performance; the processes of formative and summative assessment are typically separated. Summative assessment occurs as a performance review, and formative assessment for professional growth may or may not occur, depending on the setting. Where both occur, they are channeled through different leaders: An administrator is responsible for the summative review, while any number of support providers might be involved in professional development.

### Principals Lack Data

One key result of this traditional separation of formative and summative assessment is that very often administrators conducting formal reviews are not privy to the knowledge and perspective of these support providers. Many authors, typically from within the field of instructional supervision, have argued that formative and summative assessment are incompatible; they have raised concerns about the same person acting as both support provider and formal evaluator, or even communication between people fulfilling these different roles (e.g., Costa & Garmston, 1994; Nolan, 1997; Popham, 1988).

The dilemma is that principals' summative evaluations are, therefore, often based on very little data, limited to infrequent formal classroom observations that are almost always announced and may be quite short in duration. As introduced in Chapter 1, several issues compound the problem. Principals often lack specific content-area or grade-level expertise matched to their evaluatee, and they are often not well trained to conduct the evaluations. Principals often use unclear or unstated performance criteria, and the criteria rarely reflect national or state curriculum or performance standards of best practice. Due in part to these issues, educators have complained that teacher evaluation is uneducative for teachers (Hunter, 1988; Loup, Garland, Ellett, & Rugutt, 1996; Toch & Rothman, 2008; Weisberg et al., 2009; Wise et al., 1984). As the coach in the epigraph wryly quipped, "They give her a 3." For those unfamiliar with the hotly contested Olympic sports of ice skating and gymnastics, it is rarely clear how the judge arrived at the 3, nor whether the judge's country of origin has biased her assessment of the athlete. Similarly, teacher evaluation has historically been a foggy enterprise. At best, teacher evaluations are rarely focused on substantive development; at worst, they are meaningless. Noted one principal:

> So I come in and it's literally a Polaroid shot in time. I'm there for 50 minutes and I take my copious notes and stuff and I go back and now I meet with you and there's a form and it sort of says what were the barriers? What kept you from doing your lesson? Then what were some of the things that I saw? It's basically one way. It's sort of saying you're either doing an outstanding job or you're not cutting it and I'm giving you an A, B, C, highly satisfactory, blah, blah, blah, and tough luck.

Coaches concurred, drawing on their own experiences of being evaluated, and emphasizing the degree to which those evaluations did not contribute to their professional learning. One coach described evaluation as she had experienced it:

> Most of my conversations with my administrator when she gave me my evaluations were like "this is all the great stuff you did." It wasn't a reflective conversation. It was just her presenting her summative of me. I went into her office when I wanted to have a reflective conversation and brought up a topic, but it wasn't [ongoing].

With this system, teacher evaluation is neither about teacher learning and instructional improvement on the one hand, nor about effective quality control on the other. Rather, it is merely the proverbial hoop through which to jump for teachers, and one task among many for principals to check off their very long to-do lists.

## Coaches Engage in Ongoing Assessment

PAR presented a very different opportunity. As a result of coaches' full-time release, they could focus on PT support and formative assessment, and then base their summative assessments on their ongoing work with PTs throughout the year. The distinction between formative and summative assessment was sometimes confused by those not closely involved with PAR, especially at the outset. While the PAR coaches more often emphasized the support aspect of their role, they were not always seen by other educators in that light, as everyone tried to make sense of the new model of teacher assessment. One coach, Eva, reported with chagrin on one of her first experiences at a school as a PAR coach:

> I met with the head of the math and science department [of the school] and my PTs [from that school]. The department head says, "And here's Eva, she's your PAR person. I'll support you, she's going to evaluate you." And I said, "Well, not just evaluate, I'm also here to support you." I don't want to just be known as an evaluator!"

Coaches' ongoing support to and assessment of PTs ultimately gave coaches an intimate knowledge of PTs' teaching that differed markedly from the notorious "dog-and-pony" show of most teacher evaluation systems.

By design, PAR provided support to PTs through:

1. matching PTs to coaches by grade and subject matter wherever possible,
2. building trust and rapport with the PTs,
3. providing PTs with ongoing, individualized instructional feedback, and
4. grounding assessments in performance standards for teaching.

Grade and Subject Matching.   Wherever possible, PAR coaches were paired with PTs by grade and subject matter. This is simply not possible with traditional teacher evaluation, as it would be rare for one principal to have similar curricular or subject matter expertise as all of the teachers in his or her site. For several PTs, this matching was critical to their ability to work meaningfully with their coaches. Noted one, "The difference between my principal and [my PAR coach] is that my coach has experience in chemistry, and just in sciences in general, he was able to bring materials and suggestions to the class. The principal doesn't have that experience, her area isn't in sciences." One principal commented, "I think if somebody is teaching sixth-grade language arts and social studies, having another person who has experience in sixth-grade language arts and social studies is better than somebody, maybe an administrator who has a biology background, or someone who taught high school, just because there's so much that's distinct in each grade and each subject." This issue becomes especially severe at the secondary level, where department heads often become crucial intermediaries for providing support. It would prove difficult, however, for a department head with his or her own albeit-reduced teaching load to provide the same amount of support as a full-time-released PAR coach.

There were a few PTs who complained about the lack of a subject match with their coaches. These PTs either taught a subject for which there was no match (the half-time Japanese language teacher), taught special education (which the program was not up to speed to support until year 2), or were one of the rare cases matched to a coach by school site instead of subject matter.

Building Trust and Rapport. Most coaches felt that supporting PTs' day-to-day needs, especially at the beginning, helped develop rapport and build trust. While strong mentor programs often focus on moving mentor-mentee interaction beyond emotional support to substantive dialogue about teaching and learning, the reality remains that new teachers often do need emotional support (Gold, 1996). For coaches, part of building relationships and earning the trust of PTs was dependent upon demonstrating that they were there to support the PT, not be a burden. For some PTs, the trust needed to speak openly about teaching and learning was indeed developed by first knowing that the coach was there to help. Noted one PT: "I think one benefit is just knowing that there is someone out there [who] is on your side, who you can go to to talk things through, to problem-solve things."

One of the ways that PAR coaches met PTs' immediate needs was through providing resources—from basic supplies to release time from teaching for professional development. Beginning teachers are notoriously low on classroom materials, and are often unaware of what few resources may be available to them. Coaches were able to help advocate to get PTs' rooms in order. One PT noted, "The coach and I worked a lot on my room environment. I just didn't realize when I started that I could have [furniture and boards] changed. . . . The principal was very supportive of getting those changes made, but the PAR coach helped advocate for those changes." Coaches also focused heavily on matching PTs with needed curricular materials. One PT with experience teaching English but assigned to teach core English/social studies classes was able to utilize her coach for help with social studies:

> As much as there are other really friendly social studies teachers in this
> school, we are all in completely different parts of the curriculum and we
> have completely different teaching styles. Some are very book oriented, I'm
> a lot more project oriented. Maybe I would have figured it out, but all year

> I used [the binders of curriculum that my coach] brought to me. [Without her help], it would have been really hard not to go just straight from the textbook. . . . They're horrible books and I don't even have enough for all my kids.

A second, more experienced PT commented on the personal connection that served as a welcome into the school district:

> In the beginning, since I had some [teaching] experience, it was kind of like, I don't have to be [exaggerated sigh] coached. But, it is good, because this curriculum is different. . . . So, it's nice to have someone who comes in and kind of touches base with you and makes you feel connected and supported in the district as a new teacher.

A third PT commented more generally, "Seeing [my coach's] face helps my stress level. When I see her, I feel better."

Finally, coaches connected PTs to human resources both within and outside the district. For example, coaches often helped uncredentialed PTs through the maze of necessary coursework and testing, although the district subsequently hired someone specifically to fill that need. One coach summarized by saying, "I think we're like earthworms . . . kind of turning the soil over a little bit, connecting teachers with each other."

It is worth noting here that, in contrast to the traditional argument that formative and summative assessment should not be combined or a loss of mentee trust will result, linking the two did not appear to have a deleterious effect for PTs and PAR coaches in Rosemont. This point, worthy of deeper discussion, is the focus of Chapter 6.

Ongoing, Individualized Support and Instructional Feedback. In addition to building trust and rapport, however, the heart of the PAR program was ongoing feedback to PTs about how to teach. Ninety-four percent of all interviewees (PTs, coaches, panel members, and principals) cited the feedback and suggestions on instructional strategies given by coaches to PTs, making it the single most frequently named element of PAR in the research. The foundation of coach support to PTs rested on regular classroom observations. The support that coaches provided stemmed from this base of knowledge about the participating teacher, the teacher's skill level, and the classes being taught.

Rather than proscribe the shape of the coaches' work with PTs, the panel gave coaches the flexibility to diagnose their PTs' needs and provide support that was highly relevant. The coaches felt the imperative to honor the difficulty of being a teacher—in particular, a first-year teacher—and not waste PTs' time. One coach contrasted California's Beginning Teacher Support and Assessment (BTSA) program, which walks PTs through pre-set proscribed topics or "events" at proscribed times in the year, with PAR:

> I was a BTSA coach already. It's not that effective. It's better than nothing, you're in there [a few times] a year like a principal and you're helping them do stuff, but at the time the teacher's kind of going "Yeah, but I'm drowning over here," and you're saying, "Look at this [pre-determined teaching] domain."

A second coach concurred:

> I don't believe [BTSA mentors] get to figure out how they'd best serve their clients, the schools and the teachers that they're working with, but they're told what they have to do. And I don't think that ever works very well. I think you telling me what you think I could best do [is very different than], "Go to the school, talk to the teachers, find out what their needs are and come back and tell me." Which is what I think we're doing.

The individualization allowed PTs to get instructional support that they were developmentally ready to implement. The PTs noted that the high level of coach knowledge about their classrooms allowed coaches to give them tailor-made support, things such as bringing curricular materials that fit right in with a unit the PT was planning, being able to talk specifically about struggles with certain students, or recognizing when the PT was getting burned out and needed a break. This created an environment of individualized support that coaches often compared to a good teacher's ability to individualize instruction for students.

The content of coaches' instructional support therefore varied from PT to PT, as regular observations allowed coaches to identify the skills needed by PTs and provide the necessary support. Tables 3.1 and 3.2 provide tallies of the support provided to PTs by coaches, as reported in interviews.

Many PTs, for example, were in need of basic lesson-planning skills, and coaches filled this knowledge gap for PTs who did not have a teaching credential—and for some who did. Many coaches also focused on long-range planning with PTs. One PT highlighted a release day taken for planning: "We spent the day going over lesson plans and sort of planning out about a month's worth of work. And it was really, really positive. Having that day, it was just invaluable. When that day was done, I had a clear picture, a crispy clear picture, of what was going to happen in my classroom for the next month." Some coaches then modeled lessons with classes of students, with the PT observing. One PT noted, "She did some modeling for me of a few lessons. . . . We're not usually given time to see anyone else, to either improve your practice or inform your own practice. So, that observation, that was really critical." (Other coaches felt that without the necessary relationship with

Table 3.1. Types of Support Provided to PTs by Coaches: Number of
Mentions, by Job Type, Year 1 (N = 42)[a]

| | PTs (n = 15) | Consulting Teachers (n = 8)[b] | Principals (n = 10) | Panel Members (n = 9) | Total |
|---|---|---|---|---|---|
| Availability/ Amount of Time | 7 | 3 | 8 | 0 | 18 |
| Resources | 13 | 10 | 8 | 0 | 31 |
| Instruction | 24 | 10 | 10 | 5 | 49 |
| Curriculum | 5 | 4 | 1 | 1 | 11 |
| Relationships | 13 | 10 | 4 | 0 | 27 |

[a] Tables 3.1 and 3.2 show the types of coach support mentioned by different stakeholders in the course of semi-structured interviews. The tallies show the number of mentions (Table 3.1) and the percent of people mentioning (Table 3.2) a given form of support. They do not include multiple mentions by the same respondents for a given subcategory; number of mentions surpasses number of people in some cells in Table 3.1 only because they are totals from subcategories (listed in Table 3.2). Counts are conservative and only show specific references to the given form of support. In some cases, one comment can count for two or more categories (e.g., 'My coach talked to my principal about getting me more textbooks" would be "advocate with principal" and "materials/room"). Note that tallies for panel members are quite sparse. This is due to a lack of detail in panel member responses; rather than citing specific forms of support, they were more likely to give a holistic response about the general benefits of PAR support. Interestingly, where detailed responses were given, they were given entirely by teachers on the panel. It must be noted, however, that although panel members were given the opportunity to provide examples of how PAR affected teaching practice, they were not working directly with PTs like coaches, nor were they in school buildings witnessing coaches work with PTs like principals. For this or other reasons, their ability to speak to the issue of support concretely was far lower than these other stakeholder groups.

[b] Eight rather than 10 coaches are listed, as two coaches did not participate in spring interviews.

all the kids, modeling could backfire, and indeed, PAR programs in different school districts take different positions on the efficacy of modeling lessons.)

Two PTs did report feeling that their coaches' requests for lesson plans were too rigorous. Note that the expectations for lesson plans were not set programmatically but were determined by the coaches based on the individual PT cases. The coaches did work together to calibrate their expectations, and the panel served as a clearinghouse for examining the coaches' work with PTs.

One key factor that determined the type of support coaches provided (or perhaps, in some cases, should have determined but did not) was the prior experience of the PT, including credential status. Noted one coach: "With some of my teachers I felt much more like a peer coach and with some of my teachers I felt more like that it wasn't a peer situation, that they really wanted some leadership from me." As mentioned at the outset of the chapter, the coaches found limita-

Table 3.2. Types of Support Provided to PTs by Coaches: Percentage of People Mentioning Category Once or More, by Job Type, Year 1 (N = 42)

| | PTs (n = 15) | Coaches (n = 8) | Principals (n = 10) | Panel Members (n = 9) | Percentage of total |
|---|---|---|---|---|---|
| *Availability/Amount of Time* | 47% | 38% | 80% | 0% | 18% |
| *Resources* | | | | | |
| Materials/room | 33% | 50% | 30% | 0% | 67% |
| Release days to observe other teachers | 7% | 0% | 10% | 0% | 11% |
| Release days for planning, other work with coach | 13% | 13% | 10% | 0% | 22% |
| Resources (workshops, connecting to others in district) | 7% | 25% | 30% | 0% | 33% |
| Credential process | 7% | 0% | 0% | 0% | 6% |
| Advocate with principal | 13% | 20% | 0% | 0% | 22% |
| Advocate with district | 7% | 13% | 0% | 0% | 11% |
| *Instruction* | | | | | |
| Observation | 53% | 38% | 20% | 0% | 72% |
| Lesson planning | 13% | 0% | 10% | 13% | 22% |
| Feedback and suggestions on instructional strategies | 40% | 63% | 40% | 25% | 94% |
| Standards | 13% | 0% | 10% | 25% | 28% |
| Organization/systems | 7% | 0% | 10% | 0% | 11% |
| Modeling (lessons, interaction with students) | 33% | 25% | 10% | 0% | 44% |
| *Curriculum* | | | | | |
| Long-range planning | 7% | 13% | 0% | 13% | 17% |
| Curriculum-specific support through grade and subject matching | 27% | 38% | 10% | 0% | 44% |
| *Relationships* | | | | | |
| Familiarity with class (students, curriculum) | 13% | 0% | 0% | 0% | 11% |
| Emotional support/dealing with stress | 13% | 25% | 10% | 0% | 28% |
| Flexibility | 20% | 38% | 0% | 0% | 33% |
| Open and honest communication/relationship | 20% | 38% | 20% | 0% | 44% |
| PT-specific assistance | 7% | 25% | 0% | 0% | 17% |
| Introduction to district (feel connected) | 13% | 0% | 10% | 0% | 17% |

tions to relying on their training in cognitive coaching with teachers having little or no prior teaching knowledge. This credentialed teacher, for example, wanted more directive support from her coach:

> I felt like when I talked to my coach about [an instructional struggle early in the year] she was trying to lead me through it and lead me to a conclusion. But I was in a position where I was kind of at a loss. At the end of the meeting I said, "Well, I still don't know what I'm doing." And that was frustrating for me because I wanted someone to just tell me what to do instead of try to pull it out of me, because I was like, "I don't know!" That was hard.

One coach described this dynamic and her support to a very novice uncredentialed teacher:

> There were times when people were so new at something, like [one PT] for instance, where he just needed me to say, "Do this, this, and this." Most recently, we were talking about the teaching of reading. I was able to say, "Look, this is what primary reading looks like, you need to accomplish these things and you usually do them in this mix. Now we have to think about how we are going to adapt that for grade eight." And I went and got him materials, I got ideas on adaptations, and I was able to go back in and just present it to him. "*Here! This is what we're going to do.*" And he said, "Oh, this is really helpful," because this is a cookbook, this is a recipe for how I do this thing that I just don't know how to do.

In contrast, this PT with prior teaching experience and a credential described a release day with her coach that involved higher-level development:

> We went over how to organize literacy centers, and how to organize groups. We sat down and kind of literally wrote out a schedule. I needed someone to help me get started with doing the small reading groups and the rotations, because I was really nervous about what are the other kids going to be doing at their desks while I have these kids up here [with me]? I was real scared, I think, to do that. So, her sitting down with me made a big difference. We got that started. I just needed someone to push me through it, I guess.

Some PTs needed to see that the coach could provide assistance tailored to the PT's preferred style of teaching, not impose a certain teaching paradigm upon them. Strong and weaker PTs alike praised their coaches' abilities to distinguish between "style and content." Noted one strong PT: "I specifically liked that he didn't push his own agenda. He came in with ideas, but when he saw that I had my own ideas, he went with it. He was very flexible in that way." A less accomplished PT felt the same way: "There would be times when she would say, 'That's not necessarily the way I would do it, but that's okay, because I recognize that as a style thing,' and she [would] then be able to refocus back on the content of what was going on, what were my learning objectives, that sort of thing." Ultimately, the individualized structure of the program allowed coaches to be creative with their support as necessary, drawing on their mastery as teachers.

Not all PTs were equally impressed by coaches' mentoring range; one complained that his coach was overly focused on skills and content while he preferenced critical thinking. He was a "red flag" case, the Rosemont vernacular for a PT who is potentially not meeting standards, which likely fueled his coaches' approach. In addition, individualized support meant that to some degree, coaches could not necessarily be clear with PTs about the specifics of their support at the outset. For some PTs, "individualized" meant unstructured, and they found that frustrating.

Finally, a few experienced PTs expressed resentment at being in the program at all. One strong teacher with 3 years of prior teaching experience wanted a more reflective level of coaching, and saw very little benefit to PAR participation. Unlike those who praised PAR's individualized structure, this PT felt her support was not individualized enough:

> I think the experience was very much akin to what a student must feel like in a first-year teacher's classroom. While my coach attempted to tailor her services to meet my needs, she very often would show up at meetings with this sort of a one-size-fits-all package . . . very much like a new teacher would create curriculum that was one-size-fits-all for the class. Over the course of the year I've had a few productive conversations with her. But those were in many ways almost incidental and certainly in my mind would not have been worth required weekly meetings.

Prior teaching experience, rather than the mere possession of a credential, may be a significant factor in PTs' reactions to PAR. Strong PTs who had a credential but no prior teaching experience tended to be positive about their involvement in PAR, or in fact wished they had received more attention.

Clearly, the instructional support provided by the coaches was not without criticism, as displayed in Table 3.3. The criticism, however, was far less frequent than the praise, and overall, PTs respected the coaches and were grateful for the support.

One particular case of a coach's efforts to improve a PT's instruction exemplifies the flexibility and creativity that coaches—not all, but some—drew on. Eva, a coach whom I will highlight in Chapter 5, described this challenging PT case:

> I had this one guy who was sort of uncomfortable with me being in the room, and totally very controlled. He told me straight out, "I can out-think

Table 3.3. Criticisms of Consulting Teacher Support: Number (Percentage) of
PTs Mentioning, Year 1 (*N* = 15)

|                                                | PTs       |
| ---------------------------------------------- | --------- |
| Poor Use of Time                               |           |
| Time for meetings                              | 2 (13%)   |
| Paperwork                                      | 1 (7%)    |
| Extraneous (have other support)                | 1 (7%)    |
| Not Meeting Needs                              |           |
| Not matched by content/need                    | 3 (20%)   |
| Too reflective (want more directive)           | 1 (7%)    |
| Too "one size fits all" (want more reflective) | 1 (7%)    |
| Not familiar with student population           | 1 (7%)    |
| Too demanding                                  | 2 (13%)   |

> you. I know what you are going to say to me." And I just went okay, this
> guy, I have to have a different approach. My plan for him, I knew what he
> needed, his class was orderly, very controlling like he is, he needs to feel in
> control. But he doesn't have a lot of student interaction, he needed some
> growth in a lot of areas that I thought I could help him with.

Eva was able to recognize that she couldn't gain his trust because his defenses were
up. Instead, she identified a way he could grow without feeling that she was telling
him what to do. She continued:

> I asked him [whether he] would like to be a lead coach for [a professional
> development program] that was totally interactive, and he got paid a
> thousand dollars. Well he just whooped and jumped, "Yes, wonderful." I
> thought well, he does have content knowledge, but he doesn't know how to
> get the students to interact. It's very dry in there. So basically he went, and
> he was so thrilled because it put him in a leadership position, and it forced
> him to be with other people who thought [about interactive instruction],
> and of course he's going to have to pick up what they're doing, he's getting
> paid for it. . . . His performance changed, the kids loved it. So it had to
> come through him. He had no idea, but I orchestrated that. Without
> needing to have my ego [in it], oh, I changed you.

Eva understood her job as affecting students through improving their teacher's teaching, and felt a duty to fit her support to whatever way he could receive it. She continued:

Of course we're focused on the child, of course, but right now my job is to work with that teacher. [It's not] "I'm trying to help you, but don't you mess with me, if you don't get this real quick, you know, we're thinking about that child. . . . " To impact the children, my goal was really looking at him. I could have just said, well, he's not [being interactive], the children are not going to get that, so bye! To me in a way, you didn't really finish the job.

This snapshot displays the coach as an educational leader and teacher educator. Eva saw that the PT brought skills to his classroom such as content knowledge, that perhaps he had the potential to be good for kids. Grounded in her own leadership as well as her teaching ability, she found a way to improve his teaching.

Ultimately, the ongoing observations of each PT contributed to evaluative judgments. Seeing PTs and their classrooms regularly, through both informal contact and formal evaluations including occasional unannounced visits, gave coaches the opportunity to see both growth and potential problems. Coaches could look across a year from where a PT had started, what supports the PT had needed, what had been provided, and how the PT responded with what growth. In order to make these assessments, the work of the coaches was rooted in performance standards.

Performance Standards: Protocols for Teaching Practice.  Strong evaluation systems include established standards for performance, rubrics, and evaluator training for inter-rater reliability (Tucker, 1997). The coaches' work with PTs, including assessment documentation and presentations at panel hearings, was grounded in a slightly modified version of the California Standards for the Teaching Profession (California Commission on Teacher Credentialing, 1997) (see Table 3.4). When Rosemont's program began in 2000, the California Standards for the Teaching Profession, rooted in Charlotte Danielson's frameworks (Danielson, 1996) and the foundation laid by the Santa Cruz New Teacher Project, were at the forefront of codifying skillful teaching practice.[3] My purpose is not to promote the California Standards as a framework for teaching quality, but simply to emphasize that Rosemont used a framework. Rosemont's PAR leaders added elements to their standards document to address what they saw as inadequate attention to issues of culture and diversity in the California Standards.

Coaches were not experts in performance standards for teaching at the time they were hired. The professional development retreat that panel members and coaches took together prior to the beginning of the school year included work on the use of teaching standards. The coaches then poured many professional development hours during the year into becoming experts on the standards, and into becoming calibrated among themselves in their use of the standards for evaluating to a rubric.

The coaches generated standards-based forms for their work with PTs. These included an Individual Learning Plan (ILP) specifying the standards and precise

**Table 3.4.** California Standards for the Teaching Profession, 1997, by the California Commission on Teacher Credentialing

---

*Standard One: Engaging and Supporting All Students in Learning*

1.1. Connecting students' prior knowledge, life experience, and interests with learning goals

1.2. Using a variety of instructional strategies and resources to respond to students' diverse needs

1.3. Facilitating learning experiences that promote autonomy, interaction, and choice

1.4. Engaging students in problem solving, critical thinking, and other activities that make subject matter meaningful

1.5. Promoting self-directed, reflective learning for all students

*Standard Two: Creating and Maintaining Effective Environments for Student Learning*

2.1. Creating a physical environment that engages all students

2.2. Establishing a climate that promotes fairness and respect

2.3. Promoting social development and group responsibility

2.4. Establishing and maintaining standards for student behavior

2.5. Planning and implementing classroom procedures and routines that support student learning

2.6. Using instructional time effectively

*Standard Three: Understanding and Organizing Subject Matter for Student Learning*

3.1. Demonstrating knowledge of subject matter content and student development

3.2. Organizing curriculum to support student understanding of subject matter

3.3. Interrelating ideas and information within and across subject matter areas

3.4. Developing student understanding through instructional strategies that are appropriate to the subject matter

3.5. Using materials, resources, and technologies to make subject matter accessible to students

*Standard Four: Planning Instruction and Designing Learning Experiences for All Students*

4.1. Drawing on and valuing students' backgrounds, interests, and developmental learning needs

4.2. Establishing and articulating goals for student learning

4.3. Developing and sequencing instructional activities and materials for student learning

4.4. Designing short-term and long-term plans to foster student learning

4.5. Modifying instructional plans to adjust for student needs

*Standard Five: Assessing Student Learning*

5.1. Establishing and communicating learning goals to all students

5.2. Collecting and using multiple sources of information to assess student learning

5.3. Involving and guiding all students in assessing their own learning

5.4. Using the results of assessments to guide instruction

5.5. Communicating with students, families, and other audiences about student progress

*Standard Six: Developing as a Professional Educator*

6.1. Reflecting on teaching practice and planning professional development

6.2. Establishing professional goals and pursuing opportunities to grow professionally

6.3. Working with communities to improve professional practice

6.4. Working with families to improve professional practice

6.5. Working with colleagues to improve professional practice

6.6. Balancing professional responsibilities and maintaining motivation

elements on the standards that were the focus of their work with PTs, as determined by the coaches and PTs together, or sometimes when necessary by the coach independently. Observations of PTs' teaching then generated evidence aligned to the ILP, and coaches' summaries of their observations charted PTs' progress (or lack thereof) along those standards. The coaches eventually wrote performance indicators for all of the dimensions on the standards.

Conversations between coaches and PTs about instruction were often grounded in standards language. One panel member commented:

> This is a paradigm shift, the idea that there are even teaching standards out there. You now have about 90 people who are very familiar and know they exist, have been impacted by them . . . versus "I've never heard of teaching standards," which you might have in schools that don't have PAR.

PTs noted that if not for their coach, they would have had no exposure to the standards.[4]

Because coaches observed their PTs teaching across the year, and grounded their ongoing assessments in teaching standards, they amassed a bank of data about a given PT's classroom practice. This data allowed the ultimate summative assessments to rest on the formative assessments. It also, in the eyes of at least some PTs, made for a fairer process. Noted one PT:

> Had the vice principal come up to do the evaluation, she would have had no idea what it's like on a normal basis, when the vice principal was not sitting in the back of the room. I really like the idea that my coach did my evaluations. Who better than someone who really has seen the whole picture?

A second PT noted the benefit of substantive, targeted assessment:

> I think the most valuable thing about working with [my coach] has been the evaluations, because I feel like there's a really specific target and she's clear. She uses the standards, and she shows me what they are. . . . It's a good wakeup call to have someone come into your classroom and say, you know, "Here are the things that I've noticed." And she's done that, and I think that's really helpful and important.

Finally, without naming the standards per se, a third PT highlighted the role that clear standards play in performance evaluation: "[My coach] picked out some things that she thought that I could improve on. And throughout the year, she really helped me with those things. So by the time she would do a formal evaluation, she could show how I'd improved in those things."

One PT named Timothy, featured in Chapter 5, did complain that the standards for performance themselves were unclear. He felt that the scores required for meeting standards versus not meeting standards, and hence for renewed employment, shifted during the year. To some degree, this was symptomatic of the newness of the program, and the degree to which those involved were building the airplane as it was going down the runway. The summative evaluation paperwork did change at one point relatively early in the year, and the switch may have caused some confusion.

Several principals were so impressed with the coaches' standards-based evaluations that they asked to be taught how to conduct them as well. By contrast, principals' evaluations tend to be less connected to a solid rubric, more capricious, and inflated (Loup et al., 1996). One coach, Sarah, described this exchange:

> I met with the principal of two of my PTs. She said that she felt that the teachers were much more distinguished [than I had indicated in their evaluations], and I had just put proficient and developing [on the evaluation form] and I didn't put anything in distinguished. And in talking to her a little bit more, I got the sense that she felt that her teachers were a reflection on her and her school. So, to have distinguished teachers is her goal, because then it makes her look good and her school site look good, and that's what she's interested in. And I think I can understand that, [but] that's why I think teachers have a really positive role in evaluation. . . . I think teachers are better able to assess each other more objectively.

Sarah used the text of the standards to demonstrate to strong PTs why they were not distinguished on every element, noting that she herself would not be. Instead, she tried to focus strong PTs on being proactive, asking them to focus on what they needed to do to get to distinguished. Sarah went on to describe the strength of the PAR process:

> When I turned in all my forms to [one principal], he was like, "Can you train us? When are you going to train the administrators how to do this?" I really knew how to connect it all. I knew how to connect the standards to the observations. I knew how to connect the observations to the Individual Learning Plan [ILP]. I knew how to connect the ILP to the next observation. I knew how to connect the observation to the preliminary and the summary evaluation. . . . I think [the principal] was impressed with the process, that he believed this is a good process.

A second coach echoed a similar experience:

> The principals told me that they've learned so much from reading my observations, the ILPs, and the standard summary. The way that we choose

evidence, what we see and how it's standards-based. Because if you look at the beginning of the year where it says principal's comments [on the summative evaluation paperwork], their comments, and our comments too [at that time], were like, "so-and-so is energetic and likes children." It was real non-standards-based language. I've had a vice principal ask me if I would give him a lesson or if we could go into a classroom together and compare what we see.

Indeed, by the third year of the program, the panel required one joint observation of PTs' classrooms by the principal and coach, and encouraged a second when a PT's performance was in question. (The implications of this shift are discussed in Chapter 7.) The stated rationale for the joint observations was to guarantee that the coach and principal were in agreement regarding professional development needed and/or the PT's assessment status. According to both of the panel co-chairs, however, part of the intent was also to spread the coaches' knowledge of teaching standards to the principals through conversations about observed PT practice. The district co-chair referred to the coaches as advocates for standards, saying, "They are the experts in the district on evaluation right now."

It bears noting that despite the efforts at calibration by coaches, it is certainly possible that some PTs who were nonrenewed would have been retained had they had a different coach, and vice versa. In the first year of the program, as the coaches were working on calibrating their interpretation and use of the standards, and they and the panel were beginning a discourse on the nature of quality teaching, variation undoubtedly existed between coaches. At least one panel member thought this variation was still present in the fourth year. Ultimately, however, despite the variation between coaches that may have been present, it was invariably less than the variation that historically existed between principals with traditional, non-standards-based teacher evaluation. As one principal noted, "I think there's a difference between any two people. What I like about PAR is that it does use standards. [We finally have] specific observable behaviors that are in line with rubrics, that are in line with ratings, all that is really, really good, so it's much more objective. . . . I'd have a lot of confidence that the difference between any two people evaluating one teacher is going to be really narrowed with PAR." Fluency in standards language gave coaches legitimacy with both principals and the panel, as well as with PTs, and contributed greatly to the community's confidence in the quality of the evaluations being conducted.

Put simply, coaches' ongoing assessment of PT practice was perceived by many of those involved to improve PTs' teaching. Taken together, the PAR program's components of support may, in fact, look quite similar to other full-time mentoring programs that do not involve summative evaluation. The study was not designed to look systematically at interactions between coaches and PTs. Nor did the study compare PAR support to support in other mentor programs without evaluation. It cannot be said that the support provided by PAR was better than or even as good as other high-quality mentoring programs. For those interested specifically in mentoring, this is certainly an area for further research. What can be drawn from this study, however, is that people involved with PAR believed that meaningful professional development was taking place as a form of evaluation that looked very different from teachers putting on a special show and principals flying through with a checklist.

## RETAINING NEW TEACHERS

Chapter 1 identified high rates of teacher turnover and shortage as a fundamental cause of current problems with teacher quality, and comprehensive mentoring as a support of new teacher retention (see Smith & Ingersoll, 2004; Strong, 2004). While this study did not track the retention of PTs over time, anecdotal evidence nonetheless suggests that PAR positively affected some new teachers' intentions to remain in teaching. In several cases, PTs attributed their ability to make it through the year and continue teaching to their relationship with their PAR coach. Asked whether she planned to stay in teaching, one PT commented, "I plan to stay in teaching. I may be moving so I may not be in this school and district, but the profession, yes. Thanks to my PAR coach."

PTs' survey responses on an item asking if the PAR program had helped them decide whether to remain in teaching, however, suggest that PAR may have had a minimal effect (see Online Appendix E). PTs reported a mean of 3.22 (SD = 1.23) on a 5-point Likert scale, where 3 was "uncertain" and 5 was "strongly agree" (that PAR had helped them decide whether to remain in teaching). Decisions about the allocation of PAR resources may have reduced the benefits of PAR for teacher retention. A phenomenon that arose with PAR was that panel members and principals tended to want the coaches to focus on the weakest PTs. Rosemont had a history of hiring large numbers of uncredentialed teachers that did not abate until the second year of the PAR program. In the first year of the program, this meant that coaches' caseloads included both credentialed and uncredentialed teachers. Although a credential does not guarantee a strong new teacher, and some uncredentialed teachers are themselves quite strong, as a general rule coaches ended up spending disproportionate attention "putting out fires" in uncredentialed teachers' classrooms. The union president noted, "Practically speaking, it's really hard to get principals' attention on someone who seems to be doing okay. They don't want to spend the time; they don't see it as a priority to help that person get better." The lead coach concurred: "[Principals] will push us to the neediest teachers, which is not necessarily the best thing for us to be doing." Some coaches were concerned that merely focusing on the weakest teachers was not the best use of PAR resources, believing that credentialed rather than uncredentialed PTs were more likely to stay in the district and become career teachers if provided with sufficient support.

There were several cases of credentialed PTs who were perceived as quite strong in the fall, who nonetheless hit roadblocks and frustration later in the year. The studies reporting that 30 to 50% of new teachers in urban districts leave the profession within 3 to 5 years are, for the most part, studies of *credentialed* teachers (Darling-Hammond, 1998; Haberman, 1993); to believe that stronger credentialed teachers could get by with much less support ignored this statistic. There was also some suggestion that the job of coach would become much less attractive if it were entirely one of triage, with less reflective and higher-level involvement with PTs. Although there is some evidence that PAR increased new teacher retention in Rosemont, this pressure to focus the coaches' time on the neediest teachers may have been a mitigating factor.

One credentialed PT in her first year as a teacher provides an example, as she expressed disappointment at not receiving more regular contact with her coach. The PT commented:

> It's been pretty hit-and-miss. I don't see [my coach] on a regular basis. We talked a lot more at the beginning of the year. [My coach and I] talked about the fact that I had other people helping me, and so she was spending more time with the other teachers who were here who were having a harder time than I was. And, on the one hand, I was like, oh, that's really good, because she can spend more time with them and they can get some help from her and we need to keep people in the profession so that's really good. But I also felt like, you know, just because I look like I'm doing okay . . . some days I'm falling apart.

The coach consciously focused less on this PT when urged to focus on other PTs at the site who needed more support. The coach also received strong signals from the PT that she was receiving support from others and so did not want to give much time to the PAR process. The coach also saw the importance of the new teacher developing longer-term relationships, noting, "It's about encouraging her to develop relationships with this community. The [museum] will be there next year. I won't. I have her for one year. So basically I became her evaluator." The PT's principal, in fact, believed in retrospect that the PT was strong enough to not have been in the program at all.

Given the opportunity to do it over again, however, the coach believed the PT did need more attention—even if only to help her synthesize her other support resources. The coach noted:

> We chose to take the suggestion [from the panel] of putting a lot more time into the classrooms with the fires. I don't know if I would buck [the

panel] next year but that presents some difficulty for me in the future. . . . I think a part of our job [should be] not just giving support but retention. [Part of that is] . . . saying, "Look, you are good, you can be a mentor." Maybe they don't feel it now, but I sure felt it when people . . . gave me strokes and headed me in a direction to be a mentor. So I think that's another part of our job.

The PT, in fact, reported that her coach was the only person who gave her any meaningful positive strokes. She commented, "[My coach] is the only person that's come in and actually had some firm knowledge of what I'm doing in here and been able to say that you're doing a good job." Asked whether she would remain in teaching, this strong new teacher—precisely the type we would want to stay—said no.

There may well have been strong new teachers who were more likely to remain in teaching as a result of their support from the PAR program. One principal provided an example of a teacher whose coach arranged to have her sent to a special language arts convention: "The PAR coach recognized right away that we need to keep this person here. . . . Now we're starting to motivate this person who obviously is very talented." The point is simply that some stronger PTs were not supported sufficiently to retain them, which serves as a cautionary tale to those considering the allocation of resources.

## INTERVENING WITH VETERAN TEACHERS

My discussion of the coaches' work has focused almost exclusively on beginning teachers for a couple of reasons. At the outset of the program, when I conducted the bulk of my data collection, beginning teachers made up the lion's share of participating teachers (88 to three in year 1). In addition, due to the sensitivity of employment issues and the precariousness of the new program, I did not interview the veteran teachers. Nonetheless, veteran teachers were obviously a major piece of the picture—in symbolic significance, if not numbers initially. Indeed, PAR's mechanism for removing underperforming tenured teachers from the classroom is precisely why the policy appeals to some, and why others reject it.

Rosemont's coaches collectively agreed at the outset that the work of supporting an intervention case would require greater effort than supporting a new teacher. They developed a formula whereby supporting an intervention case counted as two beginning teachers when constructing caseloads, given what they perceived as the larger emotional drain and investment of time involved when working with a veteran teacher (in Toledo, the ratio is actually 3 to 1). They also matched veteran teachers with older coaches, believing that it would have only added to the challenge if the coach were substantially younger than the intervention teacher. The guidelines for support were also somewhat different. All observations of veterans were scheduled ahead of time. Noted one coach, "You can't just drop in. It's a proscribed visit, all of them. You're not out to catch them. You're out to help them."

At the outset of the program, the intervention cases were largely those teachers who were considered clear-cut, the teachers whom administrators had been trying to remove for many years. By the third year of the program, Rosemont successfully remediated one of the four veterans in PAR that year. This still placed the district below the average of a sample of other established PAR programs, where 30 to 60% of veterans were remediated (Darling-Hammond, 1984; Hewitt, 2000; Kelly, 1998; Murray, 1999). One coach working with a veteran teacher described her experience:

> I would try to mask who it was [I was working with], but any time I'd start asking questions [at the district for resources], I'd get, "Oh, we've been trying to get rid of her for years." Well, you know, I didn't think that's what this program was about. I think the first year you end up with the cases everybody knows about, the more obvious ones.

This coach was working with a special education resource teacher, and often spoke at the Friday coach meetings about how depleted she felt from trying to help the teacher. As the coaches sometimes did, she brought her critical friend in for a joint visit on one occasion: "The day I brought her in, after we left she said, 'Oh, I can understand why you can't do anything after a morning of that!' We went to lunch and we went to the union office and debriefed. . . . You cannot go into another classroom that day." The coach described the intervention teacher's practice:

> It was painful. I just wanted to fix it, you know. She's saying [to a student], "You do this! You do it now!" Special ed kid. He couldn't far copy—he couldn't copy from the board to his paper. She didn't figure that out. "No, he can do it when he concentrates! He can do it when he thinks!" Part of what he can't do is pay attention, you know? It's his learning disability. "No, he's just lazy." Okay.

Speaking broadly about the intervention cases in the fourth year of the program, the district co-chair noted, "These tenure cases, it's half counselor and half evaluation. The coach and principal become really allied to help the person. What's a dignified and respectful exit for [someone] who's just not serving kids. Hearing the different voices helps tilt the balance. Some just have trouble letting go. Some have financial issues, obviously."

As is typical for PAR programs, as the program became established and more principals were familiar with it, the number of teachers given unsatisfactory evaluations increased. As a result, the number of veteran teachers referred to PAR increased—from eight in year 1 (yielding three intervention cases) to 21 in year 4 (yielding 12 cases). The difference between the number of cases referred and the number that became intervention cases was due to the vetting process, ensuring placement for instructional reasons only. The district co-chair commented in the fourth year of the program, "The greater number of tenured teachers [being referred] can definitely be traced back to the influence of PAR. Principals are more willing to do what it takes to evaluate a teacher out." The union president elaborated: "This trial we had, we demonstrated that we were consistent and tough, so more principals took the time to follow through with unsatisfactory evaluations. The message always has been that it's not worth their time, consolidation was easier." "Consolidation" was Rosemont vernacular for a practice that is nonetheless widespread nationally (e.g., Bridges, 1992). When a principal realizes that the work being completed by people in two different positions can more effectively and efficiently be completed with one position, or if only one position can now be afforded due to a reduction in enrollment, the principal can *consolidate* the responsibilities into one position. As a result, the "extra" employee enters a school district pool to be placed elsewhere. In practice, principals creatively use this administrative procedure to remove teachers from their school without having to go through progressive discipline or other teacher evaluation procedures.

Recall that the California legislation mandated the veteran piece but left the beginning teacher piece optional—whereas prior PAR programs began with beginning teachers. It is perhaps interesting to note, therefore, that despite the legislation, Rosemont in effect mirrored the more common pattern. Other districts started with no veterans until a certain degree of comfort was established, while Rosemont did start with a very small number of veterans. Then, over the span of a few years, the process began to take root. By the fourth year of the program, more veteran teachers were being removed from the classroom than new teachers, in contrast to year 1—the result of stricter hiring practices (that reduced the number of uncredentialed teachers hired) and more veterans being referred to PAR.

## PROFESSIONAL DEVELOPMENT
## ACROSS THE CAREER CONTINUUM

One of the somewhat less obvious but undeniable facets of PAR is that it creates much-needed job variety for experienced and successful teachers. Placing these master teachers in roles as PAR coaches (as well as, perhaps to a lesser degree, PAR panel members) provided rich professional development and, perhaps, motivation to remain in the field.[5] One coach highlighted the significance of her job change:

I've been in the classroom, I taught the same subject, I was getting kind of stale and I was getting bored with it. Even though you can do so much [as a classroom teacher], it was time for me to grow as an individual, because I was at a point where I could do it in my sleep and that's not helpful to your growth at all. So I thought, well, this way, I'll be working with new teachers and I'll get to see really good practices, and then I'll have all that to take back to my class with me.

Noted another coach, "There are specific things, I think, 'Oh, yeah, that's what I should have done,' you know? Some of them are from watching brand-new teachers, too, which is really mind blowing." Rosemont's coaches began to develop an understanding of and language to express the complex knowledge base for teaching. Noted one:

I've just really had to reflect about teaching a lot. I've had to think about coming at it as a coach. Here's somebody who has a lot of things going wrong, where do I start? What's the one thing that would help the most and what steps do I have to take? So it's forced me to think about what makes a good teacher and how is it all put together. Kind of like what's the base and what do you build on and is there structure there and so on and so on. I'm sure that's going to improve my teaching a lot when I go back into the classroom.

Despite the significance of the new role for these coaches, several nonetheless emphasized their continued professional identity as a teacher. Noted one, "And the going back [to the classroom after 3 years as a coach], I thought that was powerful. Telling [PTs], I'm going back to the classroom, I really am one of you, and I'm going back to be one of you." Another coach echoed: "I'm a teacher. I'm with a new program but I'm a teacher. I've always taught kids. This year I'm teaching teachers."

That said, two former coaches who participated in a focus group in the fourth year of the program, after they had returned to school sites, reported a definite shift in their authority. One, Caroline, returned to classroom teaching, while another, Eva, took a position as an instructional reform facilitator. (Both coaches are highlighted in Chapter 5.) Caroline described the effects on her leadership despite the termination of her PAR coach role:

PAR gave me more of a sense of being an insider in district leadership. As a result, I am less inclined to just accept dictates from on high as if they were from God. These are just human beings making decisions and they are doing it without enough information, because they are not at the site.

Unhappy with new regulations for following district curriculum, for example, she said she would talk to the instructional superintendent for middle schools, or write a letter to the superintendent and cc the instructional superintendent. Caroline described her relationship with the school principal: "I think he sees me as having a lot of power because he knows I have personal relationships with people like [the instructional superintendent for middle schools]."

Eva, working outside the classroom as instructional support staff at one school site, described her relationship with her struggling second-year principal: "I told him that he needs to utilize me more on decision making. 'You may not like what I'm saying, but I'm honest and I'm not hostile toward you.' I think he appreciated it." These two ex-coaches summarized their elevated status. Eva commented, "You're not just another teacher, you know people, you can call or email." Caroline concurred, "Yeah, and [district administrators] won't return [the principal's] calls but I'll call and get put right through." Their 3 years as part of a special cadre of teacher leaders gave them a particular currency with district leadership.

Finally, they noted that this elevated status created some confusion in their transition back to school sites. Noted Caroline:

> The flip side is [the principal will] turn to me for things. Like a teacher I coached last year ended up across the hall from me, she's not a middle school teacher [but was placed here in a mixup]. They wanted me to coach her. I said, "No way," I'm not in that role anymore. Get her a PAR coach if you think she needs one. I am happy to be her friend, and she can come across the hall for advice from time to time. And don't talk to me about her evaluation [either], confidentiality needs to be preserved.

Eva concurred, "That has come up. I've needed to make it clear, this is who I am, this is who I'm not. I have had teachers ask me to do their evaluation, instead of the principal. I have to say, 'No, I don't do that anymore.'"

Rosemont's coaches got a view of education beyond the walls of their own classrooms, with time to reflect on teaching practice and a community of experts with whom to reflect and grow as educators (Achinstein & Athanases, 2006). The role change was not without complications, but, ultimately, mentoring programs benefit mentors as well as mentees (Resta, Huling, White, & Matschek, 1997)—and PAR was no exception.

## CONCLUSION

The dominant theme in this chapter is the ways PAR moved classroom teaching from a largely individual enterprise to one both supported and assessed by a more skillful practitioner—the coach. This support and assessment benefited new teachers, who would otherwise be left on their own to find their way. In one of 11 intervention cases in the first 3 years, PAR support benefited a veteran teacher who was able to improve his or her performance and remain in teaching. The support provided by PAR also benefited the supporters themselves, as the coaches developed as leaders. Most centrally, however, this system of support and assessment benefited the students, who would presumably receive higher-quality instruction.

## CHAPTER 4

# The Work of the PAR Panel

## *Supporting and Assessing Teacher Evaluation*

I left [the spring panel hearing] feeling like, wow, we've done
the district a favor in removing people [who] have been strung
along, in terms of tenured teachers, or people [who] could have
been staying on and taking up a place, becoming tenured. I just
feel like we've really done a good job cleaning house this year.
I'm excited about it.

—Susanna, teacher on the Rosemont PAR panel

In an ironic parallel to the lack of both support and oversight that plagues teaching, principals are neither held accountable for their evaluative decisions, nor given the support that a group of colleagues can provide in the decision-making process. Alone with their observation notes or checklists, principals typically make evaluation decisions in isolation, not needing to defend their decisions to another colleague, let alone a panel of colleagues. In part because classroom practice has not been transparent, principals typically base those decisions on minimal data. One principal highlighted the situation this way: "Administrators, if you've got 35 people to evaluate your contact is going to be limited to what's required. . . . Those times are going to be like snapshots. It's kind of like this: I'm going to come at 10:00 A.M. on March the 2nd to evaluate you in your room on a lesson that you choose to do with the class period that you choose. Will you be ready? You would think *everyone* would be ready."

PAR avoids some of the opacity of traditional teacher evaluation in multiple ways. As discussed in Chapter 3, PAR opens the door to teaching practice by putting coaches in participating teachers' classrooms on an ongoing and regular basis, generating more data on which to base the evaluations. In addition, however, PAR opens the door to evaluator practice. Perhaps the most important structural change that increased the transparency of the evaluation process was that PAR created formal teams of colleagues engaged in the work of teacher evaluation. This included the coaches working as a team on Fridays, and the partnerships they had, in some cases, with principals. Most central, however, was the PAR panel, a structure for holding the coaches accountable for their interpretations of the assessment data.

This chapter examines the design and process of the PAR panel in Rosemont, asking: How did the PAR panel work? For now, I am concerned mainly with descriptive detail. The chapter first explains the legislative framework for union and district joint work on PAR, and then explains how the panel selected the coaches, supported the coaches to do their jobs, and held them accountable. In Chapter 8, I will revisit the working of the panel further, to analyze how the presence of an oversight panel affected the teacher evaluation process and personnel outcomes, as well as shortcomings of the structure.[1]

## WORKING TOGETHER

The typically confrontational nature of education's labor relations makes attempts at dismissal prohibitively costly, time-consuming, and rare. Principals historically have viewed the union as an unbeatable adversary and often do not try to fire a teacher. Instead, they engage in escape hatches such as transfers (voluntary and involuntary), resignation, and retirement (Bridges, 1992; Kahlenberg, 2006; Kerchner & Mitchell, 1988; Kerchner et al., 1997; Painter, 2000; Toch & Rothman, 2008; Urbanski, 1999). One common practice is the "dance of the lemons," passing underperforming teachers to a different school (sometimes repeatedly for years) rather than giving a negative evaluation (Bridges, 1992). Principals often know their teachers well; they may have worked together for years, and they may be friends. Especially considering the likelihood that a negative evaluation will not result in improved performance or a personnel change, principals' hesitance to create conflict—with the teacher or the union—is understandable. It does little, however, to ensure a competent teacher for every student.

PAR provides a very different model. As introduced in Chapter 2, California's AB 1X legislation required that a district's teachers union sign off on the district's proposal to the state creating a PAR program. As a result, teachers unions had the ability to prevent districts from receiving state money allotted for PAR (based on district attendance)—money that districts were in fact already accustomed to receiving for a mentoring program eliminated with the implementation of PAR.

Recall from Chapter 2 that the legislation also required that the PAR panel be co-led by the teachers union and district administration and consist of five teachers and four administrators (with the teachers union president considered a teacher) (Villaraigosa et al., 1999). As a result, teachers held a majority on the PAR panel—meaning they possessed decisional authority regarding both programmatic decisions and PT employment decisions, although panel members in Rosemont agreed to operate on a consensus model. In Rosemont, an associate superintendent, Brian, served as district co-chair of the panel together with the teachers union president,

Doug. (I will refer to Brian as the district co-chair rather than as associate superintendent, as there were multiple associate superintendents in the district.)

California's AB 1X legislation mandated that veteran teachers who had received a negative evaluation from their principal had to have a PAR program available to support them with intervention. The law left the matter of beginning teachers open for negotiation, to be determined by local education associations and their teachers unions. Although some teachers union presidents around the state wanted to keep their PAR program as narrowly defined as possible, simply in compliance with the state law, Doug was committed to including beginning teachers in the program. In his view, as in the view of Toledo Federation of Teachers past president Dal Lawrence, who generated the original peer review program in 1981, the district's administrators could not expect the teachers union to be responsible for "cleaning up" unsatisfactory veteran teachers if the union had no role in determining which teachers became tenured in the district in the first place. Given the union's ability to rescind program approval, which in Rosemont would have cost the district $1.8 million, Doug was able to ensure that Rosemont's program included both beginning and veteran participating teachers. He was very explicit about leveraging the state legislation, via the contract, in order to force the superintendent to include what Doug viewed as critical components of the policy. At the outset of program implementation, Doug explained his position:

> PAR is the right thing to do, it's a good idea, God is on our side. And God is really defined as $1.8 million. If the PAR program fails to be continued, then the district will lose $1.8 million, okay? I think that the contract language is clear, that unless we get the district's agreement to have both parts of it, the beginning teacher part and the veteran teacher part, then we will walk away. We are not willing to do the district's clean-up unless we also have some say of what gets into the system. . . . If the district and the union fail to reach bilateral agreement, the union has the right to rescind. Now that's the poison pill. And it's there to make clear our intention that these two things are linked.

Ideally, when implemented well, PAR provides a balance between teachers union and administration, where a union can hold district administration accountable for who becomes a teacher, and district administration can hold the union accountable for the performance of teachers over time.

Note that I have highlighted the role of partnership between the teachers union and school district; I did not say that positive labor relations are a prerequisite. Rosemont had far from trusting labor relations at the time that the union and district designed their PAR program, as is likely evidenced by Doug's quote above. It would be tempting to say that each party took a leap of faith in the other and they came to agreement. More accurately, they came up with a series of checks and balances as safeguards that made the leap palatable. Most districts that initiated PAR prior to California's legislation did so through what is called a "trust agreement" that lives outside the contract, but these districts also initiated PAR on their own and were not required to do so by state law. Rosemont's leaders, by contrast, edified PAR's details in the labor contract. In the level of suspicion and heightened politicization that existed in Rosemont circa 1999, the district is less like some of the rosier PAR stories that preceded it and more like many other districts around the country where educators cannot imagine implementing PAR. AFT Vice President Adam Urbanski (1999) has argued that trust is a prerequisite for PAR, and certainly trusting relations makes the transition easier, but it can be a by-product rather than a prerequisite (see also Qazilbash, Johnson, Fiarman, Munger, & Papay, 2009). Rosemont is not the only example. In Poway, California, which has "arguably the country's most fully developed peer review program" (Gallagher et al., 1993), antagonistic relations between the union and district were present at the program's inception.

Finally—and this is crucial—control of evaluation was left vague in the contract language. A distinction was made between "evaluation" and "review," with evaluation being the domain of administrators and review being controlled by "The Program" (PAR). The Program "assumes primary responsibilities for reviewing Beginning Teachers and Intervention [veteran] Teachers," while "the principal maintains evaluation responsibility for those aspects which reside typically outside the classroom" for those same groups of teachers. However, even within the definition of "review," the contract states: "The review process requires the PAR panel to examine documented interactions between the teacher, coach, and principal, reflect with other panel members, and discuss the recommendations with the coach and principal." Although referenced nowhere in the contract, the way this distinction between PAR program and principal responsibilities was translated and concretized in the vernacular of the panel and coaches was with standards language: Coaches were to have primary responsibility for evaluating performance on the first five California Standards for the Teaching Profession, which pertain to classroom performance, while the principals would hold primary responsibility for evaluating the sixth standard, which pertains to out-of-classroom performance and activities. Over time, however, principals became more involved with standards one through five.

## CREATING TEAMS OF COLLEAGUES

Given a larger amount of data about a teacher upon which to base both formative and summative assessment, as discussed in Chapter 3, PAR then creates a mechanism whereby a team of educators is in communication with one another about those assessments.

## Panel Member and Coach Selection

The PAR panel included a cross-section from across the district—classroom teachers, teachers on special assignment, building administrators, and district administrators. In addition to the teachers union president, the teachers on the panel, appointed by the union president, included an elementary bilingual specialist, a middle school language arts teacher, a high school English teacher, and a math coach. The administrators on the panel were appointed by the interim superintendent. They included the associate superintendent for the high school division, who served as district co-chair, as well as an elementary principal, a middle school principal, and the head of human resources. (In subsequent years, a new head of human resources would become the district co-chair.)

The composition of the panel was hailed by most as an asset of the program. A number of people commented that if an observer walked into the room during panel hearings, he or she would not be able to tell which members of the panel were teachers and which were administrators. Noted one coach: "I think the panel members are fantastic. I really appreciate them. I really appreciate that there are teachers there, there are principals there, there are district administrators there, and we're all having the same conversations, we're on the same level with conversations."

The PAR panel convened in the spring semester prior to the start of the PAR program, in order to begin the process of hiring coaches and developing the program. The application process for the PAR coach job involved several steps. It began with a paper application and letters of reference, including at least one letter from a teacher the applicant had mentored. After this initial screening, pairs of panel members—one teacher and one administrator—visited the applicant's classroom for a teaching observation. According to the union president, the purpose of the observations was not to distinguish between "an A and an A+" teacher, but rather to weed out any teacher with merely decent skills being presented in letters of reference as "an A." Of 24 applicants, 13 were invited in for an interview with the panel. The interview involved the applicant teaching a short lesson to the group, answering questions, and producing a writing sample. The writing prompt presented a hypothetical teaching observation, and asked the applicant to write a post-observation memo to the teacher providing feedback.

The panel conducted multiple rounds of voting to select the 10 coaches, though it should be noted that they did not have a target number of hires; rather, their conversation and voting was to select those they believed were best qualified, and they happened to end up with 10. The voting was substantive; one of the teachers Brian wanted to hire was not selected. She happened to be the only applicant with a bilingual certificate, a point that would quickly come back to haunt the team when they were left without someone qualified to support bilingual instruction. Suffice it to say, the democratic process of the panel team may not have always led to the best decisions; my point here is that, for better or worse, it was a democratic process.

The deliberations focused on a few issues. For starters, those leading the program—and therefore most familiar with it at the time of coach selection—were particularly concerned about hiring people who understood the evaluative component of the coaching role. Brian noted at the time, "A lot of applications read like a BTSA application. They hadn't really grappled with the reviewer role, that it is hard. The main question is can you look a 25– or 30–year veteran in the eye and say fish or cut bait?"

A second issue was diversity, with gender and age featuring more prominently than race. A second male coach was chosen in part so that there would not be only one man in the group. Concerns were raised about some applicants being too close to retirement on one hand, or being too young to effectively do the job on the other. The union president emphasized that they would not penalize for age by excluding applicants who were close to retirement. However, they were ideally looking for continuity, and coaches were expected to serve for 3 years and then return to the classroom. As it turned out, the youngest coach hired, Sarah, became one of the coaches to whom the panel really looked as a model. Meanwhile, the lead coach, Bob, subsequently retired directly from his PAR position after 3 years—an outcome the panel knew was likely, but they nonetheless felt he was the clear-cut choice for the role.

Finally, the panel considered things such as who would be best in the first year of a program, to contribute to its development, versus someone who would function better in a more structured and established program. Panel members were also aware they were creating a team, and had an eye on the whole composition. Noted Brian, "I want them to have conflict, it will be fruitful. . . . I am trying not to have a picture in my mind [of a coach], and then be negatively disposed to those that don't fit. Diversity is good."

In year 2 of the program, the panel added two coaches, who added bilingual and special education expertise, in addition to more elementary experience. One of the second-year hires would go on to become lead coach in year 4, when Bob retired.

Because coaches served at the pleasure of the panel, the panel could conceivably remove a coach from the job if the coach's performance was unsatisfactory. Coaches have, in fact, been removed in other districts implementing PAR, but this did not occur in Rosemont during the time of the study. Nonetheless, the performative aspect of panel hearings left coaches with the sense that their jobs and professional standing were on the line.

It is worth noting that as the first year of the program progressed, and the coaches came to fully understand the significant role of the panel members in evaluative decision making, they did begin to question the panel member selection process. This was not due to unhappiness with any particular panel member or the panel as a whole, but rather simply a belief that the process should have as much integrity as possible. Given the rigorous selection process for being a coach, the coaches, in turn, felt that there should be a similar process for panel members, rather than mere appointment.

## Panel Hearings and Meetings

Once the program began in the fall, the panel continued to meet approximately once each month for a couple of hours for a business meeting, and also met multiple times during the year for panel hearings to review PT cases.

The most significant and formal public examinations of PTs' practice, and therefore also of coach practice, were the PAR panel hearings that occurred multiple times throughout the year. Hearings ran all day for 2 days in November, January, and April—8:30 A.M. to 6:00 P.M. with a working lunch—plus a final day in early May for any appeals by participating teachers. The two January dates were actually separated by 3 weeks, with the latter day serving to revisit challenging cases presented earlier in the month. Prior to the hearings, each panel member received an updated binder with documentation of coaches' work with PTs—including summaries of observations, ILP forms, coaches' ratings of PTs, and evidence such as PTs' lesson plans.

The atmosphere was formal and somewhat tense, as a coach sat at one end of a conference table to make his or her report to the assembled panel members and other high-ranking (though nonvoting) district administrators who were present at times, such as the superintendent. Coaches reported on PTs' growth and/or problematic practice. The panel, in turn, offered suggestions of support that the coach might try, and held the coach accountable for providing sufficient support in order for the PT to have the opportunity to improve. Ultimately, at the spring hearing, coaches made recommendations regarding the continued employment of each PT.

In addition, the teachers' principal was typically present, and would contribute his or her own impressions about the PT, in particular regarding out-of-classroom matters. The dynamics of these presentations were, not surprisingly, quite different from one coach-principal pair to the next. Typically, the coach did most of the presenting, with the panel then asking the principal what he or she had to add. But many principals offered information throughout the presentations, and in a few cases, the pair truly seemed to work as colleagues, finishing one another's sentences.

There was, in fact, little clear protocol at the outset for what the presentations should look like. Over the course of the first year, however, the panel identified a few coaches whom they felt made salient points clear at the outset of presentations (including their employment recommendation at the April hearing), and then supported themselves clearly with evidence. Over time, the presentation styles converged to some degree, and by the fourth year of the program, panel members reported that the presentations had become more standardized, with more of a protocol for the process.

Since time was a factor at panel hearings, the panel members decided that 91 PTs were too many to discuss in the 2 days allotted for hearings. At the November hearing, they were able to spend only 3 to 4 minutes on each teacher doing well, and 10 to 12 minutes on weaker teachers. Following the November panel hearing, they made the decision to bring to subsequent panel hearings only those cases that were "red flags"—those PTs whose performance had been questionable at the initial November hearing. The rest of the PTs were presented in subpanel meetings called "quads," smaller groupings of two coaches (who were considered critical friends) and two panel members who met periodically.

In addition to the panel hearings held at intervals throughout the year, the panel convened for monthly 2–hour business meetings. At these meetings, panel members addressed programmatic issues and fielded coach questions and concerns from the lead coach. This was the time for panel members to talk in a more relaxed way than under the time pressure and more public nature of the hearings. Doug noted:

> Start off with just the idea of bringing into one room teachers and administrators, who are getting a snapshot of what's actually going on in the district. So much is normally not discussed. It was good to see . . . the whole gamut of issues coming out and forcing a group of people to actually discuss and deal with them. It was good to see the lack of clear differences between the teachers and the administrators on the panel in terms of how they looked at the world.

As with panel hearings, those involved tended to feel that business meetings did not provide enough time to discuss issues as thoroughly as they would have liked; at the early stages of program implementation, many logistical issues often took time away from the substantive work of teaching quality. Nonetheless, the existence of a cross-district dialogue focused on teaching quality, however imperfectly, was a breakthrough for Rosemont's district leaders.

Of 88 beginning teachers in PAR in Rosemont's first year of implementation, 24 were discussed at the panel hearing in April (see Table 4.1). Of these, eight were renewed, including one who would continue to receive extra support the following year, and one who would be placed in a different school due to an unworkable situation between the PT and the principal. Four PTs were mid-year additions to PAR, would continue in the PAR program for another semester, were deemed to be performing satisfactorily, and would therefore be revisited in the future in quad meetings. Eleven beginning teachers were not offered the opportunity to renew their contract for teaching duties in the district, including one who was released effective immediately, and one who was specifically told in writing that he was welcome to

Table 4.1. Summary of Year 1 Participating Teacher Outcomes (*N* = 91)

| | Beginning Teachers | | Veteran Teachers | | |
|---|---|---|---|---|---|
| Outcome | Renew | Nonrenew | Renew | Nonrenew | Total |
| Resolved in quad meeting | 64 | | | | 64 |
| Resolved at panel hearing | 8 | 12[a] | 0 | | 20 |
| Continue in program another semester (move to quad) | 4 | | | | 4 |
| Resolved outside of panel (reassigned, retired) | | | | 3 | 3 |
| TOTAL | 76 | 12 | 0 | 3 | 91 |

[a] Table 4.2 below provides more detail about this cell.

come back to Rosemont if he earned a teaching credential. One additional PT was nonrenewed, to be enacted by the principal rather than the PAR program due to a fluke in employment status. Finally, the three veteran teachers in the program were removed from teaching, but were resolved prior to the April hearing through early retirements or reassignment to out-of-classroom responsibilities.

The workings of Rosemont's PAR panel, as seen through excerpts from PAR panel meetings throughout this and subsequent chapters, are not intended as a model or best case. On the contrary, in places it might be easy to lodge critique about basic aspects of the discourse such as expertise in coaching or meeting facilitation. Nonetheless, close examination of the panel's early efforts with PAR helps us more deeply understand what the program looked like, as well as how (if at all) the presence of the panel affected the teacher evaluation process and outcomes. The argument is not that what occurred was ideal, but rather that it was a significant departure from standard operating procedure—for Rosemont and most school districts.

In addition, recall that after November, only PTs whose performance was in question were brought to the panel. By definition, in other words, the panel conversations are focused on potentially underperforming teachers, and may, therefore, appear negatively skewed. Keep in mind, however, that 64 new teachers being provided with PAR support were deemed by their coaches to be teaching to standards and were not discussed at the panel hearings.

## SUPPORTING THE PAR COACHES

In a prime example of what Richard Elmore (1996, 2003) calls "reciprocal accountability," for the panel to hold the coaches accountable, the panel must also provide the coaches with support to do their jobs. Elmore argues that if teachers are to be held accountable for student performance, districts and others outside of schools must, in turn, recognize their responsibility to help build the capacity of school personnel. With PAR, there is a parallel reciprocity between the panel and coaches. While principals are mostly on their own to evaluate teachers, the coaches had a community of educators with whom to discuss their work and consider decisions. Although some coaches were anxious about the performative aspects of panel hearings, they nonetheless expressed gratitude for the role of the panel and the involvement of the panel members in the work.

## Direct Support of Coaches' Work with PTs

The panel supported the coaches in a variety of ways, most easily seen through the dialogue of the panel hearings. What follows is an excerpt from the January panel hearing, at a point where the conversation was focused on one of the three intervention teachers in the program that year. The lead coach (Bob) and principal were both present, making reports to the panel. Some other coaches were also in the room. The PT was a high school science teacher. Bob described the teacher's difficulty creating and maintaining an effective learning environment, in particular with directed teaching. He linked the need for whole-class instruction to the learning goals in the PT's subject area, and outlined the low level of learning taking place for students as a result of her inability to command a class's attention. He explained that despite the teacher's efforts, he was not seeing growth in her performance. At the point where we enter the conversation, Bob is expressing the need to try something new:

> *Bob:* I've sort of hit the wall. I need to go into a whole new approach. I'm feeling like I need to do a series of demonstration lessons. We've kicked around the idea of sending her someplace to observe, and there just isn't anywhere. I know some dynamic teachers—but putting her into a place with dynamic teachers I don't think will be useful unless she can be privy to what's behind it. I'll need to be there anyway, so I might as well do the teaching. So I'm thinking I'd do a series of constructed lessons where I share with her why I'm doing the planning I'm doing, and she sees it unfold. But the revelation that kind of hit me finally is that she needs to be treated as a first-year teacher—the fundamentals aren't there.

The panel members, in turn, ask questions of the coach and the principal. Recall that Brian was the co-chair of the panel with the teachers union president, Doug, and Caroline was a coach (see Table 2.4 in Chapter 2).

> *Panel Administrator 7:* I'm wondering about two things. First, what do the students say to you? Second, do you feel that there are some students that are being responsive to you being there?

*Bob:* I've tried to be basically a fly on the wall, so I didn't change behavior. Nevertheless, I have heard some feedback from some students, some of it is actually fairly adult thinking. "Are you here to help?" [laughter] I was thinking maybe I should create a venue to hear [from them] more.

*Panel Administrator 8:* [to the principal] Do you think [the PT] would benefit from Bob's suggestion of demonstration lessons?

*PT's Principal:* I think she's very receptive, she never says, "Oh that won't work." But the follow-through isn't there.

*Panel Administrator 8:* Maybe no matter what we do, change just won't happen, but we want to try everything we can.

*PT's Principal:* I think it would be very helpful.

Panel members then chew on the idea of demonstration lessons, voice their concerns, and make suggestions.

*Panel Administrator 7:* Maybe you should teach and have her not be there, so she's not influencing the kids. You could videotape, so she could see how her students interact with someone else.

*Panel Administrator 8:* I think that's a good suggestion, because if she is there, the kids may turn around and go, "See?" They may embarrass her, which might be counterproductive.

*Bob:* She's relatively callous to that.

*Panel Teacher 5:* Well, she spent all that time as a paraprofessional, she was watching someone who could control a class. But clearly she didn't internalize it. I'm not sure where we go with that. I think it's a good idea, but is it going to work? Maybe we're just repeating. . . .

*Panel Teacher 6:* [to Bob] But I heard you say you'd spend time with her around your thinking, all the pre-planning.

*Bob:* I think that's the difference.

*Panel Teacher 4:* How would you translate the pre-thinking, the attitude, everything that will go into you developing this lesson . . . ? I think it's a good step, of reminding you of all the pre- and during and post-thinking that has to go on. But I'm not sure that translates to people just by watching. I'm a little bit worried about the modeling piece. Across the board.

*Doug:* What I've heard from Bob is that maybe we need to go back to ground zero. That there are some fundamentals here that haven't gotten through. This is very basic stuff that she would never have seen as a para, would never have had anyone draw her attention to it. Maybe she didn't get it in teacher training. . . . What I'm hearing is that there's a glimmer of progress, but it's really dim right now, and we'll be hearing about her next time.

As the conversation progresses, coaches in the audience also join in.

> *Doug:* [to coach in audience] You had a question?
> *Coach 10:* As a coach, I have a concern about going in and modeling a lesson, and then the next day the teacher comes back, and I don't know that kids will appreciate that.
> *Doug:* Caroline?
> *Caroline:* I'd be curious to see not only you talking with her about your planning but what she sees. Have her take notes. What does she see in the lesson you do? Internalizing it is yet another step, but just her being able to see it.
> *Doug:* That's another reason to tape, so if she comes away with nothing, you can go back and revisit. What we're looking for is capacity for growth.

Finally, Brian reminds Bob, and the group, of the importance of documentation.

> *Brian:* I just want to ask about the ILP [the PT's individual learning plan]. These are evolving documents. Any time you think it's appropriate to modify, update the ILP, it's important to do so. We want the ILP to be a pathway for her to improve, but it's also due process and documentation for the program. The presence or absence of ratings that can be backed up with evidence are really important.

Ultimately, growth was not seen with this teacher, and the panel voted to dismiss her at the follow-up hearing held at the end of January. The teacher, in turn, chose to retire, leaving at the end of the year.

In addition to meeting with the full panel at hearings, coaches also met with panel members in "quads," the subpanel groups of two coaches and two panel members that met periodically. Although the quad structure was born, in part, for the simple reason that the panel hearings did not provide enough time to discuss all of the PT cases, it was also envisioned as a way to provide the coaches with support. Coaches could look to quad meetings for guidance with programmatic issues, such as negotiating relationships with principals. In addition, coaches brought their most difficult PT cases to quad meetings to brainstorm and troubleshoot prior to presenting at hearings. Susanna, one of the two panel members who worked with Caroline in quads, described her role as that of a sounding board. She noted, "I feel like, if anything, I've been a reflective person for the [coaches] to come to with their cases." One coach noted:

> What the quad does is that at least you know when you are given such a short time to present the work that you've done with the PT [at the panel

hearing], you know that two members of that panel have been privy to more conversation and have been able to go more in depth with the case. I think the panel can kind of look to those two members and think, well, they know a little bit more about this story and what you've tried.

Coaches occasionally brought their critical friend—the other coach in their quad— to jointly observe a PT's classroom for additional suggestions or assessment. Doug noted, "I think we've done a very good job of minimizing the isolation of the coaches. We knew that was a risk and the structures that we've created from the quads to the [coaches'] Friday meetings seem good, we don't seem to have had any coach go nuts." Similarly, Brian commented: "I've really enjoyed the panel quads. That's a more intimate setting and I feel like I've developed stronger relationships with those coaches just by virtue of interacting with them more frequently." From a coach's perspective, Sarah commented on the benefit of the quad structure: "It was good to have that time with the quad, to get some suggestions, because I basically was doing mini-case studies of each of my participating teachers." In later years of the program, the quad structure fell away. Coaches continued to present only red flag cases to the panel, while panel members trusted the coach and principal to make decisions about stronger PTs.

### Supporting Coaches by Intervening with Principals

The panel also supported the work of the coaches, when necessary, by holding principals accountable for managing their schools. Although a few principals were resistant to the PAR process, most had elected to have PAR at their school, were grateful for its presence, and were willing to work collaboratively at the hearings. (While PAR began in those schools where principals had signed up for the program, some changes in school leadership had occurred by the time the program started.) In Rosemont, principals reported to their respective associate superintendent, either of elementary, middle, or high schools. The associate superintendent for high schools served as the co-chair of the PAR panel, but the other two often sat in on hearings, as did a special assistant to the superintendent or the superintendent herself. The panel did not hold direct decisional authority over principals as they did over coaches; while coaches served at the pleasure of the panel, the panel was not responsible for hiring and firing principals. Nonetheless, for many principals, their first visit to a panel hearing was an eye-opener regarding the authority present and therefore the significance of their attention to PAR matters.

Dialogue at the panel hearings served as a forum for identifying "red flag situations" across the district. For example, the panel identified some cases of principals failing to give beginning teachers a sufficient opportunity to succeed, such as an assignment of four preparation periods across three classrooms on two different floors of a building. Extremely challenging situations like this complicated the coach's job of diagnosing and assessing a PT's practice and potential. In such cases, the associate superintendent on the panel addressed the situation with the principal directly and sometimes required that the conditions for the new teacher be altered. The panel members were, therefore, able to hold principals accountable for providing teachers with an opportunity for success, without which those teachers' performance could not be fairly judged.

Across the board, despite the existing support structures, coaches would have liked support from the panel to be improved during PAR's initial implementation. Most complaints involved the ambiguity that often surrounds policy implementation (Baier, March, & Saetren, 1988): Coaches wanted more directions, clearer directions, and more timely directions. One commented, "It would have helped if they could have said to us do A, B, and C this way." Another, Caroline, said, "Just tell me, you know, I just want you to tell me this is the way it is." One of the questions that the panel asked coaches during the coach selection process was whether they would be comfortable operating with a lot of ambiguity, as many of the programmatic details were still being worked out. Despite this warning, coaches were often frustrated and wanted more support—often defined as clarity—in the first year of the program.

In addition to issues resulting from program ambiguity, the coaches could have used more support in coaching itself. As noted in Chapter 3, they received professional development in coaching at the outset, but it is also true that professional development that is "received" at a point in time is not a strong model for adult learning—precisely the theory behind the coaches' ongoing work with classroom teachers. A teacher on the panel explained:

> I think the program had to start under so many compromises, but the coaches did an admirable job in a difficult set of circumstances. I don't think they were given as much support as they needed and I think we went into it too quickly. I don't think that our understanding of what it would take to help someone really know what is the difference between mentoring and coaching [was sufficiently developed].

The panel hearings and quads provided ongoing, situated support to the coaches to a degree. Ultimately, however, the Friday meetings that occurred every week were not utilized as fully as they could have been for the purpose of the coaches' ongoing learning. The panel largely left the coaches to fend for themselves with the Friday time, and could have done more to structure learning experiences for the coaches around a clear framework for being teachers of adult learners.

## HOLDING THE PAR COACHES ACCOUNTABLE

Perhaps the most profound structural distinction between regular teacher evaluation and PAR is that the coaches must defend their employment recommendations to colleagues. They must come before a group of other educators and say, "I believe we should rehire this teacher and here's evidence why," or alternately, "I believe we should *not* rehire this teacher, and here's evidence why." In addition, they have to demonstrate that the PT received sufficient support and had an opportunity to improve. The teachers union president identified the role that the panel played in holding the coaches accountable at the hearings:

> The coach has to make the recommendation. The panel has the responsibility of making sure that recommendation is supportable. That's what the questioning is about, that's what the documentation is about. If a coach is making a recommendation, they have to be able to justify it to the panel and if they can't justify it to the panel, then it gets overturned or they get sent back [to gather more evidence].

Noted one coach: "I've been really impressed with the panel. I think the panel has been very clear on what they see as evidence, and what they think is growth and not growth." Another coach commented that having to come before the panel with evidence to support a recommendation to either retain or fire a PT "keeps you honest" regarding what support has actually been provided to the PT and what evidence of growth has actually occurred. The comments in the following panel hearing excerpt, directed at the coach, are representative:

> *Brian:* It sounds like [the PT] has lots of content knowledge, can bring a lot of activities to class, but it's not tied to goals and assessment.
> *Panel Teacher 4:* Except that I'm going to ask, did you provide support in those areas?

In this way, there is a double loop of reciprocal accountability, as displayed in Figure 4.1. The panel holds the coaches accountable for teachers' evaluations, but must also provide them with support. Part of supporting the coaches and holding them accountable is ensuring that the coaches have provided adequate support to the PTs, who are, in turn, being held accountable for classroom teaching.

Of the 24 cases brought before the panel in April, four cases across two coaches involved the panel seeking more evidence or otherwise challenging the coach's initial recommendation. There was no case in which the panel overruled a coach's recommendation. Nonetheless, a close analysis of the panel hearing transcripts shows that in these four cases, the coaches' recommendations actually *changed* as a result of the panel hearing. In these cases, the coaches recom-

Figure 4.1. PAR's Double Reciprocal Accountability

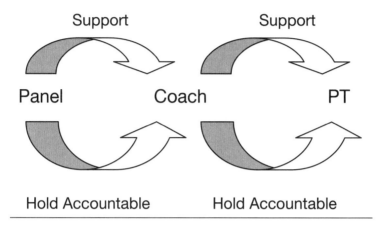

mended renewal in the written assessment documentation, but gave a wealth of negative evidence orally at the panel hearing. Table 4.2, below, builds out one of the cells from Table 4.1, providing additional details about the PTs who were not renewed.

The following exchange occurred in one of the four cases, involving an un-credentialed teacher, after both the coach and principal had discussed the PT's performance with the panel:

> *Panel Teacher 6:* [to coach] Why are you recommending that he be "renewed"?
>
> *Coach 10:* I put down renew with proof of enrollment in a credential program.
>
> *Panel Teacher 6:* It sounds like if he were in school while trying to teach, *nothing* would get done.
>
> *PT's Principal:* That's the impression I get.
>
> *Coach 10:* Well, if he were in a program, that would at least show us that he's interested in being a teacher, and maybe once he were taking classes, lights would go on about what teaching entails.
>
> *Panel Teacher 4:* I don't think at this point it's up to us to mother [the PT]. I think we make a recommendation based on what you've observed. If [the PT] has not met the requirement for rehire, then he should not be rehired.

Table 4.2. Summary of Year 1 Nonrenewed Beginning Teachers ($N = 12^a$)

| Coach's Original Written Recommendation Was to Nonrenew | Coach Recommended Nonrenewal After Challenge by Panel | Revert to Principal |
|:---:|:---:|:---:|
| 7 | 4 | 1 |

[a] One beginning teacher reverted to principal recommendation due to a fluke in employment status; therefore, technically 11 beginning teachers were nonrenewed by panel recommendation.

The coach noted in an interview a few weeks later, "I was tap dancing around giving a decision of nonrenewal, and they asked me directly, what is the evidence for keeping this person? I really didn't have enough. They held me accountable, and that was appropriate."

Similarly, in the second of these four cases, the panel identified the inconsistency between the coach's recommendation of continued employment and her verbal presentation, which revealed many concerns about the PT's performance:

> *Eva:* This teacher I've gone back and forth on, but I did recommend him for rehire based on his strength in science. He's not a very good planner or record keeper, but he does love science. . . . I asked him for his objectives or purpose, and he looked at me like I'm asking some weird question.
>
> *Brian:* If he doesn't have objectives, how does he know what to teach? [laughter]
>
> *Doug:* I'd like to see the summary evaluation reflect more of what you've just said about where he is. Everything you've written here supports the notion of reelection. In fact, where you have placed him indicates that he has met standards, and you're now saying that he hasn't.

Coaches commented on the difficulty of putting a negative assessment in writing, or of having the weight of the decision fall on them. The following exchange occurred in a third case, after both the coach and principal described the negative performance of a PT to the panel:

> *Doug:* [to Coach 10, with incredulity] Your recommendation [on the documents] was for renewal . . . ?
>
> *Coach 10:* Contingent upon [the principal's] assessment of [the PT's] professional accountability and reliability.
>
> *Doug:* There's a disconnect between the numbers you have put on this page, and the recommendation.
>
> *Coach 10:* Well, we coaches have a real hard time with putting on this paper, "do not rehire" . . . we do.

*Doug:* But that's what you're supposed to do.

*Coach 10:* I know, I know. . . . I would support not rehiring him.

*Doug:* When I was listening to you, I was listening to hear something that would justify keeping him.

*Panel Administrator 8:* Me too.

*Doug:* Where I thought you were going to go is his commitment, that he had signed up for a credential program. But it doesn't seem to make any difference.

*Coach 10:* I would say not renew him. There's a big learning that I hope will take place, he is taking classes, but I don't know that he will be any more effective than [he is now based on] what he said to [the principal], that he wants students who are self-motivated, where he just writes problems on the board.

*Doug:* I hear a recommendation of not reelect. Is there a motion?

*Panel Administrator 8:* I'll move that. . . . I would hope that this page can be revised to show that the coach supports the panel's recommendation not to rehire.

After completing the voting process, more discussion ensued.

*Susanna:* Coach 10 raised a really important issue, that coaches are struggling with needing to put down whether to rehire or not.

*Panel Teacher 5:* [to Coach 10] You shouldn't bear the burden of that at all. The weight of that shouldn't fall on you.

*Coach 10:* That's the discussion we had [among ourselves] as coaches, whether we were just presenting evidence and you decide, or whether we had to make a recommendation. That's why mine say things like "contingent."

*Observer (Special Assistant to the Superintendent):* [to Coach 10] I think you bring up a good point for us to discuss tomorrow. How can we support you better to do this? Let's face it, principals have the same problem.

The coaches, therefore, gave voice to what researchers have long observed in principals (Bridges, 1986, 1992). A disparity is typically seen between formal and informal teacher assessments. In a study of principals across Virginia, for example, principals formally identified 1.53 to 2.65% of teachers as "incompetent," but informally identified 5% as "incompetent" (and only 0.1% were actually dismissed) (Tucker, 1997). More recent studies have produced even more dismal results; in Chicago, for an example, principals gave unsatisfactory ratings to only 0.3% of teachers between 2003 and 2006 (New Teacher Project, 2007).

Conducting performance evaluations, whether in teaching or other occupations, is often a difficult process, and the PAR program was no exception. Looking back from the fourth year, Doug highlighted the issue:

> I remember that it took longer than I thought it would to get the point across to coaches that they were to have opinions. And they were to come to the panel with a judgment documented and supported, and we were then to argue with them about whether or not their conclusion was valid. Many of the folks wanted to come to the panel presenting everything and then have the panel make a decision. That's totally inefficient and also fights against the point of having them do evaluations. The point of doing an evaluation is to have an opinion.

Indeed, with traditional teacher evaluation, the evaluators (typically principals) often doubt themselves or seek to avoid confrontation, thereby failing to give either feedback that would actually help improve performance or a negative summative assessment despite cause for one. While the PAR coaches experienced some of this doubt, the results of their evaluations—in part due to the presence of the panel—were very different.

## CONCLUSION

The panel's job was to support and assess the PAR program's core work of teacher evaluation. This meant supporting the coaches in their work with PTs, as well as holding the coaches accountable. Both are relatively rare—teacher evaluators rarely receive support or face scrutiny of their work.

In dialogue with other educators, with the panel as a mirror to their assessments, and with documented evidence of teaching performance over time, the coaches themselves sometimes altered their official recommendations to match their informal assessments—and, in several cases, appeared relieved to have the panel point out the obvious. In this way, the PAR panel created formal lines of communication and reporting between coaches and panel members regarding the current teaching quality and potential future promise of PTs, which affected the coaches' recommendations. In doing so, some teachers who would have otherwise fallen through the cracks—just as they often do with traditional teacher evaluation—were removed from teaching. I will explore these issues further in Chapter 8.

## CHAPTER 5

# Two Cases of PAR in Action

> The fact is that for the first time people are actually being let go
> for mediocre teaching performance.
> —Doug, Rosemont teachers union president

This chapter looks closely at two cases of PAR in practice. Both are red flag cases of PTs whose continued employment was in question, in part because only red flag cases were presented at the panel hearings beyond November. In addition, however, such cases provide fodder for examining shifts in norms. The various elements of Rosemont's PAR program are distilled in these cases for analysis. Our focus is on two participating teachers, Kim and Timothy, who provide very different scenarios of the PAR coaches' work as evaluators. In the case of Kim, the coach relied on standards-based evaluation to document the new teacher's growth, acting as a buffer between the beginning teacher and a principal who, perhaps legitimately, wanted her gone. In the case of Timothy, the coach acted as gatekeeper, removing a beginning teacher that the principal likely would have retained. These two cases, therefore, also parallel the dual purposes of PAR, as identified by Doug, Rosemont's union president: eliminating the capricious nature of principals' firing of probationary (nontenured) teachers, and raising the bar for teacher quality. The cases provide a taste of how having a teacher evaluate another teacher is different from familiar administrator-led teacher evaluation models. Both are cases where the coach was particularly instrumental in the evaluation outcome, and therefore highlight the shifts in practice that occurred with PAR. This chapter will tell each of the teachers' stories in turn. Then, in Part III, I will draw on these cases to highlight the ways PAR interrupted educational norms.

## TEACHER LEADER AS BUFFER? THE CASE OF KIM

Betty Richards was the veteran principal of Walter Reed Elementary School. Walter Reed had one of the highest percentages of poverty in Rosemont, ranking number five in the district. After the newcomer schools, it had the highest number of limited-English-speaking students. As in many school districts, teacher segregation in Rosemont followed student segregation; as teachers gained experience, they tended to migrate to schools serving communities that had more wealth and fewer African American and Latino students.

One week prior to the start of school in September, Betty discovered that she had an open third-grade teaching position. Under the gun to find someone, she hired Kim, a first-year teacher without a teaching credential who seemed very enthusiastic. Because she was a new teacher, Kim was placed in PAR, and Eva was the coach assigned to work with her for the year.

## The Principal's Concerns

Betty compared Kim to other teachers and the comparison was not favorable. She commented, "Kim didn't want to spend the time. She much preferred to go out for coffee and socialize. In life, there are some things that hit you right away. Her class is always the first out to recess and the last in, every day. This is the gestalt that you pick up on." Betty identified Kim's lack of content and pedagogical knowledge: "Because we are a science-focused school, at the *least*, people should be interested in science, be willing to ask questions, to set up programs that do inquiry, to understand a little bit about how students construct knowledge. I felt like it would be very, very hard for her to learn it." Betty questioned Kim's ability with class management: "The first day, it was a class meeting, and already the class went amok because the kids knew, they learned that first day that school meant whenever they felt like it, they could talk about what they felt instead of content and learning things. So that still remains my question about her fit in the educational field." Betty also questioned Kim's commitment to urban students. She highlighted the school context: "We're an inner-city school, we're one of the poorest schools in the district." While the other new teachers had urban backgrounds or were bilingual, Betty complained that Kim had "been in the city for several years, but her background is from Connecticut" and "the linguistic piece was very difficult for her." To Betty, there was a cultural mismatch between Kim and the school community. Finally, Betty felt that her own involvement with Kim was reduced by PAR:

> Frankly, Kim could have used a lot more of my nurturing and experience, which I had to back off from giving because under the PAR program there's the PAR coach. She also has an onsite veteran teacher coach. And so, my God! With me, if I were in there too, I think she would be overwhelmed. Having so many people basically telling her what to do, I'm sure is very confusing.

## The New Teacher's Experience

Kim painted a very different picture. Kim's picture involved a principal who was overly negative, providing feedback in a manner that Kim was unable to absorb constructively. She described this incident from the fall:

She just was very negative, nonspecific and negative. "The kids aren't learning," she screamed at me one day in November. It was because an aide from another classroom had come in to borrow something and I said, it's back on my desk. I was on the rug with my class. She couldn't find it and she didn't speak English very well, so I got up and I left my class on the rug, just came up to the aide and was showing her where this worksheet was that this other teacher wanted to borrow. Well, Betty came in and saw the whole class sitting there not doing anything, and said, "What should you be doing?" They said, well, nothing. Because, I should have said, "Please, turn to your partner and count to a million"—that was the example she gave me. So I went into her office later and said that I wanted to apologize or to explain what had just happened. She was furious. "Well, this is just one example," she said, "the kids aren't learning, your lines in the yard are bad." Later, Eva said, "Well, she's right. You really should give the kids something to do whenever you leave them, that's just a basic teacher thing." I said, okay, you're right. Thank you. But, why did this lady have to get so mad?

Kim experienced Betty as someone who simply did not like her, gave up on her early, and was determined to have her out of Walter Reed. She noted: "It's been a really hard year. Eva was mainly a buffer in my relationship with my principal, or mediator. Because the relationship with Betty really didn't go so well. Eva helped me through it. . . . I was awfully depressed for a lot of the year." Highlighting Eva's role as "buffer," Kim described how Eva translated Betty's concerns into concrete specifics on which Kim might actually be able to improve:

I haven't actually worked with Betty at all in terms of improving my teaching practice, not without Eva there. At our first meeting, Betty went on and on, just "You're not doing a good job." And Eva kind of said, "Okay, here are the things she's going to work on." We were just trying to focus. Like, I'm going to get the kids in the yard on time, and then I'm going to work on the lesson plans. And so, that's what we did. And then we had another meeting a couple of months later and those things had improved.

Kim did not actually appear particularly focused on the stated areas for improvement beyond the big picture of lesson planning. When asked in an interview for the two teaching standards that were the focus of her work with Eva via her Individual Learning Plan, she had to pull out the actual ILP document to answer the question. Kim gave this appraisal of her future as a teacher:

I expect that I'm going to stay in teaching. Not forever. I'm already thinking about graduate school, maybe, in psychology . . . because I really like the relationship with the kids the most. More than the teaching, more than the timetables and the main idea. Right now, I'm just feeling like there's so much planning. And, again, it could just be my first year. Maybe it gets easier.

## The Coach's Perspective

Eva began the year with an opinion similar to Betty's, commenting on Kim's lack of content and instructional skill. However, Eva took on the role of steady supporter and ally to Kim—almost a good cop to Betty's bad cop, had Eva and Betty intentionally planned it that way. During the year, Eva remained focused on the district-adopted performance standards for teaching. She struggled to get Betty to put her criticism of Kim into standards language, to move away from intangibles and into concrete areas in which Eva could work with Kim to improve. In her role as coach, Eva saw Kim against the backdrop of 87 other beginning teachers—the 10 or so with whom she worked directly, as well as those with whom the other coaches worked and whom they discussed at their Friday meetings. With this perspective, and having an investment in seeing Kim succeed, Eva painted a much more positive picture of Kim than Betty did: "There were some things about Kim that really did need to be fixed; I agree with Betty there and I could see why she complained. But the principal really wrote her off, and I was saying no, she just needs more direction and more scaffolding. Kim's strength is her ability to make a connection; the kids love her. If she could learn content, she'd be in good shape." Eva contrasted the expectations set out by principals with the "scaffolding" of how to get there that she as a coach could provide:

> There's no real support [for new teachers from principals], like how do I get from A to B? And so that support is what I do. The principal just stated what should have been, this is what you *should* be doing, but didn't provide how do you get there. "You're doing really well on this, have you tried this, I want to come in tomorrow, will you try such and such . . . ?"

Eva also argued that Betty was encouraged to participate in Kim's assessment, commenting, "What she claimed was that she wanted to observe in Kim's classroom, but didn't want to interfere. And I said, 'No, this is not an interference, I don't know how many times I have to tell you, we *want* you to collaborate, we want your input, you have a lot of experience.' But somehow she sort of felt shunned. I invited her to come to an observation, she didn't."

## The Panel Decides

Although Eva was initially skeptical of Kim's chances for success, she was persuaded by the progress Kim made. Eva focused on planning, in essence teaching Kim how to lesson plan, and saw progress in Kim's lessons over time. She commented:

> My job was to go in and document [her progress]. I think I have done that. I invite anyone to do that. She has made growth. Is she where we want her to be? Maybe not. But this is standards-based evaluation, I don't want to just throw that out when she's not [yet] where we'd like her to be. The principal complains that she doesn't work hard enough. But she hasn't been that way with me. She has done what I've asked her to do.

Eva could ultimately speak far more concretely about Kim's practice than Betty when presenting to the PAR panel, given Eva's higher level of involvement in supporting Kim. Eva was able to use the performance standards document as a tool to demonstrate growth, and in doing so diffuse Betty's criticisms. Eva's ability to document Kim's progress using standards language put the more subjective nature of Betty's assessment into bas-relief. Noted one panel member:

> Betty is a successful principal, she has a set of beliefs and expectations that are basically okay, but she has gotten where she has on intuition and isn't able to articulate her intuition to a set of standards. She is used to calling the shots because that's what good strong principals do. I think she thought she had more authority than Eva due to personality, but Eva spoke with authority because her comments were grounded in the standards.

For Betty, however, Kim's progress was not sufficient to warrant keeping Kim at her school. She was looking for a certain quality of teacher, and Kim was not it. Betty argued that due to the increased challenges of second-language learners and poverty at her school, she, in fact, required higher-quality teachers. Yet, despite her litany of complaints about Kim, Betty ultimately never recommended that Kim be removed from the district. Despite her assessment that Kim fell short of some absolute standard, her recommendation to the panel was *not* that Kim be dismissed from employment in the district; she merely did not want Kim at her school. Betty explained:

> In April, at the panel hearing, I didn't propose nonrenewal—I didn't suggest she be fired from the district for next year. We focus on science, some schools focus on art. I don't think we should say that if a teacher is not good enough for one place, she's not good enough for all others—I don't buy that. Let's put it this way: I don't want to be so cold-hearted, you know? I mean, no principal wants to say, I'm the person who chopped off that person's knee caps, when who knows? There might be an epiphany that will happen this summer, 3 years hence, whatever. But I don't know where she should be now. She would not be suitable here.

Betty was very clear in her negative assessment of Kim. Yet her conclusion was merely to move Kim to a different school—the so-called dance of the lemons (Bridges, 1992). One panel member highlighted the need for professional development for principals: "They are coming in with baggage about how it's always been done. We have to look at that. What principals are used to is that because of the difficulty of the evaluation process, and the low success rate of principals with the evaluation process, it has been easier to get teachers to move to a different site."

The panel supported Eva's recommendation to renew Kim's employment, and Kim exited the PAR program. However, she was moved to a different school site, a change she welcomed.

## TEACHER LEADER AS GATEKEEPER: THE CASE OF TIMOTHY

Timothy, an uncredentialed teacher with education in English and some experience teaching math, was hired to teach science. Nancy was the first-year principal of Avery High School who hired him, and Caroline was the PAR coach charged with the task of coaching him toward success. Although everyone involved agreed that Timothy was smart and creative, his philosophy of education and his interests outside of teaching led them to the impression that he was "winging it," and his reluctance to change made them skeptical of his likelihood for improvement.

Timothy generally had positive feelings about Avery and his time there. He reported that, overall, he had a great experience, and that he learned a lot about teaching and a lot from his colleagues. He had a good rapport with his students. His supervisors saw him as talented, and recognized some exciting things that occasionally "slipped in" to his teaching. Overall, however, Caroline and Nancy did not see consistent quality from him, and, in fact, quickly came to view him as resistant to learning and change. Concerns about Timothy's performance fell into two main categories: the quality of his current practice, and his ability to develop into a successful teacher.

### Quality of Practice

Caroline and Nancy had the specific sense that Timothy put insufficient time into the job. Outside of school, he worked as a photographer. Nancy reported:

> I do think he was in overload. He was struggling with lesson plans, playing catch-up, and doing work for his credentialing program. And then on top of it, Caroline was asking for things from him. So you know, he was in overload, but he was also very involved in his photography. I felt like his priorities kind of got messed up in that he wasn't willing to make the time it takes to do this job well.

On the same theme, Caroline noted, "Timothy basically didn't spend enough time being a new teacher. He is also taking classes. He looked exhausted when I did his observation, and at other times. I tried to encourage him to do less. He is working on his credential, but he's just not being realistic about what it takes."

Caroline and Nancy viewed the degree of looseness evident in Timothy's practice as a clear problem—one linked to his time management, or perhaps personal style. Caroline noted:

> He is very loose about everything—about lesson planning, about discipline, about his appearance, about coming to faculty meetings. When I talked to him [initially] about doing lesson plans, he said it limits his creativity. I thought, "Oh no!" I urged him to keep a calendar, to write things down. He says he doesn't need to because he has a great memory. But he misses school meetings and he missed his second formal observation. He acknowledged that he had a real problem with organization. He asked for help with organization. But every single specific that I suggested he did not do! So, what do you do with that? I don't know.

Nancy agreed with Caroline's assessment, and urged Timothy to alter his behavior in order to get through the evaluation process, saying, "I told him, you know, you can just play the game. Do what you need to do to make it through [the evaluation process], and then once you're in there you can make adjustments, and he just didn't get it." This perception of looseness and unwillingness to adjust to his coach's and the panel's expectations—even when suggested by the principal as only temporary conformity—led to the assessment that Timothy was not serious about teaching and was just winging it. Noted Nancy, "I think he really felt that he was always going to make it, that no matter what, his fly-by style would do." One panel member highlighted the issue this way: "Timothy is a very intelligent man, and it's not that I don't agree with some of the cynical things he said—about standards and uniformity, blah blah—I have said them myself. But he underestimates the complexity of the job of teaching. If he is serious, we want him to go through a credential program, to get those planning skills."

## Ability to Develop

Timothy firmly believed that his skills as a teacher were sufficiently well developed to enable him to break the rules sooner rather than later, and to succeed with limited time investment. As a result, Caroline experienced him as resistant from the beginning. She noted, "I think it's that Timothy has a thing about authority," adding that "the very first time I met with him he was sitting at his desk correcting papers and he did not get up and stop correcting papers until I finally asked him to do so." Nancy concurred, commenting, "He really battles authority. I tried to give him support in science, because I was a science teacher, but he'd get defensive."

Timothy countered that what was being asked of him was unreasonable:

> Caroline had a set of demands that she received from the PAR panel [in January], for me to do one lesson plan a week. Which is not that much, which I did every week, even though I didn't like the formal nature of it, you've got to write a seven-step lesson plan, and it's got to include antici-patory set and objectives and I think that I'm in the okay when I say I know how to do that. . . . I think I've proven myself competent to the point where someone saying that you need to have weekly overviews when I'm already doing a lesson plan a week, where I'm already doing long-range plans for both subjects, where I'm already doing unit plans for both subjects, when I am also a student and working 70 to 80 hours a week, I say that is an unreasonable demand. I told her I thought these requirements were detracting from my practice as a teacher.

Despite Timothy's self-assessment, in the April hearing, one panel member ex-claimed, "These are his lesson plans? I'm sorry, these would be my notes, I wouldn't show these to anybody!" The lead coach concurred, responding, "Not under duress." Timothy lacked the self-reflection to see the need for improvement. He reported:

> If Caroline was right, if the demands were right, then I would agree. If she took the directorial role and she was right, then I would say, "Okay." I mean, I don't like to think of myself as a total anti-authoritarian person, but when somebody gets in my face and tells me what to do, I'm less likely to do it. When I believe I've shown that I am capable of doing my job and someone comes up to me and tells me to do stuff in a directorial way, I take that as an insult.

Timothy liked the idea of optional assistance that he could take or leave, noting, "I don't think that the program is all weaknesses; I think the assistance side of it [is good]." Still, he considered the review aspect of PAR an insult. He wanted free-dom to define his own practice. Yet his resistance to input, whether in the form of a suggestion or demand, was hard for Caroline and the panel to swallow, precisely because he was new to teaching. Even with 2 years of experience, he had no cre-dential and he was teaching a new subject. Noted Caroline:

> After the decision, he and I and the principal were meeting one day. He was saying, "Caroline was asking me to do things that weren't useful to me," and Nancy said, "Do you find lesson planning useful?" And even

then, even knowing that that was the substance of my case, he said to the principal, "Well, for new teachers, yeah, but I'm experienced." The whole point was he's not experienced enough.

One idea behind career ladders is that one is *not* a professional in the first years, but rather a novice or apprentice. Nancy countered Timothy's expectation of professional freedom with the notion that one can perhaps break with protocol after having proven oneself competent.

Ultimately, it was the perceived lack of willingness to be self-reflective that led to Timothy's nonrenewal. Caroline summarized:

> He has taught 2 years previously outside of the district. That was one reason I was as hard on him as I was—that was one reason why I wasn't judging him as a brand-new teacher because he's not a brand-new teacher. Where I didn't succeed was that he adamantly refused to agree with my analysis of the situation. He just didn't agree with it. He basically said, "I'm fine. I'm doing a terrific job. I don't need to change." And that was what I couldn't support. I just couldn't agree with it.

Nancy concurred: "Some things you can just let go by the wayside. Maybe his room isn't always clean, or this or that. But I think it was his inability to understand what he needed to do. Not so much even the paperwork stuff, but that there didn't seem to be enough of self-reflection." Caroline acknowledged Nancy's hesitation to take a hard line with Timothy, but knew that the attention she had given to him allowed her to speak from a place of great strength: "I think the principal is comfortable saying you're right, let's not renew this person, because she really knew how much support I had given him."

### "A Historic Decision"

Based on Caroline's recommendation and Nancy's support of that recommendation, the panel voted not to renew Timothy's contract with the district. Had Timothy not been in PAR, and had Nancy felt empowered to assess him negatively under the traditional model, the implications would have been less final: He would still have been eligible for employment in the district the following year. As an uncredentialed teacher with an emergency contract, if he were not rehired by his principal, the district would be under no obligation to employ him again, but there would be *no prohibition* against hiring him, either. With PAR, however, a nonrenewal decision by the panel put Timothy on a list at human resources of teachers not to be rehired into the district.[1] As a result, PAR appeared as a more coherent and aggressive method of monitoring teacher quality across the district. As Nancy highlighted, "I think what the surprise was [for Timothy] was that he was going to be terminated, not that he wouldn't be here at this school, but that he wouldn't have a chance to be anywhere in the district." In fact, Timothy was told in his nonrenewal letter from the PAR panel that if he acquired a teaching credential and had 1 year of successful teaching in another district, he could be reemployed in Rosemont.

Since the status quo in teaching in underserved communities across the country has been to accept (i.e., tenure) almost everyone, it is not surprising that Timothy was shocked to be faced with nonrenewal. Noted one panel member, "He may have blown Caroline off for the first semester because he didn't think this was real." Timothy, like most teachers, was not used to standards and gatekeeping in education. For this reason, the union president called the dismissal historic, commenting:

> This is the first time in this district that . . . someone has been let go from the district for just winging it, not really being a clear and present danger to children, but not really getting it about what the job entails. Not because they were evil people or molested children or anything like that. Not because someone took a personality dislike to them, not because of this, that, or the other thing. Simply because their classroom performance was mediocre.

Caroline's recommendation and the panel's ultimate support of that recommendation announced that teaching is, in fact, a complex job, one that needs to be made a priority and worked at for mastery.

What we see in this case is the degree to which such an announcement is a novelty. Doug expressed doubt that anyone would have confronted Timothy later on in his career about his performance if he had been renewed through the PAR process. A key argument made by PAR supporters, and supported in the evaluation literature, is that principals have an extremely low rate of giving negative evaluations, regardless of identified below-standard performance. Instead, they often utilize other options, such as consolidation, to move unsatisfactory teachers out of their school. Nancy agreed with Caroline about Timothy's performance, but without Caroline and PAR, she most likely would have retained him. Nancy indicated indecision and a hesitancy to make a decision that would "negatively" affect Timothy:

> It was really a personal struggle to go with the decision to nonrenew, because Caroline and I had to talk about it and she was more there than I was in the beginning because I like to look at people and see how we can work together. The first year is difficult, and I remember how difficult it was for me, so I really kind of err on the side of keeping someone and working with them. So it was a real struggle with him [for me].

Despite Nancy's fundamental agreement with Caroline's assessment of Timothy, that he was winging it and not meeting standards, she acknowledged Caroline's significant role in the employment outcome. She explained:

I did rely on Caroline because it was my first year as a principal. The fact is that I simply wasn't in his room that much. Of course I would have been in there more if Caroline weren't part of the picture. But even though I have my doubts about him—his resistance to suggestions—I might have just thought, well, I haven't seen enough, I haven't worked with him enough. That's clearly what could have happened.

Nancy indicated that she likely would not have acted on her belief that Timothy was below standard had she been solely responsible for the evaluation, without PAR.

Doug felt that, with the decision to nonrenew Timothy, PAR did a great service to the children of the district:

So the worst case, kids have been saved from a lackadaisical sort of person, and the best case, this will be a splash of clear, cold water in the guy's face and he'll come back in a year. . . . But the image of a lackadaisical emergency room surgeon, someone who really doesn't want to be there or someone who doesn't really think they have to sterilize instruments or doesn't have to follow any procedures because he has a higher calling, I wouldn't want to have that doctor operate on me. That's what we would have let happen if we renewed him. This was hard, but it was a good discussion and a good decision.

Nancy expressed a sentiment similar to Doug's: "I knew what was going to happen, he'd be here next year, and he would just slip by again."

To Timothy, he was a casualty of the political fray. He said, "I think that I got caught up in trying to counteract [the long-standing acceptance of bad teaching], and you know, I really think I got screwed by the PAR program." Caroline and Nancy expressed a very different perspective, emphasizing the potential effect on other teachers of the gatekeeping that removed Timothy. Noted Caroline:

The other teachers at his school, for instance, saw, wow, somebody wasn't renewed, you know? Somebody who seemed to be a good guy and we liked him, but he wasn't renewed. PAR really means business here. I mean, I certainly have known teachers like Timothy who go on year after year after year thinking that mediocre or less is okay and nobody ever calls them on it because their kids aren't falling out of the windows. I think we're making accountability stronger.

Nancy echoed: "I think it is a message to these other people that set the tone like he does. You know, they come in late to meetings, they sit in the back. It's like, man, this guy's going to be gone. Well, it's a message: Do you want to be here?"

## CONCLUSION

The cases of Kim and Timothy provide a bird's-eye view into PAR in action, and the differing issues and tensions that arise depending on the individuals involved. As cases of uncredentialed teachers, some readers may feel that Kim and Timothy do not represent the caliber of beginning teachers in their district. Similarly, some readers may be confident that principals in their district are "better" at teacher support and assessment than Betty or Nancy. The research on teacher evaluation nationwide suggests otherwise. Ultimately, both Betty and Nancy expressed reluctance to act on their beliefs about Kim and Timothy's teaching ability, fitting the pattern of principal behavior with evaluation. We saw PAR, in turn, alter evaluation in a variety of ways, to be explored further.

In Part III of the book, I will continue to draw on the cases of Kim and Timothy in order to exemplify four central violations of educational norms.

# *Interrupting Education's Norms*

## CHAPTER 6

# Interrupting Norms of "Being Nice"

## PAR as a Combination of Formative and Summative Assessment

It's been a very good relationship because it's been a very open one. That's one of the nice things about my coach, she encourages me to be open. So if things run badly, I can say it ran badly. In that sense I never saw her as somebody judging, which in any case she was doing. . . . I didn't see her as anybody that I had to be scared of. I just saw her as somebody who would tell me the truth and whether I was really ready to be a teacher or not.

—Rosemont participating teacher

As should be clear by now, PAR alters the typical coaching relationship by linking formative and summative assessment. This fact is central to PAR and is likely the best-known facet of peer review programs. Perhaps the most often-cited concern about PAR is a questioning of the combination of "support" with "evaluation," seen by many as a conflict of interest that will damage the coaching process (e.g., Cogan, 1973; Hazi, 1994; Huling-Austin, 1990; Nolan, 1997; Popham, 1988). Certainly not all PTs were as open and trusting as the one quoted above. Can PTs really be honest—as they may need to be for valuable support—with the person who will also be judging their performance?

Ellen Moir, director of the Santa Cruz New Teacher Center and an advocate for new teachers and coaching, has said that PAR moves us beyond the culture of "being nice" that is so common in the feminized world of education (Moir, 1999). Given the concerns that many educators have about the combination of support and evaluation, this chapter examines the interruption of this educational norm—the interruption of a culture that has perhaps preferred being nice over substantive criticism. I will not engage in all the rich contours of this debate, which would go beyond the scope of the book. I also certainly do not propose that the findings are generalizable to all or even many supervisory and evaluative settings. I am focused on one particular programmatic case, PAR, in one particular district setting, Rosemont. Nonetheless, the outcomes in Rosemont proved very interesting, and ran counter to generally accepted beliefs.

The chapter asks: To what degree do PTs trust their coaches, who are conducting both formative and summative assessments? In addition, how do PTs who do not trust their coaches differ from those who do?

## AN AGE-OLD DEBATE

The traditional supervision model challenged by PAR is predicated on the lack of a judgmental role; educators typically argue that supervision and evaluation are incompatible (see Holland & Garman, 2001). Nolan (1997) defines teacher supervision as "an organizational function concerned with promoting teacher growth and leading to improvement in teaching performance and greater student learning" (p. 100). He defines teacher evaluation as "an organizational function designed to make comprehensive judgments concerning teacher performance and competence for the purpose of personnel decisions such as tenure and continuing employment" (p. 100). In the interest of clarity, since the term *supervision* so often means different things to different readers, I will most often refer to it as *formative assessment* and to evaluation (typically conducted by a "supervisor") as *summative assessment*. Stiggins and his colleagues (2006) define formative assessment as assessment *for* learning, whereas summative assessment is assessment *of* learning.

Cogan (1973) argued that the supervisory relationship (focused on formative assessment) is based fundamentally on trust, and that without it, the supervisor/mentor will not achieve any improvements in instructional practice. Showers (1985) asserts that "the evaluation of teachers typically implies judgment," while "coaching implies assistance in a learning process" (p. 46), the implication being that judgment and assistance cannot coexist—although it is unclear how one effectively provides assistance without making any diagnostic judgments. Showers continues, "The norms of coaching and evaluation practice are antithetical and should be separated in our thinking as well as in practice" (p. 46). Odell (1987) argues that teachers in a supervisory role must be able to offer "unconditional support" (p. 75) to beginning teachers; Stroble and Cooper (1988) therefore argue that "assistance and assessment" must be clearly differentiated, as "assessment rarely coexists with unconditional support" (p. 234). Popham (1988) argued that combining formative and summative assessment will "deprive the formative teacher evaluator of the candid teacher reports so necessary if teacher weaknesses are to be eliminated." Many practitioners and scholars have, in fact, argued that not only should the two leadership functions of formative and summative assessment be carried out by different people, but that the information gathered through formative assessment should not "under any circumstances" (Popham, 1988, p. 271) be shared with the person conducting summative evaluation (see also Cogan, 1973; Nolan, 1997).

Other educators, however, have argued that formative and summative assessment can and should be combined, that they enhance one another. Only through the collection of data over time—including an understanding of the teaching context, the focus of improvement efforts, the challenges faced by the teacher, how hard the teacher is trying to improve and with what degree of self-reflection and self-assessment, and the growth or lack thereof that the teacher has accomplished—can an evaluator hope for a summative assessment to be fair and accurate. In other words, summative assessment should be the summation of formative assessment, the former obtaining its validity from the latter (Danielson & McGreal, 2000; Hunter, 1988; McGreal, 1997). Hunter (1988) disagrees with Popham's (1988) claim that "candid teacher reports" will be lost if formative and summative assessment are linked: "It is naïve to believe that the teacher will reveal problems to a supervisor and conceal them from an evaluator. Problems in performance behavior cannot be concealed. They are inevitably revealed to any sophisticated observer" (p. 277). Hunter's premise is that summative assessment is improved by linking it to formative assessment, and that formative assessment is not harmed by linking it to summative assessment. The latter is the core argument of this chapter: Most teachers in PAR did indeed appear able to engage in a trusting coaching relationship with someone who was nonetheless their summative evaluator, and those who did not were low-performing PTs.

## THE TRUST QUESTION IN PAR

To what degree do PTs trust their PAR coaches? Two types of data from Rosemont's PTs help answer this central question: interviews with 15 of 88 PTs at the end of the first year of the program and surveys returned from 112 of 143 PTs at the end of the second year of the program (a response rate of 78%). After trust emerged as an issue in some interviews during the first year of the study, I added questions assessing it to a survey administered to PTs the following year.

In short, PTs reported a high degree of trust in their coaches. On a four-point Likert scale where 1 was "strongly disagree" and 4 was "strongly agree," a construct comprised of questions assessing trust ($\alpha = 0.90$) (see Table 6.1) had a mean of 3.47 (SD = 0.82). The mean for a construct assessing lack of trust ($\alpha = 0.79$) (see Table 6.2) was 1.97 (SD = 0.85). In other words, PTs' agreement that they trusted their coach was a point and a half higher on the survey than their agreement that they did not fully trust their coach.

Similarly, in open-ended responses for program commendations and recommendations on the year 2 survey, five PTs did comment that the evaluative structure of PAR led them to less honest communication with their coach, but three times as many (16) noted that the honesty and openness of their relationship with

Table 6.1. TRUST Construct, Year 2 (PT Survey)

| Question | Content |
| --- | --- |
| 23 | I feel able to speak openly and honestly with my coach. |
| 24 | My coach supports me to take risks and try new instructional strategies. |
| 52 | I feel supported by my PAR coach. |

(3 items, $\alpha = 0.90$; mean = 3.47; SD = 0.82; $N = 112$)

(1 = strongly disagree; 4 = strongly agree)

their coach was a strength of the program. More broadly, 18 PTs commended the degree to which they were supported to grow and/or take risks as a teacher. Although some PTs certainly felt negatively about the mentorship-evaluation combination, far more PTs reported having trust in their coaches.

The interview data from year 1 PTs provide exactly the same findings as the year 2 survey data, that some PTs voice a concern about conflict of interest, but many more do not. More significantly, we learn from the interview data that, although not all struggling PTs lacked trust in their coaches, those PTs who did report a less-than-honest relationship with their coaches were all struggling teachers. The interview results are summarized in Table 6.3, below.

For 13 of the 15 PTs interviewed, the topic of possible conflict of interest was not initiated by the PT him- or herself, so instead, I directly asked the question: Did your coach's role as evaluator ever prevent you from being fully honest? For many, it was not at all an issue. Noted one PT:

> My coach had an idea of where I had started, and how much I had grown. He knew the struggles I had had, so he could look to see if I had addressed those in my lesson plans, instead of just looking at it overall. I really liked that there was some kind of benchmark, that was much better than having someone

Table 6.2. LACK OF TRUST Construct, Year 2 (PT Survey)

| Question | Content |
| --- | --- |
| 50 | I sometimes don't share my thoughts and feelings with my PAR coach because he/she is also my evaluator. |
| 51 | I am sometimes reluctant to try out new teaching strategies if my PAR coach is observing me. |

(2 items, $\alpha = 0.79$; mean = 1.94; SD = 0.85; $N = 112$)

(1 = strongly disagree; 4 = strongly agree)

Table 6.3. "Did Your Coach's Role as Evaluator Ever Prevent You from Being Fully Honest?" As Reported in PT Interviews, Year 1 ($N = 15$)

| Number of PTs | Response | How Initiated in Interview |
|---|---|---|
| $n = 2$ | Yes | PT initiated comment |
| Both = red flags<br>1 = nonrenewed (Timothy)<br>1 = renewed (Regina) | | |
| $n = 1$ | Yes | PT response when asked |
| 1 = a red flag<br>1 = nonrenewed | | |
| $n = 12$ | No | PT response when asked |
| 5 = red flags<br>1 = nonrenewed<br>4 = renewed | | |

who just comes in once and catches what's happening. So for me, it was great to have the PAR coach do the evaluation, the official evaluation.

Three of the 13 PTs who did not initiate the topic of conflict of interest acknowledged that being evaluated by one's mentor might raise problems. Of those, two felt that the pros of combining support and evaluation outweighed the cons. Noted one of them:

> I could see that [some would voice that concern]. With math, that's an area I still need to improve on, and I could have probably asked my coach more about math. And if she wasn't evaluating me, would I have done that? I might have. . . . [But] the PAR coach sees growth over time. You just have to weigh which is more important. Is it better to maybe be [more] open or is it better to really understand the teacher that you're evaluating? I think, particularly if it's only 1 year, that it's much better to have the coach be the evaluator. I feel very comfortable with my coach evaluating me. . . . It wasn't like this is the first time she's really going to sit in there for like an hour!

One of these three PTs, however, felt that the benefits of PAR support could be attained without the connection to evaluation. This PT was a struggling teacher, someone who was red flagged and ultimately not renewed for employment at the end of the year. The PT commented:

I felt like I was a little afraid to say whatever, especially because she came from the district office [sic][1] and it was really official and everything. That's a difficult question for sure. I would say that the PAR program was extremely helpful and really supportive, but I think you could also have it as the PAR program and have the principal evaluate and it would still be really effective.

The PT continued by describing a topic that he felt he could not discuss with someone "from the district office" who was evaluating him:

There are teachers that work here that grew up in [the neighborhood] and there was a real local atmosphere here and I really did feel like an outsider. I didn't know Spanish and I didn't know that much about the culture, and I think that that was a problem. I do think I really was careful about is this an appropriate thing to say to [my coach] or not. Where I can talk to, for example, the math teacher across the hall, I can talk to him about just anything as a friend or as a person, just talk to him about dealing with feeling like I'm not fitting in and so forth. I don't think I was able to talk to [my coach] about that. I have to say that's one thing that was missing is that it would have been great to just say whatever I had to say and know that I wasn't going to get penalized for it.

Reinforcing Hunter's (1988) argument that performance problems cannot be concealed from a skilled diagnostician, however, this PT's coach was well aware of the issue he identifies above, as was his principal. In interviews, both identified the PT's inability to relate to the students, and as a result, successfully manage the class.

Recall that Hunter (1988) argued that a skilled diagnostician need not rely upon a teacher's trusted secrets. The example above, like Eva's story in Chapter 3 of surreptitiously supporting an overly confident PT by putting him in a leadership role, lends credence to Hunter's claim that mentor-mentee trust is not crucial. As Eva highlighted:

You might not want to trust me and share your challenges with me at first, but it becomes very obvious. . . . So part of it will be, how do I convey to you that I see it, and that I'm going to help you. . . . It's not like a one-time deal, there's ample time to grow, if you want to. I don't think you can fail at it unless you were really not meant to be a teacher, and then it's so obvious that I don't have to gain your trust to find that out.

Despite these examples, however, the bulk of the data from Rosemont (especially PT surveys) absolutely support the centrality of trust in the mentor-mentee relationship—not so much for assessment purposes as for teacher satisfaction and retention purposes (see Goldstein, 2007b). The point here is that while trust certainly matters, in those cases where trust was not present, coaches were nonetheless quite able to diagnose performance problems without input from the PT.

Finally, of the 15 PTs interviewed, two raised the issue of a perceived conflict of interest between providing support and conducting evaluations, without being prompted by me. Both were red flagged as struggling teachers. One was ultimately not renewed for employment, Timothy from Chapter 5. The second, Regina, was renewed, but will be highlighted in Chapter 9 as a case where the panel should probably have acted differently. Timothy commented:

> If my coach had just been a support person, if she didn't have that evaluative role, my response to her would have been the same. It would have been no different in terms of how I took it. I would have taken it with a grain of salt, either way. I mean, more than a grain of salt. How do I put this? The way that she stated that my lesson planning needed work would have been different if she wasn't in an evaluation role. She used the evaluation role as leverage to make that claim. Not from the beginning. But I was meeting her demands much more when she was taking the assistance role than when she was taking the yardstick role.

Although Timothy claimed that he responded to his coach much more at the outset, and that he only became defensive after the second panel hearing in January, both Caroline (his coach) and Nancy (his principal) were already describing him as non-responsive and defensive during the first PAR hearing in November. Caroline, in fact, reported from the beginning of the year that he was ignoring all of her input.

Caroline addressed her use of evaluation as leverage in her work with Timothy:

> There was no question that I had to work to alleviate his anxiety. There came a point actually in February . . . after I had initially made the presentation [to the panel] in January and come back to him and said, "Timothy, these are the things you really need to work on," and then a couple of weeks later he wasn't working on them. I said, "Timothy, I'm really serious about this. You've got to do this because if not, I won't be able to recommend you for renewal." And he got very angry and it took us about a week or 2 to come back from that.

Taking a self-reflective stance, Caroline originally questioned the connection between support and evaluation in her work with Timothy, as her first year as a coach came to a close:

> Even though I did my darndest to emphasize the positive and say don't worry, we have plenty of time to work on this, and here are some

suggestions, it put me too much in the driver seat. And I think that was really kind of fatal in my relationship with Timothy. I think he shifted into the model of, well, I'm going to see if I can figure out how to get her off my back, not really change in the way she wants, but make it sound like I'm doing what she wants without really grappling with it. Or at certain points just resisting it. Just totally kissing it off. So at that point the evaluation role actually negatively impacted my ability to be a good coach to him, even though I tried my darndest.

Caroline reported in the spring of year 1 that if she had the choice of doing the coach job without having responsibility for evaluation, she would definitely prefer it. However, by 1 year later, at the end of her second year as a PAR coach, she recanted this position, having come to view the summative piece as a critical part of the job. Caroline and Nancy were both skeptical that Timothy's performance would have changed with a support-only mentor. The principal summarized the complexity of the issue: "There's only one time, when he knew that we were probably going to terminate him, that he let down his guard. It's tricky. He wasn't being truthful, because he was being evaluated by the same person he needed support from. Of course, in this particular case, without the threat of being dismissed, I don't think he ever would have let down his guard."

PAR's evaluative teeth may be most necessary in the toughest cases, like Timothy's. Indeed, in such cases, it may be the only way to get a resistant teacher to change. Site-based coaches, for example, often complain that they are charged with improving teaching practice, but have no authority with classroom teachers. A "support-only" mentor would have done the best he or she could with Timothy, but it would have then been up to the principal to decide. That issue has already been discussed: A principal nonrenewal would have been unlikely. Caroline, by contrast, had the time, willingness, and official capacity to act as gatekeeper.

The second PT, Regina, who was ultimately renewed, also initiated the topic of a conflict of interest, commenting:

I think for me there's a basic conflict of interest in terms of the person coaching me also evaluating me, because I don't really feel I want to share my problems in everything, which will influence the evaluation process to be more negative. I find it threatening to have someone coming in all the time and talking to me about my development, and at the same time evaluating me, so for me it's been very stressful. Not to say teaching is not stressful anyway.

This PT's coach, Sarah, acknowledged that the relationship got off to a bad start, describing one particular incident:

I had to step back a lot. I think I was so worried. I saw so many red flags that I felt in the beginning that I needed to give her specific ways of fixing those things. I remember one time in the very beginning where I went into her classroom and she had all these kids' names on the board with all the things that they weren't going to be able to do, like, José: no recess for 2 days. Cesar: no library for a week. That's how she was trying to manage the classroom. And I went in and I said, "You need to get rid of that today. I can't see that again." So I was very forceful, it really affected me. And then I had to rebuild [rapport] and I don't think we ever did really rebuild from that.

The PT's principal, Emily, strongly supported the coach, and had little sympathy for the PT's concerns about PAR. The principal believed strongly that the PAR model of combining formative and summative assessment strengthened accountability, in contrast to other support providers also working with this new teacher:

When Regina said to me, "I don't think [my coach and I] get along, I think that our personalities are different," my first question to the teacher was "Why? Are you overwhelmed? Okay, then who are some of the other support personnel that we can cut out so that you can work with this person who's really got the time, the wherewithal, the support and the dollars in terms of materials and release time and the connections to give you what you need. And my expectation is that you're going to meet standards and the rest of the folks aren't helping you meet the standards." And in my head I would be thinking they're feel-good folks and this person is helping you be a better teacher. . . .

Regina compared the intensity of her support and evaluation experience to the experience of one of her friends:

Even though the person is helping me do my job, there's still that negative aspect to it that is a constant source of worry. So I would look forward to having it out of my life, to be honest with you. I knew I would be evaluated in this job, but it is not the same process that other people that I've known have gone through. Like my friend who teaches fourth grade in another school has had the principal drop in for two evaluations a year, fairly stress-free, that's it. Mine is like an ongoing thing that I'm dealing with every week.

The comparison of Regina's evaluation and that of her friend is telling; I'll return to it.

The data, therefore, do show some truth to concerns about compromising openness and trust. Yet those who harbored this concern were exclusively under-performing PTs. In addition, it was only some of the weakest PTs, some of those potentially not meeting standards, who harbored this concern. Of the 12 teachers who did not report in interviews seeing a problem in the combination of forma-tive and summative assessment, five were "red flags" and one was not renewed for employment at the end of the year.

Having established that most PTs trusted their coaches, and that some of the underperforming PTs did not, the survey data provided additional information about those PTs who reported a lack of trust in their coach. The surveys were ana-lyzed[2] for the demographic variables of gender, years teaching, level (elementary, secondary), and credential status (pre-intern/intern, preliminary/clear, emergency). I found few differences between teachers based on these variables. The exception was for credential status (see Table 6.4). Specifically, PTs with emergency creden-tials who were either in their second year of teaching or beyond or were secondary teachers reported significantly lower trust in their coaches than other PTs. The group sizes for these comparisons were too small to report conclusively, but the trend suggests that particular attention might need to be paid to these demographic

Table 6.4. PTs' Reported TRUST by Credential Status, Years Teaching, and Level, Year 2 (PT Survey)[†]

|  |  | Credential Status [††] | | | |
| --- | --- | --- | --- | --- | --- |
| Measures |  | a:<br>Pre-Intern/Intern | b:<br>Prelim/Clear | c:<br>Emergency | Significance |
| TRUST | *Years Teaching* |  |  |  |  |
|  | 1st Year | 3.72 | 3.54 | 3.22 |  |
|  | 2+ Years | 3.75$^c$ | 3.50$^c$ | 2.28$^{a, b}$ | $F(2,101)$<br>$= 3.33*$ |
|  | *Level* |  |  |  |  |
|  | Elementary | 3.56 | 3.61 | 3.78 |  |
|  | Secondary | 3.88$^c$ | 3.46$^c$ | 2.22$^{a, b}$ | $F(2,101) =$<br>$5.01**$ |

[†] Surveys were analyzed using multivariate analysis of variance (MANOVA).
[††] See endnote number 1 in Chapter 3 for an explanation of the credential status categories.
*Note:* Superscripts indicate that groups are significantly different from one another at the $p \leq .05$ level, with a letter in one column indicating from which other column the significant between-groups difference exists.
* $p \leq .05$; ** $p \leq .01$
(1 = strongly disagree; 4 = strongly agree)

groups (although reliance on emergency credentialed teachers has declined dramatically since the data were collected).

It is worth noting that research commissioned by Rosemont in year 3 of the program, in which I had no involvement but which utilized measures from the year 2 survey, came to parallel findings. The in-house document states that "participating teachers report that their coaches' evaluation does not impact the teachers' willingness to speak honestly, take risks, and try new instructional strategies." In addition, while there were no major differences across groups based on gender, years teaching, and credential status, once again a trend was seen suggesting that emergency credentialed teachers with 2 or more years of teaching experience may be more likely to have issues with trust.

## CONCLUSION

Many skeptics of PAR criticize the combination of formative and summative assessment, believing that the evaluative aspect of the program will compromise a PT's ability to speak honestly with his or her coach. Although some PTs in this study certainly felt negatively about the formative-summative combination, the results as a whole do not support this concern. Nolan (1997) argues that "supervision should be an opportunity for risk taking and experimentation" (p. 106), and indeed, most PTs in this study reported an ability to take risks and try new instructional strategies, as well as to speak openly and honestly with their coach.

What accounts for these findings? One possibility is that the formative aspects of the program, such as feeling helped, were strong enough (i.e., supportive enough) to outweigh the summative aspects, such as feeling evaluated.[3] If sufficient attention is paid to truly supporting teachers, making professional development and formative assessment central and ongoing as described in Chapter 3, it may be possible to also evaluate without the deleterious effects typically predicted.

The issue of teacher retention is of particular concern given the current shortage of high-quality teachers, particularly in settings that serve low-income students and students of color (Lankford et al., 2002). We must ultimately, however, be concerned with differentiated retention: retaining strong teachers, and removing weak ones. This is the purpose of the summative assessment aspect of teacher evaluation. Given that one goal of teacher evaluation is gatekeeping for teachers who perform below standards (Nolan, 1997), is the fact that some underperforming teachers experienced low trust in their PAR coach necessarily a problem? Although it is certainly not true in all cases, we might expect a somewhat untrusting or even negative relationship to develop between PT and coach for some struggling PTs. The traditional supervision argument would posit that it is not possible to improve performance without trust. The interview data from this study, however, suggest that improved performance would have been very unlikely for the few teachers reporting low trust, regardless of the nature of the coaching relationship.

It is possible that with the lowest-performing teachers, coaches took a more directive role that relied more heavily on their evaluative function. It would, perhaps, then make sense for these teachers to report lower trust in their coaches. The familiar alternative of leaving these teachers a wide berth to continue weak practices hardly seems more attractive. Sarah expressed little patience for possible PT complaints: "When you're in credential school you have summative assessment. It's called finals. Why, when you're actively in the classroom with kids, why should that not be the same?" To the extent that there were some costs vis-à-vis participating teacher trust with PAR, it is ultimately a question of priorities, and some educators have begun to argue that traditional models of mentoring and coaching do not go far enough with respect to accountability issues (Feiman-Nemser, 2001; Wasley, 2001), or that supervision must be reframed to balance the improvement of instruction with the "democratic authority" to evaluate instruction and ensure quality (Holland & Garman, 2001).

Recall Regina's complaint that her friend in another school and not in PAR "had the principal drop in for two evaluations a year, fairly stress-free." I posit that those concerned with teacher quality should be more concerned with the lack of attention paid to Regina's friend than with Regina's own complaints about undue oversight. For those few PTs whose trust was low, holding them accountable is likely more important than making sure they feel trusting toward their coach. To the extent that PAR proves to be a rigorous method of weeding out underperforming teachers may simply outweigh concerns that some of those underperformers *might* have improved with a more trusting relationship with a nonevaluative coach. At least with Timothy, that was an unlikely outcome. There is also no guarantee that a nonevaluative coaching arrangement will necessarily breed trust, as some teachers are simply wary of all supervisory arrangements. For example, Stanulis and Russell (2000) identified a student teacher's reluctance to admit gaps in knowledge and ask for help due to fears of being evaluated, in what was a strictly formative mentoring relationship.

If we are serious about the dual purposes of teacher evaluation—improving instruction *and* ensuring quality—then educators might spend less time concerned with providing "unconditional support" (Odell, 1987) for teachers and more time creating the conditions for quality teaching. In any other field, this would mean ongoing assessment, serious critique matched with support for improvement, and removal when targeted goals are not met despite genuine opportunities to improve. Hunter (1988) notes:

> It is interesting that in no other enterprise do we consider helping people become more skilled, and determining that they *have* become more skilled, to be mutually exclusive enterprises. . . . Surely, teaching graduate classes does not interfere with

grading those same students. We would stipulate it contributes to a fair grade! A coach who has worked with a player usually can give a more accurate appraisal of their present skills and future potential than can a one time skilled observer. (p. 276)

Invariably, in a system historically fraught with isolation and lack of oversight, opening the doors of teaching practice to scrutiny will bother those who did not expect their practice to be scrutinized. The need to improve the quality of teachers and teaching will not allow this luxury.

## CHAPTER 7

# Interrupting Norms of Hierarchy

## *PAR as a Distribution of Leadership Responsibility for Teacher Evaluation*

> Some of the coaches couldn't even write it down, because it
> was so frightening to say: "No renewal." We've never done that
> before! You know? Have a peer say that to another peer. . . .
> But, I think that's where the strength of the program really has
> come through for me.
> —Teacher on the Rosemont PAR panel

Given the shift in teachers' and principals' roles that occurs with PAR, the policy signals a potential jurisdictional shift over the leadership function of teacher evaluation, as introduced in Chapter 1. At this point in the book, the reader hopefully has a relatively firm grasp of how PAR works. Chapter 6 addressed one of the most common concerns about PAR, its combination of formative and summative assessment. This chapter now looks deeply at what is, ultimately, the heart of the matter—control over teacher evaluation decisions. The chapter explores two related questions that are central to understanding the shift at the heart of PAR policy: How did those involved with implementing PAR in Rosemont make sense of the new role of teacher as evaluator of other teachers? Then, how, if at all, was leadership responsibility for teacher evaluation redistributed?

The notion that leadership is "distributed" across multiple actors in a school rather than housed solely with the site administrator has gained currency since the mid-1990s (see, for example, Gronn, 2002; Heller & Firestone, 1995; Leithwood & Jantzi, 2000; Ogawa & Bossert, 1995; Spillane, Halverson, & Diamond, 2001). In particular, Spillane and colleagues put forth the idea that leadership is "stretched over" two or more leaders in their interactions with followers in particular situations (Spillane et al., 2001; 2004; Spillane, 2006). In the case of PAR, those implementing the policy were constantly engaged in negotiating the ways that responsibility for teacher evaluation was stretched over the coaches, principals, and PAR panel. This chapter is specifically concerned with the novel configuration of stretching responsibility for teacher evaluation across coaches and principals (Spillane et al., 2001).[1]

Ingersoll (2003) lays out three critical issues that one must address when doing research on control in schools. The first is to define the most important decisions, which, in this case, were the summative evaluation decisions for participating teachers. Who, ultimately, was responsible for deciding who would continue teaching in the district and who would be fired?

Second, Ingersoll specifies that one must determine the criteria by which to evaluate the distribution of control. In the case of PAR, where multiple voices contributed to the summative evaluation decisions, the criterion for control is who carried the most weight in those decisions—or who held jurisdiction? We can define jurisdiction for teacher evaluation as teachers having at least 51% of the "vote" and thereby being able to control evaluative outcomes. Evaluating the distribution of control, however, is complicated by whether one's control is in fact enacted. In other words, there is both a regulative and a normative component to control. If women earn the right to vote, for example, but then simply vote the way that their husbands tell them to, there is movement in the direction of suffrage, but we probably will not see the outcomes of elections radically altered. Similarly, if teachers possess regulative jurisdiction for teacher evaluation, but systematically defer to principals' opinions, teachers' control is in fact limited by their learned normative behavior. So there are two criteria for control of teacher evaluation: regulative control (greater than 50%) and normative behavior (influence that is in fact exerted).

Third, Ingersoll advises that one must decide how to measure who has control. In this case, I have analyzed qualitative data for evidence of control, including transcripts of meetings where employment decisions were made, in addition to interviews with the teachers and administrators involved.

## MAKING SENSE OF TEACHER LEADERSHIP
## IN AN AMBIGUOUS POLICY CONTEXT

Recall from Chapter 4 that the coaches' primary complaint about the panel was the desire for greater clarity. A certain degree of program ambiguity is to be expected with the implementation of most new policies (March, 1988). Although this ambiguity is not novel, it is highly relevant to understanding how individuals make sense of—and subsequently make decisions about—their roles and relationships within new programs. Surrounded by ambiguity, the coaches and those with whom they work were not merely performing new roles but were also in the act of framing, interpreting, and constructing new roles—in effect, authoring as well as reading the new policy (Weick, 1995). They had to make sense of PAR, and as they did so, the policy itself was given shape. Spillane and colleague (2002) argue that sensemaking is the interaction of three elements: prior knowledge and experience, policy signals, and social situation, including beliefs about those experiences, signals, and situations. They note: "The fundamental nature of cognition is that new information is always interpreted in light of what is already understood and believed" (Spillane et al., 2002, p. 394).

Spillane and colleagues' (2002) framework provides a guide for exploring the potential shift in authority relations that occurs with PAR. How did those involved with implementing PAR in Rosemont make sense of the new role of teacher as evaluator of other teachers? Most educators' prior knowledge about teacher evaluation is that it is the purview of principals. To understand their interpretation of PAR, then, we must ask what policy signals they received about the new teacher evaluation program, whether Rosemont's educators supported or believed in the traditional method of principal-led teacher evaluation, and how the new alternative supported or challenged the existing social situation.

## Initial Policy Signals about PAR

Although there was widespread confusion about an array of PAR program details, the most significant for our purposes involved the summative evaluations of teachers in PAR: Who would be conducting them and how? Only a few key players, notably Doug and Brian (the union president and district co-chair, respectively), designed the foundation of Rosemont's PAR program. The other panel members had varying degrees of prior knowledge about PAR, and they, as a group, hired the coaches. This contributed to a tiered array of understandings about what the program would look like.

In addition, as discussed in Chapter 4, the contract language was left sufficiently vague to leave the control of evaluation unclear. Recall that a distinction was made between "review" and "evaluation," such that the PAR program was responsible for the review of classroom performance for teachers in the program, while the principal was responsible for the evaluation of performance outside the classroom for the same group of teachers. However, the contract made the principal a participant in the review process as well.

Finally, while the contract may have provided a jumping-off point for the initial implementation, it was only one of many messages from the environment about the policy's meaning (Coburn, 2001). In addition to the contract language, panel members interpreted the program for coaches, coaches interpreted the program for principals and PTs, and coaches interpreted the program for one another every week in their Friday meeting. Principals received policy signals from Brian as well as the superintendent. Significant among the early messages was the repeated directive to coaches from the panel to "be diplomats" and "sell" the program to principals. In addition, as the program began in August, Brian suggested that its continued survival was in jeopardy due to unclear support from the superintendent.

The acting superintendent who had approved the PAR contract and appointed the district's representatives to the panel was no longer superintendent when the program began. The new superintendent, coaches and principals were told, wanted principals to be "instructional leaders." As the superintendent explained during an interview, "It's a program I want to keep, although there are some things about it I would want us to revisit and to talk about, and that would be how to include principals in this process in a way that they're really involved in an ongoing way in the teaching and learning and supervision process. . . . Great program if it included this very important part for me." She went on to express her commitment to principals as the ultimate instructional leader of their buildings, and impatience for the "principal overwhelm" complaint:

> I believe that the final person to sign off on an evaluation needs to be the principal. And, if the principal is outside of that process, how can they sign off on something that they haven't been involved in? . . . I always say to principals who say to me [that they don't have time to do all their evaluations well], I just sort of raise my eyebrows and think, hmmm, what's that about? It is your job.

Many principals who signed up for PAR, in fact, either did not understand its evaluative aspect, confusing it with other support programs, or did not understand where the locus of control for evaluation would be, confusing it with the standards-based teacher evaluation system (STES) for principals that was being piloted by the district at the same time and had been introduced at the same principals' meeting. One coach, Sarah, summarized:

> [Principals] had no idea whatsoever [how the program was meant to operate]. They had no clue. They were always surprised and thrilled and like, wow, you're doing three formal observations, you have so much work to do! But they had absolutely no idea what it was about. They were confused about the difference between PAR and STES. They didn't understand the component of evaluation that I was responsible for. One would turn in an evaluation on the PT [in addition to the one] I did. I think a lot of them got the mentoring part, but they were surprised to see me so much, like "Oh, you're here again!?"

As a result of the ambiguity surrounding responsibility for teacher evaluation with PAR, there were two potentially (though not inherently) conflicting messages about PAR evaluation: one that handed responsibility for the evaluation of classroom teaching to the coaches, and another that told coaches to work closely with principals, who were supposed to be the instructional leaders of school buildings.

## Different Beliefs about Teachers Conducting Evaluations

Within this context of varied messages about PAR in the environment was the reality that not everyone involved supported the idea of a teacher evaluating other teachers. Therefore, I asked a series of survey questions aimed at uncovering beliefs about the proper role for teachers in teacher evaluation. One question asked respondents to indicate who should be responsible for assessing whether teaching standards are being met, while a second question asked who should be responsible for removing teachers who are not meeting those standards from the classroom (see Table 7.1). Survey responses were then grouped for the purpose of comparison as follows: administrators (principals and administrators on the panel), teacher leaders (coaches and teachers on the panel), and PTs. Everyone agreed that it is the role of site administrators to assess standards, although there were significant differences among all three groups of respondents, with administrators agreeing with the state-

Table 7.1. Attitudes About Responsibility for Teacher Assessment and Removal, Analysis of Variance by Job Type, Year 1 ($N = 90$)

| PAR Orientation Questions[†] | Full Sample | a: Adm.[††] ($n = 18$) | b: TLs[†††] ($n = 15$) | c: PTs ($n = 57$) | Group $F$-Value |
|---|---|---|---|---|---|
| 1. Whose role should it be to assess whether teaching standards are being met? | | | | | |
| District administrators | 3.15 | 3.38 | 3.73 | 2.91 | $F(2,81) = 2.57$ |
| Site administrators | 4.33 | 4.94[b, c] | 4.53[a, c] | 4.07[a, b] | $F(2,88) = 10.59$*** |
| Teachers | 4.50 | 4.38 | 4.60 | 4.51 | $F(2,87) = 0.81$ |
| The teachers union | 3.51 | 3.18[b] | 4.29[a, c] | 3.40[b] | $F(2,83) = 4.75$* |
| The community | 3.19 | 2.78 | 3.00 | 3.38 | $F(2,85) = 2.07$ |
| Universities | 2.82 | 2.38 | 2.79 | 2.96 | $F(2,82) = 1.49$ |
| The state | 2.72 | 2.53 | 3.21 | 2.64 | $F(2,81) = 1.48$ |
| 2. Whose role should it be to remove those teachers not meeting standards from the classroom? | | | | | |
| District administrators | 3.90 | 4.73[c] | 4.29 | 3.57[a] | $F(2,83) = 6.95$** |
| Site administrators | 4.40 | 4.72[c] | 4.54 | 4.26[a] | $F(2,88) = 2.19$* |
| Teachers | 3.61 | 3.53 | 4.08 | 3.52 | $F(2,82) = 2.55$ |
| The teachers union | 3.89 | 4.31[c] | 4.57[c] | 3.59[a, b] | $F(2,84) = 7.54$*** |
| The community | 2.90 | 2.56 | 2.69 | 3.07 | $F(2,83) = 1.12$ |
| The state | 2.67 | 2.63 | 3.00 | 2.60 | $F(2,81) = 0.45$ |

*Note:* * $p \leq .05$; ** $p \leq .01$; *** $p \leq .001$. Bonferroni multiple comparisons were used to test all pairs of group differences. If mean values for one column show a superscript for another column, those two groups are different at the $p \leq .05$ familywise error rate.

[†] Questions were asked on a Likert scale where 1 = Strongly disagree, 2 = Disagree, 3 = Uncertain, 4 = Agree, and 5 = Strongly agree.

[††] Adm. = administrators (principals and PAR panel administrators)

[†††] TLs = Teacher Leaders (coaches and PAR panel teachers)

ment most strongly. Yet there was similar agreement across respondents that assessing standards is also the role of teachers, with no significant differences among groups. On question 2, however, the groups reported uncertainty about whether teachers should be responsible for removing other teachers from the classroom when standards are not met, with no significant differences among groups. Instead, those surveyed agreed with the statement that it is the site administrators' role to enforce the standards that, in question 1, it had been all right for teachers to participate in assessing. Administrators, in fact, reported more agreement for site administrator responsibility than teacher reponsibility on both questions, suggesting that, despite some administrator acceptance of teacher involvement in these leadership functions, administrators nonetheless still believed that these functions are more appropriately the domain of principals. Also interesting, while teacher leaders agreed that the teachers union should both assess teaching and remove those teachers not meeting standards, administrators agreed only with the latter. In other words, administrators agreed that unions should participate in the removal of underperforming teachers, but were uncertain whether unions should be responsible for assessing teaching in the first place—a position that, suffice it to say, brings chagrin to many union leaders.

Recall from the study design that PAR was only (or mostly) in Rosemont schools where the principal had signed on; as a sample, the principals responding to this survey were, therefore, those most likely to be positively inclined toward the program. As a result, administrators' attachment to administrator responsibility for assessing and enforcing standards seems particularly salient, as it could likely be stronger for the universe of all Rosemont principals.

The survey also asked respondents to identify their ideal balance of teacher/principal involvement in and responsibility for teacher evaluation from a choice of four options (adapted from Feiman-Nemser, 2000). Respondents were then asked to talk about the choices they made on their surveys in follow-up interviews. The choices are listed in Table 7.2.

The results revealed significant variation in beliefs among the core group of policy implementers. For question 3, "Expert teachers should only be involved in the formative assessment of other teachers, not their summative personnel evaluations," teacher leaders reported significantly less agreement than both PTs and administrators, suggesting that, as a group, they were less willing to limit teachers' roles in teacher evaluation to formative assessment. This is unsurprising yet confirmatory, given the self-selection of this group into participation in PAR. In question 5, "Expert teachers should have primary responsibility for the summative personnel evaluations of teachers in PAR, with limited principal involvement," administrators reported significantly less agreement than teacher leaders and PTs. There was universal disagreement for question 6, "Expert teachers should have sole responsibility for the summative personnel evaluations of teachers in PAR, with no principal involvement," although PTs—the group least likely to be established

Table 7.2. Attitudes about Principal and Teacher Leader Responsibility for Evaluation of Teachers in PAR, Analysis of Variance by Job Type, Year 1 ($N = 90$)

| PAR Orientation Questions[†] | Full Sample | a: Adm.[††] ($n = 18$) | b: TLs[†††] ($n = 15$) | c: PTs ($n = 57$) | Group $F$-Value |
|---|---|---|---|---|---|
| 3. Expert teachers should only be involved in the formative assessment of other teachers, not their summative personnel evaluations. | 2.80 | 3.06[b] | 1.87[a, c] | 2.95[b] | $F(2,90) = 4.89$** |
| 4. Expert teachers should participate in the summative personnel evaluations of teachers in PAR, in collaboration with principals. | 3.97 | 3.81 | 4.27 | 3.95 | $F(2,90) = 0.90$ |
| 5. Expert teachers should have primary responsibility for the summative personnel evaluations of teachers in PAR, with limited principal involvement. | 3.02 | 2.06[b, c] | 3.47[a] | 3.21[a] | $F(2,90) = 7.55$*** |
| 6. Expert teachers should have sole responsibility for the summative personnel evaluations of teachers in PAR, with no principal involvement. | 1.96 | 1.42[c] | 1.57 | 2.24[a] | $F(2,90) = 5.96$** |

*Note:* * $p \leq .05$; ** $p \leq .01$; *** $p \leq .001$. Bonferroni multiple comparisons were used to test all pairs of group differences. If mean values for one column show a superscript for another column, those two groups are different at the $p \leq .05$ familywise error rate.

[†] Questions were asked on a Likert scale where 1 = Strongly disagree, 2 = Disagree, 3 = Uncertain, 4 = Agree, and 5 = Strongly agree.

[††] Adm. = administrators (principals and PAR panel administrators)

[†††] TLs = teacher leaders (coaches and PAR panel teachers)

in the norms of the district—nonetheless reported significantly less disagreement than administrators.

At the same time, despite the variation in orientation among stakeholder groups to the PAR model, the data show a convergence toward the idea of teacher leaders and principals collaborating on evaluations. Responses to question 4, "Expert teachers should participate in the summative personnel evaluations of teachers in PAR, in collaboration with principals," produced both the highest overall mean for the four questions, as well as the highest mean for each group, with no significant differences between groups. This is likely due, in part, to differing personal definitions of the word *collaboration* itself. To the extent that this term lends itself to myriad definitions, the survey item itself was problematic. The follow-up interviews provide actual insight into the meanings affixed to the term by respondents, discussed below.

### More Policy Signals: Program Ambiguity as a Response to Different Beliefs about Teachers Conducting Evaluations

According to those leading the program—Doug, Brian, and Bob (the union president, district co-chair, and lead coach)—ambiguity about how the responsibility for evaluation would be divided was key to the success of the program. Doug, who preferenced survey item number 4 above, explained:

> [Survey item number] 4 is a political statement as much as anything else. "Limited" [in number 5] is a charged word. It implies attack upon administrators, upon somehow challenging their qualifications to do the job or something like that. Four, this is the statement that I have to make and I have to keep making and I have to keep making again. Four is the only thing that you can say, because it is vague. It just says collaboration. Then it means it's open, it's embracing.

Brian's ideal balance of responsibility stretched across both answers 4 and 5. He reasoned that individual coach-principal pairs should decide for themselves how to enact the policy. In a meeting at the beginning of the year, the coaches asked Brian directly, "Who is ultimately responsible for teacher evaluations?" He responded:

> I appreciate your desire to get that clarity, but I don't know that I can give it up front. A lot of it will depend on the coach and the principal. For example, the coach must present a formal presentation to the panel, but how that gets formed is dependent on a trio of people—the coach, principal, and PT. That principal's involvement may look very different in [different schools]. What I don't want to do is start with hard-and-fast rules that we have decided for principals. That's the way to kill the program.

Finally, Bob echoed Doug and Brian's sentiments, viewing ambiguity itself as a good thing for program success. The actions of these three program leaders exemplified a phenomenon identified by organizational theorists, that intentionally increasing the ambiguity of a policy is a common method for gaining support for it among stakeholders with differing goals and beliefs (Baier et al., 1988). As a result, Baier and colleagues write, "Official policy is likely to be vague, contradictory, or adopted without generally shared expectations about its meaning or implementation" (p. 159).

Looking back on the year, one coach, Caroline, commented: "It was sort of like you were always feeling you weren't getting a straight answer. I don't think it was that [the panel was] trying to be evasive, I think it was that things hadn't been thought out sometimes, and sometimes they might have been thought out but the situation was ambiguous. But it got frustrating." Indeed, one panel teacher noted in frustration, "I haven't been involved in any conversation to say . . . what's the mission statement or the goal or what are we trying to do." She continued, "Collaboration. Well, what's the difference between collaborating with them and limited principal involvement? Collaborating—meaning we sit down together and write [the evaluation]? We sit together and go over the evidence? Limited? Limited is the way it is currently, although you could make the argument that it could be collaborative the way it is currently." Rather than view this ambiguity as a problem of implementation, we can understand it as a quite pragmatic approach to gaining the support necessary for the policy to exist, given the disparate orientations toward teacher responsibility for teacher evaluation possessed by those involved. The dilemma is that while the policy may then exist, the ambiguous context allowed for infinite interpretation and enactment possibilities.

### Who Is Responsible for Teacher Evaluation?

In response to the ambiguous context of PAR, Rosemont's stakeholders interpreted responsibility for teacher evaluation in disparate ways. Table 7.3 shows the variety of responses from different stakeholders to the interview question: "Who is ultimately responsible for the summative evaluation of a PT in PAR?" The disparity of panel member responses to this question perhaps highlights more than any other piece of data the program's lack of clarity, given the program's design and the fact that the panel made ultimate recommendations to the superintendent regarding continued PT employment.

In addition, the coaches looked to the panel as the policymaking arm of the program, as defined by Rosemont's contract language. Panel members' lack of a unified opinion about responsibility for evaluation, therefore, made clarity among other stakeholders difficult. One teacher on the panel expressed this sentiment:

> That part [evaluation] I'm not so sure about. I guess because we're in such a transitional phase, is it still the principal? Is it the principal and the new

Table 7.3. Interview Responses to the Question, "Who is Ultimately Responsible for the Summative Evaluation of a PT in PAR?"[a]

| | Response | | | | | |
|---|---|---|---|---|---|---|
| Respondent | Coach | Principal | Panel | Coach/ Principal | Coach/ Principal/ Panel | Uncertain | Total |
| Coaches | 2 | | 2 | | 1 | 2 | 7 |
| Principals | 5 | | 1 | | 1 | 3 | 10 |
| Panel administrators | 2 | 1 | | | | | 3 |
| Panel teachers | | 1 | 2 | | | 2 | 5 |
| Participating teachers | 11 | | | 1 | | 1 | 13 |
| TOTAL | 20 | 2 | 5 | 1 | 2 | 8 | 38 |

[a] Not all study participants are displayed. Due to some initial interviews occurring prior to the question being added to the protocol, and the semi-structured interview format, not all respondents were asked this question.

system under PAR with the coaches? Is it the coach? Is it the panel who actually listens to the cases and makes the decisions or ultimately makes a ruling one way or the other? So I think that part is unclear, and this is the part that is somewhat frustrating to me. I'm a panel member and I'm unclear.

Most surprising was that two panel members—one teacher and one administrator —identified the principal as still being ultimately responsible for the evaluations, demonstrating the strength of established practices and beliefs. Conversely, no principals identified themselves as the ultimate evaluator. Also interesting is that while two panel administrators identified the coach as the ultimate evaluator, and none identified the panel, two panel teachers identified the panel as the ultimate evaluator, and none identified the coach. (Panel teachers tended to express concern about too much weight falling on coaches.)

Finally, PTs, who appeared to receive rather consistent policy signals from coaches, generally identified their coach as their evaluator, both in interviews as shown in Table 7.3, and on the survey. One of 15 PTs in interviews, and 15 of 57 on the survey, demonstrated the perception of a joint effort between coaches and principals for evaluations.

Recall that sensemaking is comprised of three constructs: prior knowledge, policy signals, and social situation, and beliefs about all three of these (Spillane et al.,

2002). Although those who needed to make sense of PAR mainly began with the same prior knowledge about teacher evaluation models—namely, that evaluation is the purview of principals—we have seen that: 1) Rosemont's educators involved with PAR differed in their belief systems about the appropriate division of responsibility for evaluation between principals and teachers, with administrators less positive about teacher authority for evaluation than teachers, and all groups most positive about the idea of "collaboration" between teachers and principals; 2) those involved with PAR, other than PTs, received different policy signals about the program that left responsibility for teacher evaluation unclear, due in large part to program ambiguity; and 3) these varying beliefs and policy signals resulted in disparate interpretations of the import of the policy, most notably that even those charged with running the program held varied opinions about ultimate responsibility for teacher evaluation.

With these varied interpretations of PAR in the background, the chapter now turns to its second question: How, if at all, was leadership responsibility for teacher evaluation redistributed?

## TEACHER JURISDICTION FOR TEACHER EVALUATION

Despite both the variety of beliefs about giving evaluative responsibility to teachers and the stated preference for collaboration described above, when Rosemont's educators were asked what that collaboration looked like in practice, the descriptions uniformly assigned more involvement to the coach. For example, one coach commented, "Now, I didn't go to [principals] and say, 'Oh, let's do this summative together.' [But I gave it to them and said,] 'Here's their summative. Look it over and I want to make sure that we're on the same page.' So we talked about it. That's what I consider having collaboration." Similarly, a principal defined collaboration this way:

> The coach should have the prime responsibility, but the principal still needs to collaborate. The [principal's] writing should be limited. Collaborating would mean reviewing the [written evaluations] with the coach. [The principal] doing at least one observation, not a formal one, but at least one full informal one with note-taking [per year]. It would still be a lot less than the coach involvement with that PT.

Other responses included such language as a coach using the principal as "another pair of eyes," or the coach being "in the classroom much more than the principal." After an initial period of building trust, most principals were content to let coaches go about their work without too much communication between the two. Several coaches noted how principals wanted to talk to them more at the beginning of the year, but once they had essentially proven themselves, principals were happy to let them go about their business. One coach explained, "Once they had confidence in me it was like 'Hi,' small talk, 'Bye.' [I'd ask,] 'Do you want to meet about this stuff or do you just want me to put it in your box?' [They'd respond,] 'Just put it in my box. You're doing a great job.'" The exception was in the cases of PTs who were not meeting standards, about whom there tended to be a fair amount of communication between coaches and principals.

One principal demonstrated the role of district paperwork in demarcating jurisdiction. She commented, "[Coaches] turned in all the paperwork and gave most of the information to the panel. The principals could add things if they wanted to. But the coaches are going to be turning in the paperwork this year, not me. The district sends us scanned paperwork we have to do for the other teachers, but I didn't get any for [those teachers in PAR]." Halverson and Zoltners (2001) note that artifacts such as this evaluation paperwork are "externalized representations of ideas and intentions used by practitioners in their practice" (p. 5). The lack of evaluation paperwork given to principals displayed the idea and intention that they were not conducting evaluations of PAR PTs. Indeed, here a principal made sense of PAR and her role in it by noting simply that she did not have evaluation paperwork for those PTs who were in PAR. Another principal, making the shape of a box with his fingers, highlighted with chagrin the "tombstone-like" space given to him for comments on the official PAR evaluation paperwork. Again, the artifact suggested to this principal that his role in PTs' evaluations was minimal.

On one hand, one could argue that these characterizations of the enactment of PAR demonstrate a limiting of coach agency, since the principals were still involved, however minimally. Dal Lawrence, the former union president of Toledo who initiated peer review there in the early 1980s, has argued vehemently that principals should not be involved in the peer review process for legal reasons. His argument is that there needs to be one clear evaluator—otherwise, there is a possibility for disagreement that can cause a loss to an unsatisfactory teacher in arbitration (Lawrence, 2000). (I will revisit Lawrence's argument in Chapter 8.) On the other hand, the characterizations presented above all give primary agency to the coach in the evaluation process, not the principal.

### Timothy and Kim Revisited: Coach as Decision Maker

The cases of Kim and Timothy, presented in Chapter 5, highlight the emergent coach jurisdiction for teacher evaluation. In short, for Caroline jurisdiction meant making the decision to fire Timothy, and for Eva it meant, in essence, defending Kim from her principal. Caroline led the principal to the nonrenewal decision they made "together," while Eva spoke out against the principal's opinion. Although both principals still had a voice in the evaluations, the voices of the coaches appeared to be preferred in both examples. With Caroline, the coach's voice was preferenced by the principal herself, as Nancy was persuaded by Caroline's assessment. With Eva, the coach's voice was preferenced by the panel, which gave Eva's assessment more weight than the principal's. The preferencing of these coaches' voices over those of the principals suggests a shift in jurisdictional control and leadership responsibility for teacher evaluation.

The coaches were vested with authority for PTs' renewal recommendations in large part because of the perceived quality of the evaluations that they had conducted. For Eva, her authority rested on the skill with standards-based evaluation that the panel perceived her to have, which allowed her to concretely demonstrate growth on a performance rubric. Principals in Rosemont had not, for the most part, been trained in standards-based evaluation and, instead, were still evaluating teachers with the "45-minute observation and a checklist" model.

For Caroline, her authority rested on the amount of support she had given, far beyond what a principal can typically provide, so that Timothy's lack of growth had meaning. Those involved with the case viewed Caroline as being responsible for the ultimate decision. Although the panel members and principal clearly supported Caroline in the decision, and the panel retained in name the decision-making power with respect to making the recommendation to the superintendent, the language used by the various parties displayed the degree of agency Caroline actually had in determining the outcome of the story. She said in an interview, "I was making those decisions," and to the panel at the hearing, "I finally made the decision to nonrenew." The principal, speaking to the panel, reported that "Caroline has already made the decision." Caroline, in fact, described the panel hearing as a rubber stamp on her decision: "The only . . . suggestion I have to the panel is that they need to be a little tougher on us, especially when it comes to really nailing people down at the end when someone is going to be let go. I think that would be fair to the PT that's going to be let go. I felt it was really kind of a rubber-stamp situation."

Timothy noted that Caroline was clear about the evaluative side of her role from the very beginning, although he described it as a "necessary trailer" in her presentation of the program and not a big deal:

> She told me from the get-go, from our first meeting: "I'm going to evaluate you at the end of the semester, and then again in the spring, and then I'm going to make a recommendation about you to the panel." She said there would be a renewal-nonrenewal decision made. But that she wanted to focus much more on giving me assistance at first. And that then she would go back on areas that she felt that I was weak, and you know, I thought okay, sure.

Although Timothy referred here to a "recommendation" by Caroline, he clearly viewed her as being in the lead on his evaluation. He continued:

The communication line between the principal and myself was in effect cut off due to the fact that my PAR coach was, for all effects [*sic*] and purposes, my principal. It's the principal's job to do evaluations, and if it's not the principal's job, then what does a principal have to comment on at all, you know? My principal was part of making the recommendation to the panel, but she didn't know me that well, she didn't know my work that well. So I think that [Nancy's] evaluation was based largely upon Caroline's evaluation.

The lead coach highlighted that, in essence, someone has to step up and do the tough job, so who better than another teacher empowered with the time and resources to do it well? During the hiring process, the panel asked prospective coaches whether they were prepared to make a decision that a participating teacher be dismissed; all those hired said yes, although some laughed later in the year over the ease with which they had given that response. The responsibility for evaluation comes with a price, and Caroline clearly felt the weight of making Timothy's personnel decision heavily. A nonrenewal decision, and the interpersonal conflict surrounding it, is not easy. Caroline elaborated:

The most challenging thing for me this year was having to come to a decision to not recommend Timothy, and to speak to him and to cope with his anger and his upset and his kind of lashing out in a way. I found it really kind of traumatic. I lost sleep over making the decision and once the decision was actually made and I presented to the panel and that was all done, I really found that I had bad dreams about it. I felt like I was committing violence in a way, even though I tried to keep in mind that I'm doing this for the sake of kids and I felt in my own mind that I had weighed it very carefully. So I'm really hoping that Timothy will go ahead and become a good teacher and that having been stopped cold by my nonrecommendation will, in fact, cause him to reflect in a way that he wouldn't otherwise. But right now, it really feels like, *euw*, I did this really harsh thing to a fellow human being.

The bottom line is that, if the weight of making negative evaluation decisions were lighter, principals would likely make them more often. The coaches—who cut 14 out of 91 participating teachers that year—proved willing to carry that weight.

Distributing leadership across a school or district has the potential to lighten the burden on principals. In the aftermath of the discussion of Kim at the spring hearing, however, the panel questioned Betty's practice as a principal—not merely her behavior toward Kim, but her apparent inability to work collaboratively with the coach and to be concrete with her criticisms. The inability of Betty and Eva to work collaboratively, despite the stated expectation of that behavior by the panel, was seen by the panel as Betty's failure and highlights the difficulty presented to principals when teacher leader roles are introduced. Susanna, the panel member who worked most closely with Eva, commented:

> I just supported [Eva], saying, "You have the evidence [to support renew-ing Kim's employment]. . . . Do it. Because if you don't, it's still coming down to the principal's evaluation." I do think that the principal is key in this PAR evaluation process. Because it's not necessarily just the peer who is making the recommendation, it is also the principal. But in this case with Eva and Betty, Betty was trying to make the case completely on her own, and that didn't work either.

Betty, with years of experience and described as a "strong principal," had difficulty adjusting to the second voice of the coach and resisted collaboration. It may be that sharing authority for evaluation through PAR is harder for more experienced principals. An interesting finding in recent research (Carver, 2002; Youngs, 2003), however, is that principals with greater expertise appear to be more able to recog-nize expertise in teacher leaders, and are more likely to step back and share au-thority with them. Whether Eva was a needed buffer for Kim or an unfortunate barrier to Betty's authority as principal is at least partially informed by the collabo-ration question. When Betty appeared unwilling to participate in the PAR process as a partner, the panel viewed her as the problem.

Interestingly, the panel's decision to rehire Kim left the other educators in-volved in this case believing that Betty somehow "lost" at the hearing. Betty wanted to move Kim from her school site, yet not remove her from the district—which is, in fact, precisely what happened. It is unclear, therefore, what accounted for the reaction of those involved, who appeared impervious to Betty's agreement with the final outcome. Perhaps the novelty of a teacher's voice in the assessment pro-cess, one that countered the principal and ultimately carried more weight, left a stronger impression than the details of what was actually recommended. Indeed, Betty's negativity about Kim ultimately left the impression with panel members and the coach that the panel "backed Eva" in deciding to renew Kim for employ-ment in the district.

Regardless of rampant program ambiguity, those involved viewed the coaches as largely responsible for evaluation decisions. Although the panel held the official decision-making power with respect to making the recommendation to the super-intendent, language use revealed the degree of agency held by the coaches. As the various actors made sense of PAR, they challenged assumptions about teacher evalu-ation and authority relations in education. In Kim's case, coach jurisdiction subtly challenged the assumed authority of principals to determine a new teacher's em-ployment outcome. A principal was unable to solely decide the fate of an emer-gency credentialed teacher, as she was forced to contend with a second and perhaps more powerful voice than her own. In Timothy's case, we saw a coach collaborating as a peer with an administrator, and ultimately making the decision that has historically been the administrator's to make.

Thus far, the chapter has explored how stakeholders made sense of an ambiguous policy context, and has presented examples of the policy's enactment that highlight the shift in jurisdiction. The chapter now turns to how PAR, as enacted, challenged stakeholders' existing authority relations and teacher evaluation practices. How did stakeholders respond to the jurisdictional shift just described? We are looking at the third aspect of sensemaking: the social situation into which PAR was placed.

## The Difficulty of Naming Leadership by Teachers

Although the data show coaches holding significant authority for teacher evaluation, coaches largely avoided attributing jurisdiction for teacher evaluation to themselves. For example, one coach noted in October, "I would hope that I'm the eyes of everybody that's making the decision. . . . I don't want to say it's me [evaluating], I don't want to say it's the principal, I don't want to say it's the panel. I think it's a collaborative decision." By February, however, her language attached a sense of authority for evaluation to the role she played as the eyes of the group, suggesting a growing comfort with the role of evaluator: "I'm still clarifying [to principals] that I'm the one that's going to do the evaluation. You're going to have input. We bring in both [to the panel]. They're still not clear. I still have principals saying, 'Now who do I have to evaluate? Do I have to go in there and observe?' I say, 'No, I'll do that. I'll look, then we'll sit down and look at the information together.'" Despite articulating this sense of authority, she deferred ultimately to the panel: "I really feel that the evaluation, the part that says you stay . . . or you go, really needs to be the panel." Another coach, looking back on the year, said she had collaborated with principals, yet gave this description: "Principals gave me very limited feedback, but they gave me an impression of the person. And they were a sounding board for what I said about the person." Caroline explained why the panel was ultimately responsible for Timothy's nonrenewal:

> Clearly, the panel was responsible for the final evaluation, because . . . well, that's that whole ambiguity. What does the word *evaluate* mean? I mean, I'm evaluating all the pieces and I'm making a recommendation, but I am not really making the evaluation. It really is the panel that's doing it. And that's what I do tell [my PTs]. I say, "I make a recommendation. They make the final decision." I don't use the word *evaluation*.

The response signaled her discomfort in year 1 with holding responsibility for an employment decision to nonrenew.

Although the enactment of PAR largely demonstrated more responsibility for evaluation by coaches than principals, naming this as limiting principal power proved too radical a response, both on the survey and in interviews. Literature suggests that, due to the norms against it, educators do not often recognize leadership by teachers even where it exists (Bascia, 1998; Johnson, 1984; Wasley, 1991). The favored term *collaboration* seemed to be used as a euphemism for the reality of limited principal involvement, a more acceptable way for teachers to participate in evaluation. By and large, respondents felt that relationships between coaches and principals had been collaborative, although both coaches and principals wanted it to be more so, and were slow to acknowledge that coaches had made evaluative decisions. Different coaches defined their role vis-à-vis evaluation differently, but most seemed happy to name the "final decision" as someone else's responsibility.

Given all that is known about principals' reluctance to give negative evaluations, it should not be surprising that the coaches, especially in their first year in the role, would be slow to embrace the title of evaluator. Most coaches defined their role in interviews as one of supporter of new teachers, and tended to mention evaluation almost as an aside or afterthought. Indeed, responsibility for evaluation clearly comes with a price. Caroline described losing sleep over the decision not to renew Timothy, and having bad dreams about it once the decision was made, saying that she felt like she was "committing violence." Providing support is often perceived as nurturing. As we saw in Chapter 6, however, evaluation—typically defined as separate from professional development—is often conceived to mean rejecting the female norm of "being nice" held by many teachers (Murray, 1998; Moir, 1999).

## Negotiating New Roles for Principals

Teacher leadership requires a reframing of authority relationships. Like the teachers who assume new leadership roles with PAR, principals are also asked to engage in new roles.

Most principals are phenomenally overwhelmed by everything that they are expected to do (Copland, 2001; Marshall, 2008), and leadership by teachers not only increases teacher professionalism but eases some of the pressure on principals. Most principals viewed PAR as a welcome relief from a small portion of their administrative load. One coach described principals' reactions to her as, "Thank God someone is doing the evaluation here. It's one less thing I have to do. And, you know, this is the way it should be." One principal, asked whether he wanted to continue with the program, said, "Yes, I'd take [the coach] because she's helping me [laughter], because she's doing it. I mean, she's doing it!" Principals were very positive, year after year, in their year-end program evaluations about coaches and the support they received from PAR. Although they may have had mixed feelings about their decreased involvement in teacher evaluation, principals were overwhelmingly positive about PAR after seeing it in action. For the most part, principals' need to reduce their workload was greater than concerns about a reduction in a piece of their authority. This pattern has been seen elsewhere; although administrators in Rochester, New York, for example, were originally resistant to the idea of PAR, once it was implemented, administrators fought to keep the program in the face of district budget cuts.

Given that Rosemont's administrators were initially less favorable than coaches to the idea of teacher authority for teacher evaluation (see Table 7.2), it is perhaps surprising that principals were subsequently more willing than coaches to name coaches as responsible for evaluation (see Table 7.3). In general, Rosemont's educators believed that the quality of the evaluations with PAR was quite strong.[2] It may well be that action leads to cognition (Weick, 1995), and principals were impressed by the coaches and warmed to the PAR model.

Although principals seemed willing to grant jurisdictional control of evaluation to coaches, they still experienced tension regarding the reduction of their own role. Though quick to offer that they do not have the time to conduct evaluations well, some principals remained uncomfortable with evaluations being conducted by someone else. Principals were conflicted because they wanted to be—and the superintendent expected them to be—so-called instructional leaders. Yet they recognized that coaches were doing a better job than they could. One noted:

> [PAR is] helpful, it gets a job done and a job done well, no question about it. But to me it's a little sad. Someone is coming along and doing [teacher evaluations] and that's great because the job needs to be done, but I always see that as my job, a principal's job. It's a concession to reality, really. Essentially I have all these ideas about being a principal, getting things done, but that's just not the reality. So this is filling a role, but I don't think that's the way it should be. It's this administrator's compromise.

One principal dealt with this tension by continuing to conduct evaluations. He explained:

> What I've chosen to do here is to do informal evaluations, because technically you can't evaluate somebody twice and I don't want to interfere with the relationship [between the PT and coach]. But I also feel an obligation to get into the classrooms and to see people and so what I've done is set up a series of four evaluations, informal evaluations, observations, and then I'll do an informal summary at the end. I've told the teachers that they can share with their PAR coach if they want or they can, you know, throw it in the garbage can or whatever they want, but that I feel that I need to have that connection with them. So with that I've been happy letting the PAR coaches do what they want.

Due in part to the fact that this principal never attended a panel hearing, as well as his less-than-welcoming interactions with the coaches working with PTs in his building, coaches and panel members perceived him as uncooperative and resistant to relinquishing control. His comments above perhaps reflect some internal resistance to the reforms brought by PAR. Nonetheless, this principal's commitment to observing the teachers in his building (as well as his stated reluctance to being out of his building to attend panel hearings) is both understandable and laudable—highlighting the conflict or "compromise" raised for some site leaders by PAR's jurisdictional shift.

## A SHIFT TOWARD COACH–PRINCIPAL COLLABORATION

Despite positive sentiments among stakeholders about the program as enacted, a clear shift toward formal collaboration between coaches and principals was seen over time. In the fall, the panel felt that principals should attend the first hearing. They believed that if principals saw PAR in action, they would like what they saw and support the program; at that time, the purpose of principal attendance at the hearings was for principals to *gather knowledge* about PAR. By the second hearing, however, as evidence of a drift toward "collaboration," it was expected that principals would attend hearings. Panel members came to view principal attendance at hearings as necessary for principals to *provide input* about PTs, without necessarily being cognizant of this shift. Indeed, for the remainder of the year, principals who did not attend were seen as unsupportive of PAR and not upholding their share of the bargain (and ultimately, the principal just cited was the only one of 28 who never attended).

The summative evaluation paperwork provides a second example. It moved in 3 years of PAR implementation from including the "tombstone-like" box for principals to comment on out-of-classroom performance (standard 6), to adding a line the second year for principals to officially sign off, to formally including space in the third year for principals' comments and signatures alongside those of the coaches for each of the six California Teaching Standards.

In the third year of the program, in fact, the contract was modified to include a joint observation by the coach and principal. (This "contract attachment" was generated by a committee with representation from the teachers union, administrators union, and district office, including Doug, Bob, Brian, and principals with experience with PAR.) The contract attachment required one joint observation per year officially (in the fall for beginning teachers and in the spring for veterans), with a second informally encouraged in the cases of struggling PTs. In addition to the "required" observation, it was "desirable" that the principal also participate in pre- and post-observation conferences with the coach, and:

Hold a post-observation discussion of PT needs and next steps with the coach, specifying principal/site administrator's role and priorities to be included in the PT's Individual Learning Plan. Address and attempt to resolve with the coach any discrepancies between the administrator's and coach's assessments.

This program amendment was made, in part, to mollify the superintendent, who felt that if the coaches took this task off principals' plates, then principals were, in effect, getting a free ride. In addition, however, part of the panel's intent for the joint observations was to spread coaches' expertise with standards-based evaluation to the principals—hence the emphasis on conferencing between the coach and principal. In truth, the implementation of the joint observations was spotty: Coaches found them very challenging to schedule, and principals often failed to show up. The lead coach (following Bob) reported in year 4:

> Administrators always have things come up . . . so the principal has to cancel, or just doesn't show up. And I would say that happens for at least a quarter of the arranged joint formals. . . . We've come to just accept that [joint observations are] great when they happen. If the coach does everything within their power to try to make them happen and the administrator isn't there, oh well. We don't do them over. We give the administrator another chance. "You didn't make it to the November formal, but we'll be doing one in February. Hopefully you can come to that one." But sometimes they don't. . . . No one is coming around and saying, you didn't do the joint formal, this whole process is invalid . . . It's expected that it will happen, but if it doesn't, it doesn't throw the process off.

Panel members reported similar impressions of inconsistent implementation of this program change. Coaches, in a continuation of their role as support to principals, often tried to help principals in their new dealings with the panel. The lead coach noted, "I make sure a principal knows, okay you weren't there to do the joint observation with me, be sure to be in the classroom some time before the panel [hearing] so that you'll have something to say about the classroom." When the joint observations did occur, coaches still took the lead completing the evaluation paperwork. They also gathered principals' reactions to observations and communicated them to PTs, in cases when principals did not attend post-observation meetings with PTs.

In addition to codifying participation by the principal in PAR review, however inconsistently implemented, the contract attachment also formalized procedures for cases of disagreement between a coach and principal regarding a PT's evaluation:

In the event that significant discrepancies exist between the administrator's assessment and the coach's assessment of the PT's performance on any of the Essential Elements of Standards 1–5, the administrator and coach are obligated to document and supply relevant evidence for those differences. The PAR Panel may direct the site administrator and the coach to conduct a second joint formal classroom observation, if it is needed, to resolve those differences.

In the event that significant discrepancies still exist after the second joint formal classroom observation or other steps recommended to resolve the situation, both the administrator and the coach must attend the next Panel presentation. Both the administrator and coach must present their assessments and supporting evidence to the Panel. The differences in opinion and evidence will be included in the record, and forwarded with the Panel's recommendation to rehire or not to rehire to the Superintendent. The Superintendent will review the recommendation and the record of evidence, and will make his/her final recommendation to the Board of Education.

Significantly, the contract attachment stipulated that if a principal disagreed with a coach's assessment for standards 1–5, he or she had to be prepared to support his or her case with documented evidence from classroom observations.[3]

With the year 3 contract attachment, Rosemont leaders essentially appeased the concerns of all key stakeholder groups. The superintendent felt more comfortable with a clear, formal role for principals in the process. Principals felt better knowing that if they disagreed with a coach's assessment, there was an avenue to voice that disagreement (even if, in reality, such cases were extremely rare). Most coaches felt better having a clearly spelled-out role for principals, so that individual principals were limited in their ability to ignore the PAR process or otherwise be uncommunicative with coaches. Similarly, panel members considered formal rules for principal involvement—and coach/principal disagreement—a natural step in the development of the program, part of working out the kinks. Those participating in year 4 research conversations uniformly viewed this codified increase of principal involvement as a positive program development.

Finally, results from the research on Rosemont's PAR program solicited by the district in year 3 provide interesting context for the contract developments. Growing out of the survey questions asked in year 1, as displayed in Table 7.2, subsequent researchers established that administrators, coaches, and PTs all reported that their "ideal choice of evaluator" was "mainly coach in collaboration with site administrator" (see Table 7.4).[4] In other words, increased codification of principal involvement in the PAR process existed alongside a reported positive attitude for coach jurisdiction. In the case of administrators, this represented an *increase* in positive attitude from year 1 survey responses.

Table 7.4.  Attitudes About Principal and Teacher Leader Responsibility
for Evaluation of Teachers in PAR, Year 3 (Reported as Rounded
Percentages of Respondents Giving Answer)

| | Respondent | | |
| --- | --- | --- | --- |
| | Participating Teachers (N = 133) | Coaches (N = 16) | Site Administrators (N = 33) |
| *Ideal choice of evaluator* | | | |
| Site administrator only | 9 | 0 | 0 |
| Coach only | 6 | 13 | 3 |
| Mainly site administrator with coach | 17 | 19 | 30 |
| Mainly coach in collaboration with site administrator | 69 | 69 | 67 |

Ultimately, a number of factors that have been raised in the chapter contributed to more codified involvement of principals in the PAR process—and therefore a related drift away from coach jurisdiction for teacher evaluation, however
ambiguous it may have been. Most notably, although principals were overwhelmed
by their jobs and welcomed PAR as a relief from a piece of their responsibilities,
the norms against teachers holding authority for personnel evaluations challenged
movement in this direction. The transition from authoritarian to participative leadership is a difficult one for principals (Kerchner & Koppich, 1993), who are expected to be instructional leaders but are nonetheless asked to move over for teacher
leadership (Little, 1988). Several principals were seen to be conflicted about their
disengagement from the evaluation process, despite their support for PAR.

In addition, central office administrators often oppose the type of organizational changes brought about by teacher leadership and peer review (Kerchner
& Koppich, 1993). The superintendent and an administrator *on the panel* were
seen as not fully supportive of PAR's key concept of teacher responsibility for
teacher evaluation, instead viewing principals as ultimately responsible. After
establishing positive district-union relations and signing PAR into contract with
the prior superintendent, the union president then had to start fresh with a new
superintendent who accepted PAR because her predecessor had signed it into
the contract, but who did so warily given her convictions about instructional
leadership by principals. The result was mixed signals about not only the details
of the program but about the program's prospects for continuation at all. These
mixed signals went to coaches as well as principals who were already worried
about their jobs (many of whom were dismissed later that year). Despite the

pragmatic attraction of lightening principals' responsibilities and evidence of a more rigorous evaluation process with PAR, the superintendent's stance contributed to the shift toward "collaboration."

Coaches recommended nonrenewal of PTs at unprecedented rates, although they were reluctant to be held singularly responsible for the decisions that they had, in effect, made. Hence, Caroline decides to nonrenew Timothy, comments on the degree to which she felt that the hearing was a "rubber-stamp" situation, but reports in the same interview that the panel was ultimately responsible for the decision. This desire not to be the one blamed for a nonrenewal led to collaboration.

Finally, as demonstrated, program ambiguity was an intentional strategy by those spearheading the PAR program in order to secure its support from potentially opposed administrators. Although increased program clarity and coherence would certainly have pleased the coaches, a more coherent program might have created a dead program. The lesson, though not new, is that a shift toward greater program coherence can come over time, as support is secured. Administrators, as we saw, were very positive about PAR once they had been exposed to it. The dilemma was that by the time Rosemont might have been ready to give PAR greater coherence, it had already started to become more "harmless" than originally conceived vis-à-vis teacher authority for teacher evaluation, like so many teacher leadership policies before it. In the vacuum created by the lack of a unified definition of PAR, people regressed to what was familiar—namely, principal involvement in teacher evaluation—still confirming Little's (1990) finding that districts move quickly to blunt the effects of new teacher leadership policies.

## CONCLUSION

This chapter has highlighted expanded roles for the coaches: as gatekeepers who chose to recommend nonrenewal of some PTs; as buffers between PTs and principals unable to help them improve; and as colleagues of principals, who collaborated on decision making. Conducting evaluations was difficult for coaches, and seeing themselves as evaluators also proved difficult. The transition to being one's brother's keeper is not easy. Nonetheless, coaches, in varying degrees of collaboration with principals, conducted summative evaluations and made decisions about the continued employment of other teachers. They reported those decisions to the panel, which was responsible for the "final decision" to be recommended to the school board. However, out of 91 PTs, there was no case of the panel voting against a coach. In the fourth year of the program, in fact, the district co-chair commented that "I don't think there's ever been a time when the panel overruled a coach." Yet, despite this reality of teachers evaluating their peers, the desire of most of those involved was for more collaboration between coaches and principals, although descriptions of collaboration often looked like coach jurisdiction. Over time, the program shifted toward more codified collaboration between coaches and principals.

This shift toward increased principal involvement over time must be viewed in the context of the perceived technical improvements to evaluation that came with coach jurisdiction in the first year. The fact that stakeholders were positive about the program and believed improvements in evaluation were occurring makes any shift away from coach jurisdiction particularly salient.

It is understandable that PAR principals and coaches wanted to work together—especially given principal isolation and coaches conducting evaluations for the first time. Despite being understandable, however, the push for collaboration can be viewed in light of the body of literature that shows little change resulting from teacher leadership policies over time. Formal, regulative structures (Scott, 1995) or artifacts (Halverson & Zoltners, 2001) like a teacher evaluation policy are "deeply ingrained in, and reflect, widespread understandings of social reality" (Meyer & Rowan, 1977, p. 533). Education's social reality has not previously included space for teachers in the leadership role of evaluators, and the deeply ingrained notions of appropriate roles for teachers was challenged by PAR policy. In the end, though, PAR's ambiguity made it a somewhat weak challenge. The undefined responsibility for teacher evaluation gave currency to the attractive idea of sharing responsibility. Collaboration is a legitimate approach to leadership, but institutional theory and prior research on teacher leadership policies suggest that the model of teacher leader–principal collaboration may be just a stop on the way back to principal jurisdiction for teacher evaluation.

Chapter 8, however, looks at the phenomenon from a different angle. Rather than focus on the balance of authority between coaches and principals, Chapter 8 throws the net wider to include the panel as part of the picture. Given that teachers made up the majority of the panel, it could be argued that teachers—panel teachers in addition to coaches—continued to hold jurisdiction for teacher evaluation, regardless of the increased role for principals. With this framing, "collaboration" becomes the professional learning community in which teachers engage in collective responsibility for professional standards, together with administrators.

## CHAPTER 8

# Interrupting Norms of Isolation

## PAR as a Site for Professional Learning Community

> Teachers and those of us in the teaching profession need to
> figure out what teaching standards are so we can articulate
> them to the public and to the universities who are training
> teachers. We can't just say we want good teachers. What does
> that mean? That's one thing I love about the standards in any
> area, teaching and content areas. They require talking to other
> people. There is no way you can say, "Okay, here's a standard,"
> and then everybody just follows it. Someone will always say,
> "Well, what does that mean, and how would you know it when
> you see it, and what would I be doing, and what would you be
> hearing, and what would the students be doing, and what would
> a parent who came in the room say?" It requires that communi-
> ties talk together.
>
> —Teacher on the Rosemont PAR panel

I argued in Chapter 4 that the PAR panel is a crucial element of the PAR process. In this chapter, we go deeper to examine how the PAR oversight panel made a significant difference in the evaluation process. Specifically, this chapter examines how the structure of the PAR oversight panel, as seen through panel hearing excerpts, generated transparency in the evaluation process, breaking down the isolation that typically surrounds both the practice of teaching and the practice of evaluating teaching. The chapter explores how this increased transparency enabled a particular form of professional learning community, one that created collective responsibility for professional standards and increased accountability for personnel outcomes.

Significant shifts in organizational structure occurred to support the PAR coaches in their role as evaluators. Like allocating time, linking formative and summative assessment, and giving teachers responsibility for the evaluation of other teachers, another structural shift that occurred in Rosemont was altering the solitary nature of the work of the teacher evaluator by creating a community of colleagues. The argument presented in this chapter is that making the typically solitary practice of teacher evaluation transparent to colleagues fundamentally alters the nature of educational accountability.

It should be emphasized, if it is not clear already, that the PAR process broke down the traditional isolation of educational practice more broadly than the specific work of the PAR panel. The isolation of classroom teaching was broken down through the work of the coaches with PTs. The isolation of principals' work was broken down where coach-principal relationships became collegial. The isolation of the evaluator role was broken down as coaches engaged in regular conversations with one another about their caseloads each week at their Friday meetings. The panel filled a unique role, however, as the formal site of teacher-administrator collaboration and cooperation, group dialogue, and evaluative decision making. As such, I am focusing here on the ways in which the panel generated a professional learning community, building on the data presented in Chapter 4.

It is also perhaps worth noting at the outset of the chapter that the PAR evaluation process was certainly not entirely "transparent." Indeed, as we saw in Chapter 7, responsibility for personnel decisions was quite ambiguous—which is to say, not clear, and, therefore, not transparent. The decision process was spelled out: PAR coaches made a recommendation to the panel (which included principal input, especially from year 3 on), the panel passed their recommendation to the superintendent, she passed her recommendation to the school board, and the school board had the final say. Yet, within this protocol, many practitioners felt awash in ambiguity; coaches and even some panel members complained that responsibility for "the final say" was unclear. My argument in Chapter 7 may, therefore, seem to contradict the current argument that the process increased transparency. The distinction, however, is between the decision-making process (how decisions happen) and responsibility and accountability for those decisions (March, 1994). This chapter will argue that PAR increased the transparency of the decision-making process; the teacher evaluation process involved more eyes engaged in more scrutiny of more data. At the same time, as we saw in Chapter 7, PAR generated ambiguity around ultimate responsibility for evaluation decisions, as that responsibility was "stretched over" (Spillane, 2006) coaches, principals, and the panel before being passed to the superintendent. James March (1994) argues that decisions happen through complicated processes in which it is often not possible to specify where or how a decision occurred. Although individual ownership of accountability for teacher evaluation decisions may have been ambiguous, the argument taken up in this chapter is that the actual evaluation outcomes demonstrated that accountability nonetheless occurred, regardless of this ambiguity—and perhaps even partly because of it, as we will see.

## CREATING TRANSPARENCY AND PROFESSIONAL COMMUNITY

The PAR evaluation process in Rosemont, and in particular, the presence of an oversight panel, appears to have broken down isolation and increased transparency in two central and related ways. First, panel members were involved in teacher evaluation in addition to coaches and principals, creating a professional community of educators who were focused on the examination of practice. A communal teacher evaluation process involving dialogue increases transparency because it forces what would otherwise be an isolated evaluator to explain his or her assessments to others—thereby bringing the evaluation into the light of day. Second, there was a paper trail to document the assessment work that had occurred, and that data provided the focus for professional conversations. Documenting the assessment of teachers increases transparency because it allows the above communal conversations to focus on teachers' practice—on observed behaviors rather than opaque evaluator opinion.

## Time and Space for Professional Conversations

The need to reduce teachers' isolation and open the doors of classroom practice has become axiomatic (e.g., Feiman-Nemser & Floden, 1986; Little, 1982; Miles & Darling-Hammond, 1998; Rosenholtz, 1989), often referred to as a need to alter the "egg crate" model of schooling that isolates teachers in separate classrooms like eggs in a carton. Although PAR opens the doors of teachers' classroom practice, transcripts from the panel hearings show that the doors to support provider and evaluator practice were opened as well. Both the work of teaching and the work of evaluating teaching were opened for examination by the panel. Recall from Chapter 4, for example, the conversation about the coach considering model lessons for the veteran science teacher who was an intervention case. The panel members considered whether modeling was likely to be a successful strategy for working with the teacher, and if so, how it might best be done. At the center of the conversation were questions about the content of good teaching practice—effective planning and execution of whole-group instruction—and how to break that down and teach it to someone whose practice is below standard in that area.

Little (2003) identifies the markers of "teacher learning communities":

> . . . the groups demonstrably reserve time to identify and examine problems of practice; they elaborate those problems in ways that open up new considerations and possibilities; they readily disclose their uncertainties and dilemmas and invite comment and advice from others; and artifacts of classroom practice (student work, lesson plans, and the like) are made accessible. In all these ways, the groups display dispositions, norms, and habits conducive to teacher learning and the improvement of teaching practice. (p. 938)

Because the PAR panel included administrators as well as teachers, it could perhaps be considered an "educator learning community" instead of the more standard "teacher learning community," but the similarities are evident. The panel had set, reserved time to meet and discuss problems of practice. They discussed the problems of practice in ways—however new and tentative—that involved disclosing uncertainties and dilemmas (*"we coaches have a real hard time with putting on this paper, 'do not rehire' . . . we do"*). The coaches brought forth artifacts of PTs' classroom practice and artifacts of their own practice (such as Individual Learning Plans and observation summaries), around which to focus conversation and inquiry. In short, the panel members and coaches engaged in dialogue regarding the technical core of their work—the practice of teaching, coaching, and assessing. This engagement was, indeed, somewhat messy, as those involved worked to figure out the nature and boundaries of their task. In doing so, however, they may have avoided (perhaps unintentionally) what Seashore Louis (2002) warns is a tendency to develop professional learning communities "like a new reading curriculum"—as superficially adopted ideas with short shelf lives rather than as internally developed programs with depth and commitment. A teacher on the panel gave this example:

> I think by the end we nailed it down. There was so much ambiguity [at first]. I think by the end when you look at reports like Sarah's, where she bullets, "Here's the standard, here's the three things that I'm going to look for that would be a demonstration that you've mastered the standard, and then here's what's happening at each of those." Very clear. But we didn't get to that point until after we'd gone through some serious adjusting. But I think we could have. Oh, maybe we couldn't have. Maybe that's just the whole point that you have to sort of go through it before you know.

Although panel members and coaches complained about lack of clarity and ambiguity along the way, they were forced to face core questions of practice: What do we consider good teaching? What does it look like in a novice versus a veteran, and in a credentialed versus an uncredentialed novice? In addition, what do we consider good coaching, and good assessment of teaching? How do we generate data about observed teaching practice so that a group of educators can discuss the data and make appropriate decisions? For many of the educators involved in PAR in Rosemont, this was the first time they were able to engage in such conversations, and certainly it was the first time they engaged in them as a group of administrators and teachers from across the district, as colleagues. One teacher on the panel noted, "As a new panel member, I have enjoyed being a part of this new adventure. It has put me, along with this team of panel members, in a learner mode. It's been very exciting."

Betty Achinstein (2002) has documented how professional learning communities are sometimes understood to mean everyone getting along (i.e., being nice), rather than engaging in the conflict needed to redesign our schools for the success of all students. Challenging, substantive, and critical conversations are needed to focus improvement efforts.

In the first year of the program, despite the reduction from presenting all 91 PTs after the November hearing, to only presenting 24 PTs at subsequent panel hearings, most of those involved tended to feel that the hearings did not allow sufficient time to go into the depth they would have liked. Some coaches, although sympathetic to the amount of work involved, wanted panel members to be more informed. One commented, "[Panel hearings] felt generally okay but rushed. I would like it if in the future they could read the documentation a little more carefully. I know it's a lot, but it would help them listen to the stories a little better, and ask better questions of us." As we saw in Chapter 7, some coaches reported feeling that the panel was essentially a rubber stamp on their decision about a PT. Eva commented on the deliberations over one of her PTs:

> In every case pretty much it was what the coach recommended, and maybe it should have been that. But when I think about the questions they asked about [a PT that I recommended for nonrenewal], they didn't really hold my feet to the fire. They just didn't really go after me in ways that they could have. . . . There would have been more a feeling of somebody really advocating his side.

Caroline echoed the sentiment: "They can only go on the data we present. But I really think when it comes down to telling somebody, 'No, we're not going to let you return,' I think they need to have read chapter and verse and really thought about it." Although Rosemont's story reveals movement in a direction toward increased transparency and accountability, there was certainly room for growth. PAR involved a much larger number of people in a more transparent teacher evaluation process and broke down some of the isolation around both teachers' practice and evaluators' decisions. Nonetheless, coaches clearly felt that even more transparency was needed.

## Generating Data to Focus Professional Conversations

The panel creates a very critical distinction between traditional teacher evaluation and PAR. We simply do not know how traditional teacher evaluation might be affected if principals had to defend their evaluative decisions to a board of colleagues or supervisors. Being required to defend one's decisions with evidence naturally alters and guides the decision-making process. Unlike PAR coaches, principals cannot be matched by grade and subject area to all the teachers in their building. However, it is conceivable that if principals were required to defend their evaluative decisions to some sort of oversight panel, and were given the time and training that would support making those decisions, some of the changes documented here might also be seen. Similarly, teachers making evaluative decisions might look quite like principal evaluations without the oversight of the panel. It is entirely possible, for starters, that without PAR panel oversight, the coaches might not have dismissed teachers at such an unusually high rate; we saw in Chapter 4 that the panel played a critical role in the cases of four of the 11 new teachers who were removed. Similarly, if principals had to defend their evaluative decisions to such a body, higher rates of dismissals might occur.

In short, the pressure of the panel hearings, and specifically, the panel's expectations that the coaches' assessments would be standards-based, simply created more data and documentation. These data, in turn, focused the work (i.e., the conversations) of the panel. Gathered around the accumulated evidence of PTs' teaching practice and the coaches' work to support them, panel members, coaches, and principals explored how best to proceed with each PT presented. Doug, the teachers union president, noted:

> We're trying to institute standards for teaching, so that people will be playing on a common playing field, with common rules. Hiring and firing decisions would be made centrally. They would be based upon standards rather than the whim of a particular individual. Who has defined what good teaching would be [until now]? Who has defined what the standards would be? Who has defined that has been the individual principal at the 100 sites? So, we have had kind of like Italy before Garibaldi. We have 100 separate standards. None of them written, of course.

The superintendent also emphasized the importance of agreed-upon standards:

> Can it really be that [a coach and a principal] are on opposite ends of the spectrum of whether a teacher should be retained or not? I've got to believe that as professionals we are going to have the same criteria, we're going to be using the same observation forms. We're going to be looking for the same end results, which is student learning and how that interaction with that teacher is occurring in those classrooms. And so the data [are] going to be the basis on which the decision is made. It's not just what the coach says versus what I say as a principal. It's based on evidence. Somebody is being very subjective if they can't look at the evidence and come to the same conclusions.

As we saw in prior chapters, coaches tended to speak with more authority than principals at panel hearings precisely because of their greater facility with standards language. Their recommendations carried weight to the degree they were transparent—clearly documented, supported by evidence, and grounded in practice rather than personality.

Elmore (2006) argues that there is a profound misconception in education regarding the meaning of the word *professional*. Professional is often understood in education to mean "autonomy," and anything that compromises autonomy—such as an oversight panel, or proscribed standards for practice—is viewed as antiprofessional. Yet professions are made up of people who have autonomy within proscribed protocols of practice, and in a profession, people who do not follow the protocols are excluded from practice.

Part of the historic problem with teacher evaluation, therefore, is that without clearly defined standards for good teaching practice, there is subsequently no clear agreement among educators about how teaching should be evaluated, and about who should be included and excluded from membership. The result is the ubiquitous "I know good teaching when I see it" that has plagued much of traditional teacher evaluation.

Neither PAR nor the panel inherently codifies teaching practice, and the program could exist (as a thinner version of itself) without standards-based evaluation. Indeed, some PAR programs look much like traditional teacher evaluation (see, for example, Feiman-Nemser, 2001). Yet the work of PAR in Rosemont was intimately tied to standards for good teaching and to conversations about the meaning of the standards—even as those involved were still figuring out the meanings of the standards and how to converge in their interpretations of them. As the panel teacher noted in the epigraph, standards created the focus for the professional conversations about practice that, over time, created professional community.

## COLLECTIVE DECISION MAKING
## ABOUT PROFESSIONAL STANDARDS

Through their dialogue, and over the gathered documentation, the panel could hold the coaches and one another accountable for their assessments of PTs' classroom performance. Although one might argue that superintendents are similarly responsible for holding principals accountable for the support and evaluation of teachers, and that school boards are in turn responsible for holding superintendents responsible, we know that administrators typically do an ineffective job with these tasks, as already discussed. In Rosemont, by contrast, accountability actually seemed to occur. The coaches had to demonstrate to the panel that participants had received sufficient support to make success a possibility. They then had to defend their recommendations to keep or dismiss a teacher by providing evidence demonstrating growth or lack thereof on performance standards. The resulting personnel decisions were a marked departure from the norm.

After a century of a hierarchical educational system that places administrators above teachers in the chain of command, many people believe that teachers cannot be trusted to conduct teacher evaluations. The Rosemont case shows that, at least under certain conditions, this concern is unfounded. First, the presence of the panel turned personnel decisions into group rather than individual decisions. Second, these group decisions generated collective responsibility for professional standards.

The PAR panel created group personnel decisions based on the professional dialogue that occurred and the data produced by the coaches regarding PTs' classroom practice. A dispersion occurred that allowed a group rather than an individual to make personnel decisions, as responsibility for teacher evaluation was stretched over a variety of educators. Coaches were responsible for the support and evaluation of classroom teachers (increasingly in partnership with principals as the program progressed), while the panel held the coaches accountable for that support and evaluation in a case of distributed accountability. Although the coaches' recommendations certainly weighed most heavily, the panel structure created conditions where a group of people rather than an individual ultimately participated in making employment decisions.

Involving more people in the teacher evaluation process through PAR appears to distribute both the responsibility for teacher evaluation and the onus of accountability. Individual coaches doubted themselves when it came to giving a negative evaluation, just as individual principals do. The group, however, served as a window through which assessments regarding observed practice shone clearly, transparently, unobscured by that doubt. In the face of colleagues who shared their opinions of practice, the coaches became more able to make the tough decisions necessary for accountability. When it came time to make decisions, the group was more confident in its decision-making process (March, 1994) precisely because there were more people involved, with more eyes on the evidence of practice. The coaches were engaged in making decisions about professional standards, but, as we saw in Chapter 4, in those cases (or in most of those cases) when they seemed likely to fall short, the panel served to compensate.

In Chapter 4, we saw that the panel challenged coaches' recommendations for renewal in some cases when the evidence did not warrant renewal. Given the historic tendency in education to perpetually give satisfactory evaluations, it is not surprising that accountability for unwarranted retention (rather than unwarranted dismissal) was seen at the outset of Rosemont's PAR program. It might be expected that over a larger sample of PT cases over time, the reverse could also be true; we might expect the panel to challenge coaches who recommended dismissal when the evidence demonstrated that participating teachers were meeting standards or showing sufficient growth.

Ultimately, consensus diffused responsibility for the harder decisions. As coaches could take refuge in the "group" decision, they could go to PTs and say, "The panel decided this." Even as their recommendations were the central factor in the panel's decisions, this ability to share or deflect responsibility appears to have contributed to increased dismissals; quite simply, the coaches were not on their own.

Recall from chapter 7 that Dal Lawrence, the original mastermind of peer review in Toledo, has argued that one person must ultimately be responsible for evaluation (Lawrence, personal communication, 2002). Lawrence argues that if this responsibility is spread out—and he was concerned about shared responsibility between coaches and principals—then the district opens itself to a loss in arbitration should a teacher appeal a dismissal. In other words, two or more people may disagree about performance, and any disagreement could be used to create doubt about the decision and therefore pave the way for a teacher's successful appeal. An alternate perspective, however, is that multiple opinions can (and should) be considered as part of a professional dialogue, and then the group has to stand behind one decision. A panel certainly needs a clear decision-making and voting process, as well as an agreement to stand together behind the group's decision.

Some readers may see a lack of responsibility, with no one person wanting to be held accountable and the buck stopping nowhere. The fact is, however, that the group as a whole demonstrated a willingness to act on low performance where historically there has been little, displaying collective responsibility for professional standards. It also seems likely that the collective dialogue undertaken by the PAR "professional learning community" generated better decisions about teaching practice and employment.

## BUILDING SOCIAL CAPITAL

PAR in Rosemont provided what Richard Halverson (2003) calls redundant opportunities for closure of the accountability system. He explains: "Closure happens when actors have opportunities to interact, create trust and develop reputations around selected practices. Closure involves creating feedback loops for information and social interaction in organizations. Social capital is developed in organizations and interactions that present redundant opportunities for closure" (Halverson, 2003, p. 22). Traditional teacher evaluation, by contrast, could be considered an open system, because there are few structured opportunities for site administrators to interact with other actors around the practice of teacher evaluation. Principals and assistant principals may discuss the evaluations of teachers in their building; more often, they divide the caseload of teachers between them. Many elementary principals and principals of the growing number of small high schools have no assistant principals. In short, principals are without colleagues on the matter. One coach, speaking to broader issues than teacher evaluation, highlighted the phenomenon: "I've enjoyed working with principals, but I think the district needs to have like a principal support group or something. Because they're very alienated. Any time I go in to meet with a principal [about a PT], they talk for at least half an hour just about their job." PAR, however, created interactions and feedback loops that generated more attention to, scrutiny of, and communication about individual teachers' teaching practice.

The social capital generated between the teachers union and administration through the workings of the PAR panel was an important by-product of the program. In many ways, in fact, the interaction of the teachers union, district administration, and PAR program components in Rosemont defined the development of the program. As discussed in Chapter 4, Doug felt strongly that the trust between the union and administration that would have been needed initially to place the program outside the contract, in a trust agreement, was not in place. The creation of a professional community among panel members, however, created the opportunity to build that trust between teachers and administrators—and, by extension, between the teachers union and district administration. It is certainly true that Doug and the superintendent, and other district administrators involved with PAR, leveraged aspects of the program for particular ends (i.e., the inclusion in the program and more rigorous evaluation of beginning teachers, the dismissal of underperforming veteran teachers). It is also true, however, supporting Halverson's (2003) argument, that their joint work with PAR over time built a trust that altered the very nature of the need to "leverage" and negotiate certain issues. Emily, Regina's principal from Chapter 6, summarized: "I have a pretty strong belief that we're not being political in that panel. I see that everybody is in there looking at each teacher and really trying to be open-minded and leaving all the crap at the door."

Principals believe teachers unions to be the most significant barrier to the dismissal of teachers (Painter, 2000). Rosemont's district administration took a large step toward removing this barrier by forming a partnership with the teachers union. Many principals were surprised to find the teachers union president not only sitting at the table at panel hearings, but arguing for teachers' dismissals. Emily highlighted the change with PAR:

> It takes forever to move teachers out if they're not doing the job. It's really hard as an administrator by yourself without PAR to do that. They grieve you and you have to do progressive discipline. All your eggs need to be in a row and the union really sort of comes at you. And this way, [with PAR,] I'm working collaboratively with the union. It's a whole different feel and there's a sense that the union and I agree that we need teachers who use best practice, and we're working together to have best practices occur, and we're not opposed in terms of keeping some person in there who is not utilizing best practice. I feel like we're all on the same team and it's about children and the kind of teaching they get.

In turn, district administrators were able to hold principals more accountable for quality control, since principals could not blame the teachers union.

## CONCLUSION

PAR's teacher evaluation process appears to have been strengthened by the increased transparency seen in Rosemont with its PAR oversight panel. Mechanisms affecting the individual evaluator were modified by the presence of the group, in the form of the oversight panel. Isolated decision making was modified by the presence of a professional learning community, and the relatively limited amount of data on which principals' evaluations were based was replaced with a collection of standards-based evidence gathered over time. As a result, the group was probably wiser than any one individual, but was certainly more confident. The group proved to be more likely than an individual to uphold professional standards of practice—which is to say, to act in the best interests of children.

## CHAPTER 9

# Interrupting Norms of Negligence

## *PAR as an Accountability Mechanism*

> The 11th Commandment is you don't speak ill of another
> teacher. I taught for 7 years next to this nice person, just an
> awful teacher, and I could hear her through the wall, hear the
> kids and stuff and I would go over and have to quiet them
> down, just to kind of bring some sanity to it. But it was like the
> elephant in the living room. Nobody would talk about how
> awful she was.
>
> —Rosemont principal

Instructional leadership is often defined as creating and maintaining the conditions for high-quality teaching (see Murphy & Seashore Louis, 1999; Spillane et al., 2001). All too often, though, instructional leadership is absent, especially in our highest-needs schools and districts, leaving metaphoric elephants all over the living room. Powerful norms exist to ignore these elephants, held both by teachers who will not "speak ill" of one another, and by principals who fail to uphold their quality control responsibilities. This complicit negligence clearly does not serve children.

By contrast, instructional leaders must design organizational structures that promote high-quality teaching. Yet existing school district structures typically occur simply by default or by inheritance from prior leaders (Halverson, 2003). Actively designed new structures are rare, and designing a new structure for teacher evaluation interrupts a century-old and taken-for-granted institutionalized facet of school district life. Peer assistance and review would be interesting to explore if for no other reason than its existence as a case of organizational change. The Rosemont story, however, suggests a fairly significant shift in teacher evaluation outcomes as well as process.

Creating and maintaining the conditions for high-quality teaching certainly involves far more than firing underperforming teachers. Providing teachers with sufficient support so that they have the opportunity to be successful is perhaps the most critical piece of the teacher quality challenge (Fideler & Haselkorn, 1999; see Darling-Hammond & Sykes, 1999), and the support provided to classroom teachers through PAR was discussed in Chapter 3. Nonetheless, removing underperforming teachers has been a historic weakness in public education.

159

By contrast, PAR in Rosemont squarely attended to matters of quality control. The effort was certainly not without flaws, but by all accounts, it was far more rigorous than the evaluation of teachers in the district prior to PAR implementation. This chapter focuses on the ways in which PAR interrupted norms around accountability—namely, the lack of responsibility for quality control that often plagues public education. In doing so, it summarizes to some degree the chapters that precede it, explaining the phenomenon of PAR's higher level of accountability as an accumulation of the design elements and normative interruptions explained thus far.

## MORE CONFIDENT DECISIONS

Principals often doubt themselves when making evaluative decisions (Bridges, 1986), and how could it be otherwise? The problem of making a decision has accrued through the various prior problems. Principals do not have sufficient time to spend on evaluations, or the needed grade-level or subject-area expertise, and therefore often lack the ability to be involved in professional development in an ongoing and substantive manner. As a result, they are uncertain that the teacher under review has been given an opportunity to improve. They typically lack standards on which to rate teachers. They make the decision alone, without the benefit of an organizational structure that provides collaboration with colleagues. Finally, they know that a negative evaluation will involve a timely and costly battle with the teachers union, which they may likely lose.

One extreme case involving a middle school PT whose performance was clearly below standard highlights this phenomenon. The PT was nonrenewed, and in the appeals hearing before the PAR panel in which he was entitled to present his case, he was asked what different methods he would employ if he were to return to his classroom. He responded, "I would take over the classroom right away—that it was my world—and that if [the students] were entering it, they would be following my rules. I would also yell and scream a lot more; it seems to work very well." The teacher's principal—who was also a member of the PAR panel—was relieved by the outcome of the nonrenewal, yet revealed in her interview that, even in this case, she most likely would not have been confident enough to make the decision to nonrenew:

> I needed [the PT] to be gone. I think it was easier for that to happen because he was in PAR. Without PAR, he might have slid through and be back next year, because I wouldn't have been able to give him the one-on-one all the time that the coach did. It would have taken a lot of time to identify all the problems and do all the documentation. And as a new principal, doubting myself, because he's a first-year teacher, maybe I didn't do enough. And he might have grieved. That's always a legal weight.

This principal acknowledged that doubt surrounds the accuracy and defendability of what might be considered the clearest of evaluations.

It has been said that public schools and school systems are "large bureaucracies without strict bureaucratic controls and highly professional organizations that lack collegial forms of collaboration and control" (Rowan, 1990, pp. 354–355; also Bidwell, 1965; Weick & McDaniel, 1989). Indeed, teachers are rarely fired for teaching poorly (e.g., Loup et al., 1996; Tucker, 1997). As we have seen, teachers are more likely reassigned to other school sites (Bridges, 1992).

Just as the problem of making a decision accrues through the prior problems, so the solution accrues through the prior solutions. Due at least in part to several factors—that is, the amount of time devoted to supporting the PTs, the coaches' content-specific expertise, the ongoing nature of the evaluations, the link between the evaluations and teaching standards, and the shift from one evaluator standing alone to a group of peers participating in the process—the coaches, principals, and panel members had an increased sense of confidence in the quality and accuracy of the evaluations. Finally, by virtue of the union-district partnership, there was no reason to fear legal battles over individual outcomes. Perhaps one of the most significant findings in the study is that, across the board, coaches were seen to be willing to recommend nonrenewal of a PT. This is not to imply that coaches were eager to recommend nonrenewal, or that they did not agonize about such decisions when they had to be made. Certainly, the role of evaluator is fraught with tension. Nonetheless, coaches rose to the challenge—not in all cases, but at a much higher rate than principals.

Those involved with PAR in Rosemont felt confident enough in the soundness of the evaluative decisions to make them and stand behind them—despite being steeped in a culture where teachers do not speak ill of one another and nonrenewal decisions rarely take place. It is important, however, to note the difference between confidence in evaluations, or perceived quality, and the actual quality of the evaluations in this discussion. I did not examine the teacher evaluation paperwork. Given the level of analysis, the data from this study can speak only to the perceived quality of the PAR evaluation process, and not to the appropriateness (i.e., the reliability and validity) of the evaluations conducted or the employment decisions made. People involved with PAR, including principals, believed that higher-quality evaluations were being conducted than those that traditionally occurred.[1] It is possible that PAR provided the mechanism for strong rationalizations about personnel decisions that may not have been sound. However, PAR's data-driven rationalizations, whether they were completely sound or not in year 1 of implementation, would nonetheless likely be an improvement over principals' traditional rationalizations that were not based in evaluative data.

Coaches were recommending nonrenewal, principals and panel members had confidence in their recommendations, and the teachers union was part of the process rather than against it. As a result, the 11 new teachers nonrenewed for employment in year 1 of the program were a stark contrast to the automatic granting of tenure that often meets new teachers after a set number of years of service (Bridges, 1992; Peterson, 1995). In addition, the three out of three veterans encouraged into retirement by the genuine threat of nonrenewal stood in contrast to the perennial acceptance of below-standards teaching, as well as the widespread belief that tenure means inability to fire rather than inability to fire *without cause* (Baratz-Snowden, 2009; Goldstein, 2009b).

These numbers constituted a major change in accountability when compared to prior dismissal rates in the district, supporting findings in prior PAR studies (Darling-Hammond, 1984; Kelly, 1998; Murray, 1999). In the year immediately before PAR, only three teachers *out of a teaching force of almost three thousand* (0.1%) were nonrenewed, an identical figure to that reported in the Tucker (1997) study in Virginia. Although there were teachers removed for various reasons such as tardiness or drug problems, Doug could not recall, and the district had no record of, any other teachers being dismissed for issues of teaching quality in the years prior to PAR.

The full import of the higher dismissal rates is seen in the context of a year of attempted support. Far from a draconian or capricious decision, a PAR dismissal represented a concerted collaborative effort to help a teacher improve that ended with a decision that the teacher's improvement was beyond the ability of the district. Coaches and panel members often noted that they were fulfilling a responsibility to the students of the district, in effect "stepping up" to do a difficult job that had to be done.

## SUMMARIZING THE DESIGN ELEMENTS OF PAR

Table 9.1 summarizes the differences between traditional teacher evaluation by a principal, as reported in prior studies and the participants in this study, and evaluation with PAR in Rosemont. Coaches had more time to devote to the process of teacher evaluation (Chapter 3). Coaches' summative evaluations rested on extensive formative assessment (Chapters 3 and 6). The coaches held primary responsibility, or jurisdiction, for employment decisions (Chapter 7). The process of evaluation was less isolated and more transparent, involving a community of colleagues (Chapters 4 and 8). PAR existed as a partnership between the school district and the teachers union, drastically altering the traditionally adversarial labor relations that surround teacher evaluation and dismissal (Chapters 2 and 4). Finally, those charged with making employment recommendations in PAR had more confidence in those recommendations (this chapter, above). As a result of these interconnected factors, Rosemont's educators changed the nature of quality control in their district.[2]

Table 9.1. Summary of Literature and Findings

|  | Traditional Teacher Evaluation | PAR in Rosemont |
| --- | --- | --- |
| Time | Minimal | Extensive |
| Professional development | Separate from evaluation | Linked to evaluation |
| Jurisdiction | Hierarchical (principal) | Professional (teacher leader with principal) |
| Transparency | Isolated process | Collective process |
| Labor relations | Adversarial | Collaborative |
| Decision making | Hesitant | Confident |
| Accountability | Low | High |

This was certainly not a comparative study; the intent here is merely to revisit in summary the key arguments made thus far, alongside conventional wisdom regarding traditional teacher evaluation. It is worth reiterating that teacher evaluation by a principal would most likely look very different than it currently does if principals were given the same time to conduct evaluations, the same training, and the same collaborative support as the coaches in Rosemont. In other words, it would be a grave simplification, and certainly not my intent, to claim that master teachers are better able than principals to conduct teacher evaluations. Rather, the PAR program presented here addressed structural barriers in the system of teacher evaluation that allowed the coaches to achieve results that principals are typically unable to achieve.

In addition, remember that PAR programs look different in different locales. Paper-driven "PAR" programs exist that look much like traditional teacher evaluation, simply substituting the administrator with a teacher/coach. Conversely, "PAR" programs exist that involve coaches in formative but not summative assessment. The findings reported here are based on one particular PAR program and speak to PAR's promise; they are by no means universal.

## PAR'S DISTRIBUTED SYSTEM OF ACCOUNTABILITY

The design elements of PAR that interrupt certain closely held norms, summarized in Table 9.1, can be understood as an interlocking and simultaneous "system of practice," one that distributes accountability across an array of district stakeholders in order to shift patterns of accountability.

A distributed perspective on leadership generates a focus on leadership practice, and that practice is viewed as the product of interactions among leaders, followers, and their situations (Spillane, 2006; Spillane et al., 2001). "Situation" refers to more than the mere context in which leadership practice occurs; it involves the tools and routines generated by leadership practice, sometimes called "artifacts" (Halverson & Zoltners, 2001). The accumulated artifacts that exist across an organization together form a system of practice: "A local system of practice refers to the network of artifacts, taken together, that both shape the given context of instruction and point toward opportunities for school leaders to alter instructional practices" (pp. 2–3). Although classroom teachers are actors *within* the instructional system of practice, leaders are actors *on* it (Halverson, 2003).[3] Leaders exert indirect influence on the local system of practice through the design and implementation of artifacts (Halverson & Zoltners, 2001). In the case of teacher evaluation and PAR, district leaders designed and utilized key PAR artifacts to increase accountability within and across the system—the accountability of classroom teachers for teaching, the accountability of teacher evaluators for evaluation, and the accountability of district leaders for teacher quality and instructional leadership.[4]

In Figure 9.1, solid lines represent the formal accountability relationships and dashed lines represent the informal accountability relationships that were present in Rosemont's implementation of PAR, while the arrows show the direction of the accountability enacted. Through four lines of formal accountability, district leaders distributed responsibility for the quality control of teaching. (Although I have put a dashed line from principals to PTs, we saw in Chapter 7 that as the program progressed, principals' role in PAR became more formal; one could argue that this, too, should be a solid line. I have left it a dashed line since the bulk of responsibility for assessment, even after the joint observations were codified, still sat with the coaches.)

Figure 9.1. Distributed Accountability in the PAR System of Practice

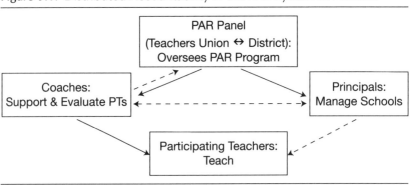

The relationship most likely to be highlighted in discussions of PAR is the one between coaches and PTs, as coaches hold PTs accountable for the practice of teaching. Yet several other formal accountability relationships were present within Rosemont's system of practice for PAR, as we have seen. The panel held coaches accountable for their practice of providing teacher support and evaluation. In addition, the panel, albeit to a lesser degree, held principals accountable for their practice of managing a school, where that responsibility overlapped with the support and evaluation of the PTs. Finally, the teachers union and district administration, as joint members and co-chairs of the PAR panel, held one another accountable for maintaining a focus on teacher quality.

For classroom teachers in PAR, the influence on and assessment of their instructional practice therefore flowed through these multiple accountability relationships. The PAR panel members, as the conveners of the program, influenced the practice of teaching and learning through their work directly with coaches and, to a lesser degree, with principals. Coaches influenced the practice of teaching and learning through their work with PTs. For PAR to exist at all, the teachers union and district administrators entered into an agreement to influence the practice of teaching and learning as partners.

Figure 9.2 displays the distribution of accountability presented in Figure 9.1, adding the relevant supporting program components or artifacts employed by the

**Figure 9.2.** Distributed Accountability in the PAR System of Practice with Related Artifacts Displayed

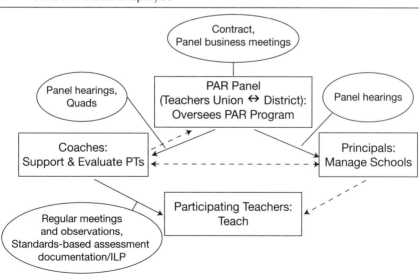

leaders of Rosemont's PAR program. Rosemont had a long history of mistrust between teachers and administrators. The redundant opportunities for closure provided by the PAR artifacts—the repeated meetings between the coaches and PTs, among the coaches themselves, among the panel members themselves, and between the panel, coaches, and principals, as displayed in Figure 9.2—contributed to creating trust among the educators over time. As Emily commented in Chapter 8, they were increasingly "leaving all the crap at the door." In short, the panel members and coaches, together with principals, engaged in dialogue around the technical core of their work—the practice of teaching, coaching, and assessing. During panel hearings, an array of district leaders worked at the same time in the same space to ensure teaching quality.[5] Through their dialogue, and over the gathered documentation, the panel aimed to hold the coaches, principals, and one another accountable for their assessments of PTs' classroom performance, thereby "closing" the system (Halverson, 2003) with formal lines of communication and reporting.[6]

## CREATING A QUALITY STANDARD

The cases of Kim and Timothy, and also Regina, show the benefits, and limitations, to these redundant opportunities for closure of the system—PAR's ongoing, formally established time and space for professional conversations about the assessment of teaching *across the district*. According to Doug: "The current [teacher evaluation] system is totally skewed toward duck and cover. It allows teachers to duck and cover and hide, it allows administrators to hide. This whole system of peer assistance and review was designed to provide an answer to that problem. Bringing out the issue of hiring and firing and dealing with it directly, and putting professional growth on the table, is what this whole system is about."

One outcome of the panel hearing conversations over time was that they forced a cross-section of Rosemont's educators to grapple with their definition of teacher quality, and to enforce a standard across schools regardless of which children were being served. As Doug pointed out, these conversations were a first. A good part of this reflection on practice involved simply grappling with the teaching standards, with having standards-based evaluation for the first time. Another recurring theme was the panel's attempt to establish a districtwide quality standard, meaning a bar that teachers would need to clear in order to teach in Rosemont, rather than separate standards at each school. In particular, they began to grapple with equity issues and the fact that there seemed to be different teacher quality standards based on the population of students being served. Through the dialogue at panel hearings, panel members began to hold principals accountable for the learning of all students in the district—not only those at their school. As a result, principals were being guided to change their long-standing practice of passing underperforming teachers to other schools rather than firing them.

## Revisiting Kim: Standards-Based Assessment

Accountability for teaching quality requires clear measures for teaching performance. Teaching standards, or protocols of practice—however imperfect—provide these measures. As we have seen, standards-based reform was an innovation being initiated via the PAR program by the coaches.

Some principals resisted the shift. For Betty, the progress documented by Eva was not sufficient to warrant keeping Kim at her school. Betty may, in fact, have been concerned about Kim for all the right reasons, a principal merely trying to staff her high-needs school with the best teachers possible. Brian, the district co-chair of the panel, framed the issue:

> The "this teacher isn't good enough for my school" has been a prejudice with Betty all along. I pushed her very hard about what do you want from this teacher, from Kim. She said she wanted clear lesson plans, and wanted them delivered to her on a consistent basis. That was the main theme. And I feel that evidence was provided. There was pretty impressive progress. Part of this is about nailing the principal down, and if the principal doesn't want to be nailed down because that principal for whatever reason doesn't want a certain teacher, we can't make them change their opinion.

Ultimately, the panel was engaged in setting clear standards for teaching, and expecting assessments of teaching performance to be based on those standards. Principals were used to greater freedom in their assessments—Betty, for example, referred to the "gestalt" of teacher evaluation, of the *feeling* of a teacher's quality. Although she expressed a sentiment with which many educators agree ("I know good teaching when I see it"), the panel was saying that such an approach to assessment was no longer acceptable.

Some readers may be concerned that PAR was a hindrance to the principal's ability to have high-quality teachers for her school site (regardless of whether she used standards-based evaluation language or not). Kim herself admitted to being overwhelmed by the requirements of the job, lending some credence to Betty's concerns. Despite whatever progress Kim may have demonstrated, Betty was still responsible to the community and to the superintendent for educational outcomes. Despite demonstrated growth on standards, a principal could argue some absolute bar that must still be cleared. A focus on growth over time may be acceptable for students, but not for the teachers charged with their education.

On the other hand, beginning teachers who are *not* overwhelmed are rare (Gold, 1996), especially those without teaching credentials. Indeed, the panel debated the issue of standards all year, wondering how to adjust the standards rubric intended for credentialed beginning teachers when scoring interns and pre-interns such as Kim. Ultimately, mediating contextual information in this case is the fact that Betty did choose to hire a first-year uncredentialed teacher, and perhaps should have expected the performance level that she got. There were also clearly counter-productive effects of Betty's negative interactions with Kim.

In addition, Betty's criticisms must be viewed in the light of her demonstrated flawed understanding of the PAR program and the standards. She commented,

> This [standards] document will nickel and dime you to death in that if teachers are only allowed to choose one aspect that they want to improve on, you can go 20 years and, you know, poor teachers will not be fired. Not only that, but often the qualities that make for good teaching and learning have nothing to do with what's written here, have a lot to do with one's own willingness to commit time, how much time are you willing to prepare materials, are you willing to call parents after school?

First, Betty's complaint that PTs can only be evaluated on an area they have se-lected for improvement was simply wrong; PTs and coaches together chose two areas for improvement, which focused their work and played a prominent—but by no means sole—role in summative evaluations. As for the merits of teaching standards, it is beyond the scope of this book to address that debate—though cer-tainly some criticisms are valid. Yet Betty criticized the document for not speak-ing to professional commitment (effort), when, in fact, her domain in the PAR evaluation process, standard 6, addresses precisely such teaching elements.[7]

I asked several panel members about this issue in the fourth year of the pro-gram. They emphasized the ongoing challenge of standard 6, "developing as a pro-fessional educator."

> *Panel Teacher 4:* Principals are not as articulate with standard 6. Lots of principals are trying to articulate it.
>
> *Bob:* They'll say "these line items don't do it" [on standard 6 as written], but if asked to identify which ones would, they don't want to, they want the loophole, they don't want their authority taken away.
>
> *Brian:* There has always been an uneasy relationship with standard 6. Coaches don't coach for it, and the panel can't nonreelect based solely on standard 6 because it's professional conduct, it's blurry.
>
> *Bob:* "This person isn't a good fit for our school."
>
> *Doug:* Principals don't have enough training in discipline procedures, how to document professional conduct. That's where they could make their case, but they fall back on "It just doesn't feel right." If it were documented, principals could present the information to the panel, but the panel wouldn't really need to deal with it because the district could nonreelect for professional reasons alone. It's a separate process.

> *Brian:* If standard 6 is the only area where the teacher is not meeting
> standards, the panel would tell the principal to pursue [disciplinary
> procedures]. That's why HR is present on the panel. . . . Look, in the
> case of Betty, when she said Kim is not good enough for our school
> but okay for the district, the panel really rejected that. Just as a school
> is not a collection of classrooms, a district is not a collection of
> schools. We want common standards, and teachers who can be
> successful anywhere. A few teachers have gotten caught in that—they
> were not successful on the Eastside [high poverty], they might have
> been on the Westside [high wealth]—but on balance it's a good policy
> to have.

Brian noted that this shift in expectations regarding a districtwide standard of practice had forced them to pay more attention to the teacher hiring process.

Brian highlighted Kim's case as an example "where the panel worked admirably":

> The panel provided the forum for a cross-section of district people to hear
> what the principal had to say and for the principal to get pushed on making
> a [recommendation about continued employment in the district] and
> coming down on one side or another. Now, the principal may not have felt
> very comfortable about it, but I think having that experience is a way in
> which the principal is also accountable as well as the coach.

Betty was not removed from her job, or otherwise reprimanded, for her inability to engage in meaningful quality control. Rather, panel members voiced the belief that principals would get re-educated or "recultured" over time.

## Revisiting Timothy: Ending the Dance of the Lemons

Although the "not good enough for my school" theme was present in Kim's case, it was more commonly raised by site administrators serving wealthier communities like in Timothy's case. Timothy's middle school was on the "Westside" of Rosemont, serving a predominantly White and high-wealth community. Nancy, the principal, commented on the discussion that took place about Timothy at the panel hearing:

> This is a good school, a lot of people want to be here. There are other
> schools that would take Timothy, and what Brian and [other panel
> administratorss] had said was, look, we have to have that quality for every
> school. I really had to think about it when the question came up: Do you

want him at any school? I think that's what the bottom line was when it came down to it, and [the panel's question] forced me to look at the big picture of this school district, that if we want this school district to service all its kids, we have to have high-quality teachers everywhere who are committed.

Panel members were able to use their authority to prevent principals from engaging in the typical dance of the lemons. Rather than pass inadequately performing teachers from one school to another, the panel began the process of reculturing principals vis-à-vis teacher evaluation. Principals were prevented from thinking strictly in terms of their own school, but rather were asked to make decisions on behalf of all children in the school district. Noted an administrator on the panel:

I think that [principals' hesitance to dismiss a teacher] is something we need to get to. I think this is a carry-over from past practice and principals have found that rather than evaluate a person negatively, especially a junior teacher, it's easier to consolidate them at the end of the year and let them go someplace else. That way, the principal doesn't feel that they're putting an end to anybody's career, but they're also moving the problem to another place.

"Edge" is considered a critical leadership disposition (Reeves, 2003), and speaks to a person's ability to make a tough and unpopular decision when he or she believes it is the right decision to make. Principals, as we have seen, are often extremely reluctant to give an unsatisfactory evaluation, and they tend to be very reluctant to remove a teacher from teaching. Nancy relied on Caroline, and even Betty did not want to "chop off anyone's knee caps"; she simply wanted Kim out of her school. Standard operating procedure with teacher evaluation has made it easier for principals to move teachers to another school—where they will presumably teach poorly to some other principal's students—than to take the action necessary for dismissal. PAR began to undo this practice.

## FALLING THROUGH THE CRACKS, STILL

Timothy represents the pattern of raising the bar for teacher quality seen in Rosemont, but there were certainly exceptions; not all mediocre teachers were identified and removed. Regina emerged as a particularly poignant case of a red flagged PT who was renewed but perhaps should not have been. She was introduced in Chapter 6 as the PT who was listing the names of students along with their respective punishments on the board, and who complained about the pressure of PAR relative to the experience of her friend in another school without PAR. Her coach, Sarah, commented:

I think PAR strongly affects accountability. If Regina were an island, if she were on her own, doors closed, I never walked into that classroom, the names on the board would have continued for the rest of the year, I guarantee it. She was required to meet the standard or at least show growth with the standard. It's the only reason why she changed some of the practices she was doing because that does not meet standards.

Nonetheless, Regina was an example where the panel likely did not enforce the level of accountability that they should have. Both Sarah and Emily, Regina's principal, were highly respected by the panel, which may have contributed to the panel's easy agreement with their recommendation to renew. From the spring panel hearing:

> *Sarah:* In standard 2, she is getting closer to meeting standard. . . . The main issue is standard 2, an environment of fairness and respect. Her students . . . [are] just not very respectful to each other, to her. Her classroom is not one you walk into where you say this is a good climate. It's borderline. It was a bad climate, they were out of their seats, throwing papers, those things are not happening anymore. It's the bare minimum.
>
> *Panel Teacher 5:* Does she like the children?
>
> *Sarah:* [opens mouth]
>
> *Emily:* No. [laughter] I'm sorry, Sarah, she doesn't. She's angry at them.
>
> *Sarah:* She has resentment, yes. She resents—
>
> *Emily:* —that they're naughty.
>
> *Sarah:* She resents them, but she tries. She works very hard—she has gone to every [professional development session]. She always meets with me, takes on my suggestions, is very concerned about her professional growth and development. . . . If you look at her lesson plans, they are typed with every single step written out.
>
> *Doug:* Let's hear from Emily.
>
> *Emily:* Every bone in my body says she doesn't have the right stuff. However, it's her first year, she works really hard. There is something to the fact that the chemistry of this class is really bad. I feel that she deserves another shot at it with support. . . .
>
> *Doug:* So your recommendation is for retention?
>
> *Sarah:* If there are ways of supporting her next fall.

A discussion ensued about the support that could be provided to this PT for the following year. Recall that "BTSA" refers to California's statewide mentoring program (Beginning Teacher Support and Assessment), which, in Rosemont, provided far less intensive support than that provided by the PAR program. Continuing:

*Doug:* She is a BTSA candidate.

*Sarah:* Having been a BTSA coach [myself], she needs more support than that.

*Emily:* BTSA is too advanced for her.

*Sarah:* I want to make that clear. I did not write BTSA down because BTSA is not enough.

*Doug:* Well, I'm having a little trouble with that. Because if the recommendation is for that much support, what is the recommendation, really?

*Brian:* Intensive support.

*Doug:* But we know that that doesn't exist [in the district].

*Brian:* Yet.

*Doug:* But if we're saying she can't function without intensive support, then we're saying she can't function.

*Panel Teacher 4:* No, where she's scored on the documents, she's meeting standards.

*Doug:* She's not meeting classroom management standards, and what she is doing, she's doing with intensive hand-holding.

*Sarah:* If she's not going to get the type of support I'm saying she needs, then I need to come back tomorrow or a different time when there's more time, because this is a case where I'm not sure.

Ultimately, the recommendation was to rehire the PT with continued support, "as yet undefined." The PT was, in fact, assigned a full-time (non-PAR) mentor the following year, an anomaly in Rosemont, although her performance problems continued. During an interview a few weeks after the panel hearing, Sarah reflected on the case:

> I'm still wondering if we did the right thing. . . . I did present evidence that didn't sound too good and [the panel members] didn't ask for more. They didn't have questions about it. There wasn't communicated a strong concern or a strong, hmmmm . . . I thought if there were more questioning it would draw out what the FINAL final [recommendation] would be. I came in with a recommendation, and I know for some coaches that recommendation changed. It kind of sounded like because [the principal] and I were like, "We both see it this way, we both think these are her strengths, we both think these are her weaknesses," they were like "Okay, fine, all right, time's up."

The tension between the time needed to fully question practice and "the press simply to get on with it" (Little, 2003, p. 240) is a common facet of professional communities of practice. Sarah identified the dynamic between the coach and the principal as a key factor in the outcome. In this case, she and the principal had a close working relationship, and although both believed that the PT did not "have what it takes" to be a teacher, they both wanted to err on the side of "compassion." She speculated on how the outcome might have been different with a different principal, specifically another PAR principal with whom she was working at the time:

> I tell you one thing, if Regina were at [a different school] with [a different principal], she wouldn't have made it through. That's how the collaboration kind of infests itself. [The other principal] would have been like, "Sarah, she's not coming back here," and I would have been affected by that. Whereas Emily and I worked on the other end, our decision was rooted mostly in having compassion for this person and giving her more time and not going with our gut instinct of this person isn't effective. . . .

Finally, Sarah reflected on her own process and development in her new role, and the implications for accountability:

> I needed support in the opinion. It's like somebody needed to shake me up a little bit to get to [a nonrenewal]. Now what I need to do next year is I need to bring a lot more coaches into those classrooms or I need to bring another coach consistently into that classroom, or I need to get the principal in the classroom a lot more. Why, why do I need that? I don't know. I think I just do right now. But maybe next year I won't because I've had a learning experience. It would be interesting to look at the statistics of how many first-year teachers are let go by administrators, and compare that to what we did and see if there's a difference, because I don't know if there's a difference or not. Had I let Regina go, I think there might have been a difference. Had I chose to let her go.

Sarah was unusually perceptive and candid regarding her own hesitance to give a nonrenewal recommendation. At least half of the coaches, however, commented on the significant role that the panel played when it came to getting them to recommend dismissal. Coaches believed that the panel needed more time for hearings, but another factor was certainly their own reluctance to recommend dismissal and their desire for the panel to remove some of this burden, as historic norms in education precluding teachers from passing judgment on other teachers played out (Little, 1982, 1988).

In addition, however, Sarah suggests that principals' habituated behavior regarding teacher evaluation had an effect, to the extent that principals and coaches worked together on the task. In light of the developments described in Chapter 7—namely, that the formal involvement of principals in PAR increased over time—Sarah's insight is particularly salient. Sarah acknowledged that as she constructed her coach role, she made sense of the jurisdiction granted to her by modifying it and redefining it as stretched over the coach-principal unit. The role of the panel was to be, in effect, the check and balance to the work of the coach. In this case, because Sarah and Emily carried a lot of weight with the panel and presented a unified recommendation, the panel did not dig as deeply as they should have—as deeply as Sarah asked them to, had they fully listened.

## CONCLUSION

All too often, negligence exists in place of instructional leadership in education, especially in our highest-needs schools and districts. Rather than ignore the elephant in the living room, educators in Rosemont began a genuine conversation about it. In many cases, these professional conversations—the assessment of teaching and the assessment of evaluating teaching—led to higher accountability for teaching quality. We also saw that in some cases, it did not. Ultimately, though, PAR's design elements combined to create a distribution of accountability that served to interrupt long-held norms of negligence.

# PART IV

# Developing Teacher Leadership for Teaching Quality

## CHAPTER 10

# Implementing PAR

It is a paradox of teacher leadership that it requires administrative leadership to be effective.
—Mark A. Smylie, Sharon Conley, & Helen M. Marks,
"Exploring New Approaches to Teacher Leadership"

This chapter turns to some of the key lessons learned from the Rosemont case. The chapter examines the practical challenges and important considerations in PAR implementation. Leaders interested in implementing PAR should carefully consider a number of issues.

Although the biggest challenge to implementing PAR is perhaps that people believe there are simply too many challenges, there are some very real factors to take into consideration. District leaders must ensure quality—both of the coaches who will be the face of the program, the panel members, and the standards for good teaching against which participating teachers will be judged. District leaders must figure out how to pay for PAR, which will involve a concerted commitment to harnessing resources for the improvement of instructional practice. District leaders must build bridges to mentoring programs, where the deepest local knowledge of teaching practice is likely to be found. Perhaps most significantly, district leaders must reframe both labor relations and instructional leadership, changing the nature of how administrators and teachers can lead together.

## ESTABLISHING PROGRAM QUALITY

The core elements of PAR program quality are the coaches, the panel members, standards for the assessment of teaching, and a framework for coaching.

The perceived quality of Rosemont's program appeared to be based largely on principals' and panel members' confidence in the coaches. The coaches, in short, are the face of PAR across a district. Coaches should be selected very carefully, and coaches must be regarded as master teachers. As discussed in Chapter 4, Rosemont's selection process included a paper application, classroom observations by two panel members, and an interview with the panel. The coaches were also required to demonstrate prior success mentoring a peer, including a letter of recommendation from a teacher whom they had mentored. Once selected, it was imperative that coaches receive training in coaching methods, standards, and assessment.

The coaches also had to be above reproach. Given the authority that coaches held with respect to employment recommendations, it was critical that the selection process appear unbiased and without favoritism. Coaches had to remain vigilant with respect to confidentiality. They needed to rely exclusively on conferring with one another, not discussing the details of their work with friends, and they also needed to be vigilant about keeping evaluation paperwork under lock and key. Once returning to the role of classroom teacher after serving as a PAR coach, some coaches found that they had to implore principals to maintain confidentiality and cease confiding in them regarding personnel matters.

Given the substantial role of the panel in determining employment outcomes, it would seem that panel members should also pass through a rigorous selection process. In Rosemont, this was not the case. While the coaches did not raise complaints about any panel members in particular, and tended to respect the panel members as a whole, they raised the vague process for panel member appointment as an issue of program integrity. I agree. Districts implementing PAR would be wise to have clear selection criteria for panel members, including knowledge of good teaching and knowledge of coaching strategies.

Rosemont's program rested on a working definition of good teaching—a slightly modified version of the California Standards for the Teaching Profession. For evaluative decisions to be beyond reproach, they must be standards-based. Effective peer assistance and review requires agreed-upon standards of practice and performance rubrics, which form the foundation of the work between participating teachers and coaches. Ideally, however, content as well as performance standards would form the basis of PAR assessment. While some of the PAR coaches drew on content standards for their work with PTs, this occurred on an individual basis; content standards did not occupy a formal programmatic role in coaching or assessments, despite their adoption across core subjects in California.

Educators in many districts have not reached—or even sought—agreement around a definition of quality teaching, nor made their implicit priorities and values explicitly clear. These are necessary steps for a transparent evaluation process. Educators may not find themselves in agreement when they do make their values explicit, but creating these conversations is a crucial step in establishing a strong PAR process.

Finally, quality coaching requires a knowledge base of its own. Achinstein and Athanases (2006) define the following key domains of mentors' knowledge that require extensive development: "formative assessment, pedagogical learner knowledge, antiracist mentoring, mentoring stances, adapting curriculum to local needs, subject matter expertise, curriculum of mentoring, political literacy, and leadership development" (p. 178). Those implementing PAR should seek to develop this knowledge base in coaches, albeit with the awareness that most of the literature on coaching is not aimed to support people also conducting summative evaluations. We could add knowledge of summative assessment, as well as the development of "edge" (Reeves, 2003)—the leadership disposition needed to enact summative assessments—to Achinstein and Athanases's list.

The leaders of Rosemont's PAR program set out to provide the coaches with training in coaching. The year 1 coaches were given a multiday workshop on cognitive coaching before they began their jobs, and, when cognitive coaching proved insufficient for their PTs' needs, the coaches brought a second trainer in to work with them at some Friday meetings midway through the year. Just as workshops are inadequate professional development for teachers, however, it is also true that Rosemont's coaches would have been better served by ongoing, situated learning. This was, in effect, the whole point of the Friday meetings. However, for the most part, the coaches were on their own to structure and lead this time. While this allowed them to use the time to meet their immediate needs, it is also true that their work with PTs would likely have been enhanced by devoting a portion of each Friday to the structured development of coaching skills. Some of the coaches, as well as some of the teachers on the panel, expressed this, and chalked the shortcomings up to a symptom of "building the airplane as it's going down the runway."

## PAYING FOR PAR

The main cost involved with PAR is the replacement cost of coaches who leave the classroom. Additional minor costs include stipends and substitutes for teachers on the PAR panel and release days for PTs to observe other teachers. In Rosemont, these costs were covered by funding from the state per the AB 1X legislation.

The costs for PAR must be compared to the costs for traditional teacher evaluation. Officials in Rochester, New York, for example, estimated that with regular teacher evaluation, they spend one-half to one full day of principal time for each probationary teacher each year, as well as an additional half day of clerical time (T. Gillett, personal communication, November 2004). There is a corollary, albeit lower, figure for tenured teachers. One must factor in any current expenses for induction and mentoring programs that would be terminated with PAR, or folded into the PAR program. Finally, the legal costs for removing an unsatisfactory veteran teacher range between $50,000–$200,000, depending on the state (Kaboolian & Sutherland, 2005), and it usually takes 3 to 6 years for the litigation to run its course. Kaboolian and Sutherland (2005) report that effective peer review programs reduce litigation costs associated with terminating tenured teachers, but highlight the complications for a comprehensive cost comparison. They note that peer review programs weed out weak teachers while they are probationary, avoiding the expense of termination later, after the teachers become tenured; peer review programs also improve retention, avoiding the expense of recruiting, hiring, and orienting even more new teachers. These cost savings are hard to measure (Kaboolian & Sutherland, 2005).

When AB 1X was passed, it allocated roughly $100 million in state money for PAR. Recall, however, that California's legislation marked the first time that a state implemented PAR, and districts have allocated existing resources to fund PAR programs. That said, money is of course an issue in PAR implementation. Noted Doug, "If I had my way, PAR would take teachers through the second year of teaching, and decide whether they get tenure. But there's nowhere in the country that does that, mainly because nowhere is there enough money."

## BUILDING BRIDGES TO MENTORING PROGRAMS

As explained earlier in the book, PAR programs exist that look much like traditional teacher evaluation, without the focus on professional development seen in the Rosemont case. Rosemont's PAR program benefited greatly by resting on a decade and a half of mentoring efforts in California, in particular by the Santa Cruz New Teacher Project and the statewide Beginning Teacher Support and Assessment (BTSA) program. Rosemont's coaches were able to enter an already existing state conversation about performance standards for teaching and effective coaching strategies, and some of them had already served as BTSA mentors. Strong PAR programs require not only courageous teachers who are willing to engage in self-regulation, but also deep knowledge about the complexity of teaching that is very often housed among those who may be PAR's biggest adversaries.

As examined in Chapter 6, many educators adhere to the notion that formative and summative assessment must be separate in order to ensure trust between mentor and mentee. Although that concern was not supported by this research, those interested in PAR must attend to it or face certain resistance. This resistance can be particularly strong among those focused on induction and mentoring, who often view summative assessment as harsh treatment for new teachers.

California's state-level PAR narrative highlights this phenomenon, as opposition to PAR from within the state mentoring program played a role in undercutting the development and spread of PAR. In the fall of 1998, Senate Bill 2042 introduced sweeping changes to teacher credentialing in California. SB 1422, which had established the BTSA program for new teacher induction at the state level in 1992, required that a panel be formed to study teacher credentialing in the state. SB 2042 was the result of that panel's findings. In turn, SB 2042 provided for the appointment of an advisory panel, which spent 3 years (1998 to 2001) developing program standards that would flesh out the new credentialing legislation. The result was a two-tiered credentialing program, which included induction as a formal second tier of teacher credentialing.[1] Recall that AB 1X, legislating peer review, was passed in 1999. The SB 2042 advisory panel, therefore, developed the credentialing program standards simultaneously with—though completely separate from—the implementation of AB 1X. It may also be worth noting that the $83.2 million in state funds for the existing mentor program being transferred to PAR potentially threatened BTSA, as districts had previously had discretion to use the mentor money for their BTSA programs.

The resulting SB 2042 program standards, presented to the California Commission on Teacher Credentialing in September 2001 (to be implemented by 2003), included a clause that prohibited *any* of the formative assessments generated for induction and credentialing purposes from being used for summative evaluation purposes. In other words, all new teachers would be required to participate in induction in order to earn a professional clear credential, and none of the documentation generated as part of that induction process could be used for summative personnel evaluation (though one could certainly argue that determining whether or not someone earns a credential is itself summative in nature). This meant that either districts had to run two separate parallel programs, with credentialed new teachers simultaneously participating in both—not likely at a time when money was drying up, nor a parsimonious way for new teachers to receive their induction support—or these new teachers could not be evaluated by PAR coaches.

This was not simply a matter of California's left and right hands not communicating. In effect, the architects of the SB 2042 provisions succeeded in undermining the expansion of AB 1X and PAR to new teachers throughout the state, partially a standard turf battle, but also partially the result of deeply held beliefs about formative and summative assessment that ran counter to PAR.

These legislative developments had immediate and concrete results for PAR implementation in places like Rosemont, where new teachers had been included in the program. In Rosemont's year 4 (2003 to 2004), coach caseloads were still made up of both new and veteran teachers, but coaches no longer conducted summative evaluations of new credentialed teachers. They did, however, continue to conduct evaluations of *uncredentialed* new teachers, as uncredentialed teachers were not included in the SB 2042 provisions. Recall that coaches were frustrated already with the partial implementation of PAR across the district, and the fact that they supported and evaluated some, but often not all, new teachers in a school. After the SB 2042 developments, they only evaluated some of the teachers whom they were supporting. More frustration resulted as coaches felt that the new teachers' uneven experiences were an "equity issue" and not "fair."

At the same time as the SB 2042 standards were put in place, the state budget for PAR was cut by 75%.[2] Districts were then allowed to roll leftover money originally allocated for PAR into the general fund. In Rosemont, the superintendent chose not to do so, in large part because administrators in the specially designated high-needs schools being served by PAR reported on surveys that PAR was invaluable and should not be eliminated. Nonetheless, what remained, still called "PAR," was certainly narrower in scope than its original incarnation.

Concerns about combining formative and summative assessment are very real. Although this research did not validate such concerns, educators who want to implement PAR will need to grapple with this issue and seek strategic alliances—possibly at the state as well as the local level. One moral of the Rosemont story is certainly the power of competing conceptions of how best to assess new teachers and induct them to a career in teaching.

## REFRAMING LABOR RELATIONS

A crucial piece of the story of PAR in Rosemont, as elsewhere, was the teachers union. Although both the American Federation of Teachers (AFT) and the National Education Association (NEA) officially support PAR, union locals are often not aligned to national leadership. In Rosemont, the union president was an advocate of PAR who pushed for the policy prior to the AB 1X legislation. Doug's willingness and ability to forge a positive relationship with school district officials, however, and then his willingness to vote to nonrenew teachers through PAR, was and is contrary to many people's perception of teachers unions.

American teachers, as indicated by internal NEA and AFT polls, report wanting their union to attend to professional issues of educational quality, as well as "bread-and-butter" issues such as salary (Koppich, 2006). A thorough discussion of the future of teacher unionism goes well beyond the scope of this book (see Koppich, 2006). Suffice it to say, there is clearly tension between those attached to traditional unionism (often older members) and those who expect their professional association to be engaged in questions of educational policy and quality (often newer entrants to teaching).

This tension played out in Rosemont. In the third year of PAR implementation, Doug was voted out of office as union president. Voting, after all, was not limited to those with firsthand knowledge of the PAR program. Some teachers characterized the president as "too soft" on management, and indeed the replacement president was a more traditional unionist who took a more adversarial approach with district administrators. Clearly, there is a need to legitimize cooperation between labor and management in order for professional unionism to flourish (Koppich, 2006). In the meantime, superintendents interested in PAR, or professional unionism more broadly, should recognize the risky political environment faced by union presidents. Superintendents may need to grant concessions in contract negotiations that union presidents can sell to their members, offsetting potential negative reactions by some teachers—in particular veterans—to these policy changes.

In addition, school districts may want to begin PAR programs with new teachers only, since the idea of apprenticeship is far less controversial among teachers than peer evaluation for veterans. In California, where the state legislation specifically targeted veteran teachers, Rosemont and other districts across the state were required to skip the trust-building phase of PAR. Despite this, Rosemont began with very few veterans and gradually expanded this aspect of the program. The expansion to include intervention cases can occur more successfully once a program has been in place for a few years, and teachers and administrators have grown familiar with the idea of teachers evaluating other teachers.

However, even if a majority of educators in a given district—both teachers and administrators—were prepared to shift the conception of unionism towards a reformist professional model, legal issues potentially remain. With an acceptance of cooperation between labor and management in place, a professional model of unionism would then require an expansion in the scope of bargaining to encompass educational policy (Koppich, 2006), and the precedent of the infamous *Yeshiva* decision (*National Labor Relations Board v. Yeshiva University*, 1980) is often perceived to present a roadblock.

In 1980, the United States Supreme Court ruled—in favor of Yeshiva University in New York and against the National Labor Relations Board (NLRB)— that faculty members at the university did not have the right to collectively bargain because they were, in effect, managers who set policy. (Under the National Labor Relations Act, exceptions are made for "managerial" and "supervisory" behavior.) In *Yeshiva*, the NLRB argued that faculty could not be considered managerial because the University's Board of Trustees held ultimate authority for policy decisions. The Court, however, held that the faculty's recommendations on matters of hiring and tenure, curriculum, and so forth were upheld by the University's Board in the "overwhelming majority" of cases, and therefore the faculty acted in a managerial capacity (Iorio, 1987, p. 100).

As Julia Koppich (2006) writes, "Although this case is not entirely analogous to the situation of public school teachers, the *Yeshiva* decision has had a chilling effect on subsequent considerations of expanding scope to include traditionally managerial (or quasi-managerial) responsibilities" (p. 225). In short, K–12 public school teachers and their unions have often been afraid to extend their leadership into such realms as, for example, the evaluation of other teachers, for fear of having their collective bargaining rights taken away. It is not, however, entirely clear why this is so. The National Labor Relations Act pertains to private-sector, not public, employees. Labor relations between school districts and their employees are governed not by the NLRA but by state and locally determined statutes. Although local lawmakers could choose to be influenced by the Court's rationale in *Yeshiva*, they need not be. George Margolies, writing in 1987 when he was legal counsel to the superintendent of public schools in Washington, D.C., considered it a "sizeable leap" to argue that *Yeshiva* should "send up warning signals to teacher unions in the elementary/secondary sector" (p. 106). Similarly, Dal Lawrence, union president in Toledo, Ohio, asserted that it "would stretch one's logic to assume that *Yeshiva* has anything to do with public elementary and secondary schools" (1987, p. 114). Both men warned, however, that *Yeshiva* would be used as a red herring by those opposed to labor relations reform in K–12 public education.

Given the chilling effect of *Yeshiva*, it is compelling to consider the core issues. The question of shared authority raised in the *Yeshiva* case is particularly interesting, given the discussion in Chapter 7 regarding ultimate responsibility for teacher evaluation. Some administrators have argued that in the case of PAR, coaches are supervisory (they implement policy), and teachers on the PAR panel are managerial (they set policy) (Iorio, 1987). The Court ruled that review by a higher authority, such as the Yeshiva University Board of Trustees (or Rosemont's school board), does not negate the managerial or supervisory status of the employees whose decisions (or recommendations) are being reviewed. Iorio (1987) argues that there was no shared authority in Toledo's PAR model, as their PAR agreement clearly specifies "final responsibility" in the hands of the consulting teachers.[3] Rosemont, however, presented murkier conditions; responsibility for teacher evaluation decisions was much less clear. As a result, and especially once the involvement of principals in PAR formally increased, Rosemont would appear to present less of a challenge to labor relations statutes.

The unfortunate Catch-22 of the *Yeshiva* paradigm is captured by Margolies (1987):

> Yeshiva University . . . may have won the battle, yet may still lose the war. . . . [T]he faculty now has reason to be skeptical when management seeks their participation in decision-making, knowing that an increased collegial role . . . will result in a denial of any role to an exclusive bargaining representative. This can only prove detrimental in the long run to the goal of providing quality education to our young people. (p. 109)

Schools are served when leadership is shared by teachers and administrators (Ingersoll, 2003; Leithwood & Mascall, 2008). Yet the *Yeshiva* decision—whether relevant or not for public elementary and secondary school teachers—leaves some teachers worried that they must choose between their right to bargain collectively and leadership roles in educational improvement efforts. For reform unionism to flourish, the statutes governing district labor relations must address these concerns—they must clearly protect teachers' rights to bargain collectively even as teachers engage more substantively in local policy decisions and implementation.

This is, to some degree, what happened in Ohio and California with those states' forays into peer review. Ohio changed the relevant teacher-bargaining statutes to legalize the evaluation of members of a bargaining unit by other members of the same unit, after Toledo, Cincinnati, and Columbus had implemented peer review. California, rather than alter this aspect of collective bargaining law writ large, created a separate law "specifically about peer review, which held that a member of a bargaining unit who evaluated another member of that same unit remained a unit member and could not be declared a supervisor" (Koppich, 2006, p. 226). One might argue that a more progressive law would have allowed teachers to be declared supervisors (or managers) while retaining their right to bargain collectively.

Finally, Lawrence (1987) argued that legal challenges regarding a union's responsibility to fairly represent its members present a much larger issue for the implementation of PAR than concerns about teacher-supervisor relationships. Toledo has successfully weathered lawsuits claiming failure to represent a member properly, charges of unfair labor practices filed with the State Employment Relations Board, and complaints filed with the Ohio Civil Rights Commission. At least two additional school districts, Rochester, New York, and San Francisco, California, have weathered lawsuits brought by teachers dismissed through PAR. In both of those cases, the courts sided with the school districts and upheld the dismissals.

Legal and regulative barriers may, indeed, stand in the way of implementing PAR in many districts. These are not insurmountable barriers, however, and an alliance of teachers unions, administrators unions, and relevant local and/or state lawmakers can forge a path of labor relations that are in service to educational improvement.

## REFRAMING INSTRUCTIONAL LEADERSHIP

Despite the largely positive response to PAR in Rosemont, shifting norms in the way required by this policy is very difficult, as explored in detail in Chapter 7. Despite the confidence in coaches' abilities and the perception of high-quality evaluations, most people—principals, panel members, and coaches themselves—wanted principals to be more involved in the PAR process.

To some degree, I have chosen not to take a position on the formal involvement of principals in the evaluation of teachers in PAR. On one hand, I certainly view Rosemont's movement towards more "collaborative" evaluation in light of the body of literature that shows the blunting of teacher leadership policies over time. On the other hand, I am inclined to respect the opinions of the educators who actually implemented PAR, who believed the process worked better with formal principal involvement. I also believe that the significant role of the panel— and teachers' majority on the panel—is a mitigating factor that still renders this a story of profound leadership by teachers. The issue is less whether principals are involved—most scholars of school improvement would say that they have to be— but how.

At the center of negotiating these new role relationships is our conception of instructional leadership. Rather than define an instructional leader as one who directly provides the instructional support for teaching and learning, theories of distributed leadership (Heller & Firestone, 1995; Leithwood & Jantzi, 2000; Ogawa & Bossert, 1995; Spillane et al., 2001) suggest that an effective instructional leader can generate the conditions for a focus on instructional matters, actively involving the leadership of those around her. Principals cannot be experts in all subject areas and grade levels, and are therefore not equipped to provide direct support to and conduct the assessments of all teachers in their buildings. They can, however, be instructional leaders who create and maintain the conditions for high-quality teaching by promoting the leadership of the best teachers around them. With this framing, principals with PAR enact instructional leadership by communicating regularly with coaches, meeting with the panel, and conducting the personnel evaluations of those teachers who are not in PAR. As we saw, even once joint observations became part of the program in Rosemont, the coaches still held the bulk of responsibility.

Central office administrators have been found to be opponents to the type of organizational change brought about with teacher leadership and peer review (Kerchner & Koppich, 1993). In Rosemont, the absence of committed support for PAR from the superintendent affected principals. Even a principal who believed in the core concept of teacher responsibility for teacher evaluation would be foolish to step back from teachers' evaluations in the face of conflicting policy messages that included a boss telling him not to. Superintendents who want to implement PAR successfully need to send a clear message to principals regarding the local conception and definition of instructional leadership. If superintendents make it clear that they value principals who successfully distribute leadership, principals' skill sets will surely change over time. Districts can also promote the development of leadership preparation models that foster a collective model of leadership (Spillane, 2006), such as programs that admit teams of teacher leaders rather than individual aspiring principals.[4]

## CONCLUSION

Some school districts may lack the contextual factors to make PAR possible at this time, or simply prefer not to shift authority relations in the ways that PAR does. Certain design lessons may be transferable to a more traditional teacher evaluation system. District leaders, for example, might consider structures like the PAR oversight panel to support principals' evaluations of teachers and hold principals accountable for their evaluative decisions. As leaders across school districts begin or extend conversations to improve the local quality of teaching, however, these conversations will hopefully promote the collective responsibility of teachers for professional standards.

## CHAPTER 11

# Teachers at the Professional Threshold

> Professionalism is not an end state for an occupation; rather it is a
> continual process of reaching for useful forms of accountability.
> —Linda Darling-Hammond, *The Right to Learn*

> [W]e do not have the right to be called professionals . . . unless
> we are prepared honestly to decide what constitutes compe-
> tence in our profession and what constitutes incompetence and
> apply those definitions to ourselves and our colleagues.
> —Albert Shanker, *The Making of a Profession*

Peer review is potentially radical on at least two fronts. First, Rosemont's program was a bold case of teacher leadership that involved teachers conducting the evaluations of other teachers. At the same time, peer review in Rosemont proved to be a fairly bold case of accountability, given the personnel outcomes that suggest more rigorous standards for teaching practice.

In Chapter 1, however, I referenced Linda Darling-Hammond's (1990) caution that increasing teachers' authority without increasing expertise leads to bureaucratization, not professionalization. I identified this as an appropriate test of Rosemont's PAR policy: The program could be considered a success if it grew both teachers' professionalism and their professionalization. Was Rosemont's PAR program both complex in its approach to teacher support and assessment, and courageous with accountability? In this final chapter, I revisit this test in light of the Rosemont data.

## DEVELOPING A SHARED KNOWLEDGE BASE FOR TEACHING

It is difficult to exaggerate the significance of the expert role teachers assumed (and were granted) in Rosemont. The PAR coaches became the district's experts in teacher evaluation, and their source of leadership with principals and panel members was largely their perceived expertise with assessment.[1] Quality assessment, of course, must rest on knowledge of teaching, and in Rosemont, this was defined by the California Standards for the Teaching Profession. The coaches were the most fluent and versed in the teaching standards and how to apply them to the formative and summative assessment of teaching.

Prior research has documented that subject matter expertise is a source of leadership among teachers (Little, 1995; Spillane, Hallett, & Diamond, 2003). In the case of PAR in Rosemont, subject and grade-level expertise were a source of leadership for the coaches with PTs (in addition to their fluency with standards and their availability) and by extension with principals. With the panel, however, this expertise was largely embedded within the coaches' expertise with the performance standards (see standard 3 in Table 3.4), which may not have been sufficient in emphasizing the role of content knowledge in coaching.

The coaches' growing expertise with the assessment of teaching was a source for building knowledge across all those involved with PAR. The panel relied on the coaches' expertise, and principals, when they collaborated with coaches, learned from it. We saw that many principals held the coaches' assessment documentation in high regard. The coaches inducted the PTs in their caseloads to professional standards, and spent a year helping the teachers realize those standards in their practice.

In addition, the panel members and coaches had to grapple with developing their local standards of teaching practice—in effect fleshing out the California Standards. Over time, they grew their knowledge of what quality teaching looks like for teachers with different levels of experience and education, as well as appropriate methods for supporting classroom teachers to meet standards—although, as discussed in Chapter 10, more attention could have been given to developing a knowledge base for coaching.

These teachers and administrators working together as colleagues, with teachers as experts, was in itself a reform. The fact that teacher expertise was the focus and foundation for employment decisions about who should be retained and who should be removed was a powerful indication of movement toward professional accountability.

## POSSESSING CONCERN FOR CLIENT WELFARE

The coaches and panel members defined their function as improving the quality of teaching for the clients of the district—students. They expressed the belief that PTs could improve, and their commitment to helping them do so. If a PT's performance was ultimately not meeting standards, however, they saw their job as recommending dismissal of the teacher. Although firing someone from employment is extremely difficult, coaches mollified themselves with the reminder of the greater good of improving teaching quality for students. It was the professional identity of those involved that enabled them to put client welfare, or at least their perception of it, at the forefront of their work. For Rosemont's coaches in particular, for whom the renewal or nonrenewal decision weighed heaviest, client welfare came before possible loyalty to a fellow teacher with whom they had worked for a year, as well as the path of least resistance of continued PT employment.

The emphasis on the firing of new teachers as "good news" may seem, at best, cold-hearted or, at worst, irresponsible at a time when improving teacher retention is critical to improving teacher quality in urban schools (e.g., Lankford et al., 2002). In a professional model of evaluation that includes a serious concern for client welfare, however, the goal cannot simply be retention, where we strive to keep anyone with a pulse in teaching. The goal is *differentiated* retention, where we strive to retain high-quality teachers (or those who show the potential to grow into high-quality teachers), and seek to remove from classrooms those teachers who are not performing up to standards and who show little promise of doing so. New teachers are more likely to stay in both teaching and their current settings if they are provided with the support they need (Smith & Ingersoll, 2004), and the data presented here suggest that PAR may provide that support. It is nonetheless also important to take the responsibility for quality control and gatekeeping seriously or continue to deprofessionalize teaching and fail to serve children adequately.

At the outset of the book, I asserted that teacher quality is the central civil rights issue in education. Recognizing that public education is a public good, Rosemont, like all districts employing peer review, had an oversight panel that included district officials to which coaches reported their recommendations in addition to the usual superintendent and school board oversight. Also recognizing, however, that current methods of accountability and gatekeeping appear to be failing gravely where our students are most in need of high-quality teachers, more meaningful accountability was found in creating standards to which members of a profession could hold one another. The fact that concern for teaching quality took precedence over historic patterns of concern for individual teachers' continued employment indicated movement toward professional accountability.

## ENACTING COLLECTIVE RESPONSIBILITY
## FOR PROFESSIONAL STANDARDS

Professionals are empowered by virtue of the authority granted to them by society to not only specify but also enforce protocols of practice. In other words, a key part of professionalism is oversight, where structures are in place to guard and defend standards of appropriate practice. As displayed in Figure 1.1 (Chapter 1), collective responsibility for standards is a component of (and, therefore, a lever for) both professionalism and professionalization. The Rosemont story demonstrates teachers' ability and willingness to hold colleagues to professional standards (professionalism), as well as a shift in the locus of authority for personnel decisions (professionalization).

Teachers' internal commitment to upholding standards—their willingness to make tough calls regarding employment decisions and their competence in doing so—is a crucial component of professionalism. Some coaches were able to come before the panel and recommend dismissal of a PT; others were hesitant despite the evidence they presented, as seen in four cases in particular, as presented in Chapter 4. In these cases, the panel questioned the coaches' practice, meaning they pushed the coaches to reconsider their assessments. The hearing transcripts reveal that teachers on the panel, including the teachers union president, were as vocal as administrators (if not, in fact, more so) regarding holding classroom teachers to high standards. The willingness of these educators to hold colleagues accountable was directly related to the transparency of the group process. The presence of more eyes and ears and opinions, and the presence of more data on which to base those opinions, created a more confident decision-making process on which a collective professionalism could rest. The coaches and panel members were seen to be willing to hold PTs to established standards for teaching practice.

Just as teachers' willingness to uphold standards is central to professionalism, teachers' authority in matters of gatekeeping and quality control is a crucial component of professionalization. PAR granted teachers such authority through both the coach and the panel roles. Doug, the teachers union president, highlighted the significance of PAR:

> If you want to become a beautician, you are entering a profession and the profession of being a beautician is controlled by beauticians. The governor appoints beauticians to the commission that determines the standards for entry into the profession of being a beautician. What a radical notion that members of the profession would define the criteria necessary to exhibit that profession. Education, though, is too important to be left to teachers. You have to be an administrator, or better yet, a politician, to define what good teaching is. There are lots of us who don't think that that's valid, and we're fighting it, and PAR is part of that fight.

Certainly, part of the significant shift for teacher professionalization with PAR resulted from coaches making employment decisions in place of principals. Coaches' authority was vaguely defined at the outset, and the program changed over time to formally include principals, but coaches' role as primary authority for evaluative decisions was, nonetheless, seen in the data.

In addition, since the PAR panel in Rosemont, and by state law across California, was comprised of five teachers (including the union president) and four administrators, an analysis of the panel's role in PAR evaluation is also ultimately a story of shifting authority relations that placed teachers in new positions of leadership. PAR in Rosemont was not teacher evaluation without hierarchy, but it began to replace the hierarchy of individual administrators with the "intelligent hierarchy" (Leithwood & Mascall, 2008) of a panel—a joint panel of teachers and administrators that gave teachers a majority voice and weighed the input of teacher

leaders (the coaches) most heavily. Both of these shifts—coaches holding responsibility for teacher assessment and panel oversight—rested on the courage of the
teachers involved to step into unknown territory, and the courage of the local administrators and state politicians who granted teachers the space to do so. This
collective responsibility of teachers for professional standards was at the heart of
Rosemont's movement toward professional accountability.

## TEACHER PROFESSIONALIZATION IN ROSEMONT

As argued in Chapter 1, professional autonomy without professional expertise leads
to bureaucratization rather than professionalization. With PAR in Rosemont, the
data show an increase in autonomy connected to demonstrated expertise, as district leaders appear to have granted authority for evaluations to coaches based
upon perceived coach knowledge and skill. Principals and panel members came
to view coaches as very qualified to conduct teacher evaluations. Coaches, having demonstrated their knowledge, concern for client welfare, and commitment
to self-regulation—in other words, their professionalism—were granted a degree
of authority that was critical to professionalization.

Ultimately, the role of the teachers union as a force for professionalism and
professionalization was crucial. Lawyers hold collective responsibility for professional
standards through the bar. Doctors hold collective responsibility for professional
standards through a board. The professional association of teachers, their union, has
not historically held any equivalent power. An oversight panel for teacher evaluation co-led by the teachers union president, however, clearly signals a substantial shift
in the potential role of teachers unions in setting and maintaining standards. Principals were sometimes surprised to find the teachers union president "on their side" at
PAR panel hearings. Teachers opposed to PAR typically complained that the union
should not be involved in "management" responsibilities. The central role of the
teachers union on the PAR panel, however, clearly fostered accountability. By putting the teachers union and district, or teachers and administrators, together in a
professional community of educators focused on relatively objective measures of the
quality of teaching practice, the teachers union moved from defending individual
teachers to defending the profession of teaching.

This self-regulation, central to professionalism and professionalization, has
been slow to occur in education. Policymakers, practicing educators, and the public
tend not to believe that teachers are capable of regulating themselves. Yet with PAR
in Rosemont, teachers' work expanded to include quality control and gatekeeping,
and the evaluation process benefited.

Patricia Wasley (1991), in her work on teachers who lead, identified three areas
that lead teacher positions might provide. First, lead teacher positions could provide
stimulating career options that allow excellent teachers to grow without leaving

the classroom. Rosemont's coaches returned to their classrooms following their tenure with PAR, and they did so with deepened knowledge of teaching and elevated professional standing in the district. Second, Wasley posited that lead teacher positions could provide school cultures that foster learning for adults as well as students. In Rosemont, the adult learning occurred between specific coach-PT pairs and among the teams of coaches and panel members, not across a school. Districts that have had PAR for many years, however, where most teachers at a school have gone though the program, do report a change in school culture. Third, Wasley posited that lead teacher positions could provide opportunities to reduce the conditions of isolation and autonomy in which teachers have traditionally worked. We saw that PAR in Rosemont systematically, and by design, reduced the isolation of participating teachers and those charged with assessing them through substantive, ongoing conversations about teaching practice.

To Wasley's list I would also add a fourth category: Lead teacher positions could provide opportunities for teachers to take on formal roles as experts. In teaching, historically, there has been no institutionally legitimate role for teachers as experts. Indeed, Lortie's "schoolteacher" not only lacked an institutional claim to expertise in the abstract knowledge of teaching, but in day-to-day operations and content knowledge as well. In Rosemont, PAR positioned the coaches and the teachers on the panel in roles as experts with significant control over consequential decisions.

The transition to being one's brother's keeper is, indeed, not easy. Nonetheless, coaches conducted summative evaluations and made decisions about the continued employment of other teachers. They reported those decisions to the panel, which was responsible for the "final decision" to be recommended to the superintendent. However, the panel members considered the coaches to be the district's experts in teacher evaluation, and in 4 years of the program, there were no cases in which the panel overruled a coach's recommendation.

The role of a PAR coach is very different from that of resource specialist or mentor teacher or other professionalization roles that officially elevate teachers to expert status. The gatekeeper function—holding responsibility for decisions about the quality of performance of others in one's profession—is central to demarcating professions from other occupations. PAR differs from other teacher leadership policies because it transcends the role expansion of the individual teacher leader to signal role expansion for the profession of teaching. Smylie, Conley, and Marks (2002) note that current models of distributed leadership "depart from the individual empowerment, role-based models of teacher leadership that dominated the 1980s and early 1990s. They reframe teacher leadership as a more collective . . . and organizational enterprise" (p. 163; also see Lambert, 2002).

Rosemont's teacher leaders were seen to occupy a liminal space where their possession of jurisdiction for teacher evaluation was unclear. They were not only engaged in but responsible for quality control in extremely important new ways.

However, the superintendent's lack of clear support and a new union president who did not enthusiastically embrace the program (although who came around with time), a significant withdrawal of state funds for the program due to a budget crisis, the competing state credentialing legislation that greatly reduced the number of teachers who could be evaluated through PAR, and the national shift of attention away from teacher professionalism policies and toward student standardized testing all contributed to a reform that was, ultimately, unfinished.

Districts like Rosemont are the testing ground. Although the fate of PAR, both at the district and state level, was not overly promising, the stories told along the way should hearten those who believe that educators' collective responsibility for professional standards can improve the quality of education for children, and challenge those who do not. As state and national policy makers seek better mechanisms for teacher evaluation, they will invariably (and hopefully) generate models that combine measures of student learning with the assessment of observed teaching. Peer review can be a potent piece of that puzzle. In the end, children are the only firsthand clients of K–12 education, and they are without question the group of constituents least able to organize for their right to expert quality service. There is perhaps no stronger mandate for both professionalism and accountability.

# Afterword

Since states and the federal government adopted accountability policies about a decade ago, schools have found it increasingly difficult to ignore incompetent teachers and mediocre teaching. Meanwhile, within the schools an enormous cohort of veteran teachers has retired and been replaced by a new generation of teachers, who bring their own expectations for their work in schools. These new teachers dread isolation and hope for productive work with colleagues. They seek flexibility in their teaching, but not complete autonomy. They want guidance and advice, knowing that their work will be assessed. They want to be paid for their effort and recognized for their accomplishments. Many see teaching as a short-term career, but say that they may continue if they experience success with their students and see opportunities to progress professionally.

These teachers' views differ substantially from those of the generation of teachers they replace, who were hired in the late 1960s and 1970s when the school was the only professional organization likely to hire women and men of color. Then teaching's traditional recruits had few professional options and remained clearly subordinate to administrators. Today, new teachers today compare their schools with other organizations for which they might work—businesses, engineering firms, law firms, management consulting companies—and are less accepting of teaching's traditional norms and the schools' hierarchical, static structures. They want to be members of a profession that recognizes and rewards expertise and accomplishment, that encourages them to develop over time and to exercise influence beyond their classroom.

As Jennifer Goldstein's rich and careful analysis of the case of Rosemont explains, Peer Assistance and Review (PAR) provides the means for improving students' education by advancing such professional goals for teaching. PAR, which addresses many of the concerns of new teachers today, is gaining credence and credit as a strategy for improving the quality of a district's teachers. As Goldstein makes clear, the program is not easy to implement, for it challenges the deeply embedded structures of public schooling and the firmly defended professional norms of teachers. However, in our recent study of seven programs at the Project on the Next Generation of Teachers, we too found that PAR has great potential for far-reaching change (www.gse.harvard.edu/~ngt/par).

Districts such as Toledo and Rochester, which adopted PAR in the mid-1980s, demonstrate that the program can succeed over time despite budget cuts and labor-management strife. Programs in Cincinnati and Syracuse illustrate how PAR is supported by a standards-based evaluation system, which has replaced the archaic observation checklist still used by too many non-PAR districts. PAR districts also upend the view that all teachers are alike by appointing expert consulting teachers ("coaches" in Goldstein's discussion of Rosemont), carefully selected and supervised to mentor and evaluate other teachers. In Montgomery County, the consulting teacher is but one differentiated role in an expanding career lattice designed to capitalize on the talents and skills of the district's best teachers. Like others, PAR programs in Minneapolis and San Juan, California, demonstrate how teachers and administrators collaborate, both within the schools and on the PAR Panel, to ensure high quality. PAR does not simply substitute teachers' judgments for those of administrators, but facilitates and reinforces their shared responsibility for improving teaching. Each PAR program is designed to be responsive to the district's local context, but all provide intensive assistance to teachers as well as assessments that can, and often do, lead to dismissal.

A renewed interest in PAR is emerging as policymakers increasingly demand evidence that schools hold teachers to high standards and districts seek to improve evaluation, meet the induction needs of new teachers, and expand the responsibilities of expert teachers (Sawchuck, 2009). The American Federation of Teachers recently awarded a coveted Innovation Grant to networks of districts in New York and Rhode Island that propose to develop standards-based evaluation systems and PAR programs. For the new generation of teachers, these developments augur well for a transformed teaching career—one that is collegial and grounded in expert knowledge, one that provides meaningful assistance within the classroom, one that holds teachers to high standards of performance, and one that creates career opportunities for those who choose to remain in teaching. The existing breadth of districts' experiences with PAR can encourage and inform those who decide to pursue the reform, while Goldstein's deep analysis of PAR in Rosemont can help reformers understand both why this work is so challenging and so very important.

—Susan Moore Johnson

## REFERENCE

Sawchuck, S. (2009). Peer review undergoing revitalization. *Education Week*, available online, retrieved January 6, 2010, from www.edweek.org/ew/articles/2009/11/18/12peerreview_ep.h29.html

# Available Online:
# Methodological Appendixes

The following five appendixes are available online at http://www.tcpress.com/pdfs/ GoldsteinApp.pdf, and provide the methodological details summarized below. Interested readers are invited to read Appendix A for a greater understanding of the research, and to utilize Appendixes B–D as meets their needs. The data tables in Appendix E are included due to their breadth; the survey items cut across the content of multiple chapters.

## Appendix A
Appendix A provides a narrative explanation of the study's design and methods, in greater detail than the summary included in Chapter 2. This appendix discusses how and why Rosemont was selected as the case district, the study's design, qualitative methods and analysis, and quantitative methods and analysis.

## Appendix B
Appendix B provides the coding schema (or "coding tree") used to analyze the interview transcripts and observation notes, discussed in Appendix A as part of qualitative data analysis.

## Appendix C
Appendix C provides the following interview protocols:

- Fall Year 1 coach and panel member protocol
- Winter–Spring Year 1 principal protocol
- Spring Year 1 participating teacher protocol
- Spring Year 1 coach and panel member protocol
- Spring Year 1 superintendent protocol
- Spring Year 2 coach and panel member follow-up protocol

## Appendix D
Appendix D provides the following survey instruments:

- Year 1 coach, panel member, and principal survey

- Year 1 participating teacher survey
- Year 2 participating teacher survey

## Appendix E
Appendix E provides the descriptive statistics for survey items addressing perceived effectiveness of PAR in Rosemont, as reported on the Year 1 surveys.

# Notes

## Chapter 1

1. Scholars often disagree about what type of teacher expertise and which qualifications matter most, but many agree that teacher qualifications do affect student learning. Teacher qualifications include things such as possession of a master's degree, certification status, years of teaching experience, teachers' test scores, selectivity of teachers' undergraduate institutions, and whether or not the licensing exam was passed the first time taken.

One recent study in Illinois, for example, created a rich index of teacher qualification factors by which to rate schools, including teachers' years of experience, credential status, college selectivity, and test scores and passage rates. The study demonstrated that twice as many students at high-poverty high schools with high teacher qualification index ratings met state standards as students at similarly high-poverty high schools with low ratings (Peske & Haycock, 2006).

Given the significance of teacher qualifications to student learning, it is especially dire that children most in need of highly qualified teachers are least likely to receive them. In a study of all teachers in New York state over fifteen years (1984–1985 to 1999–2000), non-white, low income, and low-performing students, especially those in urban areas, were found to consistently attend schools with less qualified teachers (Lankford et al., 2002). Other studies have shown similar results in California, Wisconsin, Ohio, and Illinois (Esch et al., 2005; Peske & Haycock, 2006).

2. Koretz (2008) reports that our current value-added models produce error-prone estimates of teacher effectiveness, providing a valuable but "seriously incomplete" view of student learning (p. 20). Student achievement tests only measure a subset of educational goals, namely, achievement, and they only measure achievement in a subset of subjects and a subset of skills in those subjects. The intense focus on testing as part of accountability has, quite ubiquitously, generated rampant narrowing of instruction, test preparation, and a resultant artificial inflation of test scores (Koretz, 2008).

3. This knowledge needed to teach well is often referred to as "pedagogical content knowledge" (Shulman, 1986), the interaction of subject area knowledge, teaching skills, and knowledge of students.

4. The so-called "second wave" of education reform was launched by a set of reports that emphasized increasing the influence of teachers. All appearing in 1986 were: *Tomorrow's Teachers* by The Holmes Group; *A Nation Prepared: Teachers for the 21st Century* by the Carnegie Task Force on Teaching as a Profession; *What's Next? More Leverage for*

*Teachers* by the Education Commission of the States; and *Time for Results* by the National Governors Association.

5. Educational administration literature has historically referred to formative and summative assessment as "supervision" and "evaluation" (e.g., Hazi, 1994; Iwanicki, 1998), although this literature lacks agreement as to whether supervision is properly an administrative role (e.g., McGreal, 1997; Nolan, 1997). While the most commonly invoked purpose of evaluation is the need to ensure a quality standard (summative assessment), various authors (Costa, Garmston, & Lambert, 1998; Danielson & McGreal, 2000; Wise et al., 1984) have encouraged educators to move beyond this narrow definition of evaluation to include the supervisory aspects of professional growth (formative assessment).

6. Englund (1996) ultimately argues that both professionalism and professionalization lead to the routinization of teaching work, and that "the concept of teaching as a profession tends to obscure a necessary discussion of the future competence of teachers" (p. 84). Yet the definition put forth by Abbott and others of professions argues to the contrary. Professional work is by definition dynamic and unroutinized. Although I reject his conclusions, I find Englund's distinction between professionalism and professionalization extremely useful given the common blurring of these terms.

7. Van Maanen and Barley (1984) use the term *occupational self-control*.

8. Ingersoll (2003) analyzed the administrator questionnaire of the 1990–91 and 1993–94 Schools and Staffing Survey (SASS). See his Chapter 3 note 15 for the list of decisions.

9. To be clear, it is not my intention to take the word *bureaucratic* in its common pejorative. It is worth remembering that Weber's (1968) bureaucracy was an antidote to fiefdoms, a way to establish organized meritocracy where previously there had been only local favoritism (see Benveniste, 1987, for further discussion).

10. I am making the distinction here between the national teachers unions and their local affiliates, because both the American Federation of Teachers and the National Education Association have officially endorsed the idea of peer review: the AFT in 1984 and the NEA in 1997.

11. See Grant and Murray (1999) for a defense of positioning teachers and principals as separate occupations.

12. In addition, studies of the social distribution of leadership have illuminated the ways that teachers' influence in school leadership extends far beyond formal roles (Leithwood & Mascall, 2008; Spillane & Diamond, 2007).

13. Benefits included less conflict between teachers and students, between teachers and principals, and among teachers, as well as reduced teacher turnover. Notably, these benefits were seen to be significantly larger than those found with increasing teacher control over instructional matters, such as establishing curriculum and grading standards.

14. The normative and cognitive pillars are closely related and can sometimes be combined (Scott, personal communication, spring 1998), as they will be here.

## Chapter 2

1. See peer review case studies of Toledo (Darling-Hammond, 1984; Gallagher et al., 1993), Poway (Gallagher et al., 1993), and Rochester (Grant & Murray, 1999; Koppich & Kerchner, 1999; Murray, 1999).

2. While most scholarship on teachers unions characterizes union involvement in education reform as a relatively recent development, it should be noted that Bascia (1994, 1997a, 1997b, 1998) sees this involvement as inherently and intrinsically linked to what unions have always done. She has argued that the perceived dichotomy between professionalism and unionism is a false one, rooted in a failure to understand the continuity between traditional union work and calls for teacher professionalism. Bascia (1998) highlights the irony of teacher- or practice-centered education reform that fails to include the centrality and contribution of teachers unions: The connection between teachers' working conditions and the quality of schooling only came to the fore in the policy world with the second wave of education reform in the 1980s, but unions have to some degree always made this argument (and often been criticized for being self-serving in doing so). Rather than posit drastic transformations, Bascia argues that "union reform" should be viewed as part of a continuum of teachers' ongoing efforts to exert control over their work lives.

3. Technically, the legislative language of AB 1X named the program the "California Mentor Peer Review and Assistance Program," but this was never used in practice.

4. Toledo's peer review program, by way of contrast, presents nearly identical numbers for the dismissal of beginning teachers—roughly 10%. The percentage of veterans who have been dismissed in the nearly three decades of the Toledo program is much lower, although still well above the national average. In Toledo's program, significantly, the coaches (who are called "consulting teachers") are responsible for the formative but not the summative assessment of veterans.

## Chapter 3

1. The California context in 2000 included "intern," "pre-intern," and "emergency" credentialed teachers, in addition to credentialed new teachers. Interns had demonstrated subject-matter competency, but no teaching credential, and were enrolled in a credential program. Pre-interns had neither demonstrated subject-matter competency nor a teaching credential, and were enrolled in a credential program. Emergency credentialed teachers had none of the above—no demonstrated subject-matter competency, no credential, and no enrollment in a program to earn the credential. In any of these categories, despite likely need for teaching support, a given teacher may have already been teaching in Rosemont for one or more years, and were therefore not "new" by the PAR definition. Teachers were supposed to be in their first year of teaching, or in their first year of teaching in Rosemont (despite prior teaching experience elsewhere), to be considered for PAR participation.

2. The combined group of principals, panel members, and coaches ($N = 34$) were asked to rate PAR's effect on the principals' ability to do their jobs well, with a mean of 4.41 (SD = 0.56), where 5 was a very positive effect.

3. As data-based decision making has taken center stage, some argue that teacher evaluation based on frameworks like the California Standards for the Teaching Profession does not place enough emphasis on the ongoing assessment of student learning, in particular via achievement test scores. Toch and Rothman (2008) report that evidence from recent research suggests alignment between students' test scores and their teachers' ratings using standards-based, comprehensive evaluation models.

4. Asked to rate PAR's effect on the use of teaching standards in the district, principals, panel members, and coaches ($N = 34$) had a mean of 4.60 (SD = 0.63), where 5 was a very positive effect.

5. When asked to rate PAR's effect on building the teaching expertise of the PAR coaches, the combined group of panel members, coaches, and principals reported a highly positive effect—a mean of 4.66 on a 5-point Likert scale (SD = 0.55) (see Appendix E).

## Chapter 4

1. For an article-length discussion of the role of the panel, see Goldstein (2009a).

## Chapter 5

1. Although this was the intended outcome, the reality at the outset of PAR implementation was that there were some glitches, and one PT who was non-renewed did accidentally resurface in the district the following year.

## Chapter 6

1. The coaches were not from the district office but rather reported to the PAR panel.

2. Surveys were analyzed using multivariate analysis of variance (MANOVA). This approach allows a layered comparison of differences between groups for multiple variables.

3. See Goldstein (2007a) for a discussion of items measuring "help received" and "felt evaluation."

## Chapter 7

1. Since PAR does create formal leadership roles for teachers, namely PAR coach and panel member, it is perhaps a less esoteric model than that envisioned by some of the theoretical work on distributed leadership. Nonetheless, the potential jurisdictional shift at play overlaps with distributed concepts of leadership and makes it an important lens through which to understand PAR.

2. Asked to rate PAR's effect on teacher evaluation in Rosemont, the coaches, panel members, and principals ($N = 34$) had a mean of 4.60 (SD = .70) on a 5-point Likert scale, where 5 was a very positive effect.

3. As of year 4, principal-assessed standard 6 (professional conduct) still posed challenges to the panel in terms of appropriate and adequate evidence, and its weighted relationship to standards 1–5.

4. Changes in both the survey questions asked and response scales prevent parallel comparison between year 3 responses in Table 7.4 and year 1 responses in Table 7.2.

## Chapter 9

1. Rating PAR's effect on teacher evaluation in the district, the combined group of principals, panel members, and coaches ($N = 34$) had a mean of 4.60 (SD = 0.70) where 5 was a very positive effect.

2. For a concise, article-length discussion of the factors that distinguish PAR from traditional teacher evaluation, see Goldstein (2007a), Goldstein and Noguera (2006), or Goldstein (2008).

3. What I am calling the "instructional system of practice" is more commonly referred to in distributed leadership literature as an "instructional activity system." Halverson's (2003) systems of practice, and indeed, much of this branch of the distributed perspective, rests on activity theory, in which activity systems tie actors, outcomes, and mediating artifacts into a unified system of action (Engeström, 1996).

4. There is a subtle but significant difference in the emphasis in James Spillane's and Richard Halverson's work. Halverson focuses on the agency of leaders (i.e., how leaders use artifacts to influence practice), while Spillane focuses on the triadic interaction of leaders, followers, and situation (i.e., how these three create the conditions of practice by influencing one another) (see also Leithwood & Jantzi [2000] and Ogawa & Bossert [1995]). Both are relevant for the discussion at hand, although I am emphasizing Halverson here. In addition to asking how district leaders utilize artifacts to increase accountability, we might also ask how do the PAR artifacts contribute to defining the interactions between district leaders (both administrators and teachers), and between district leaders and followers.

5. When Rosemont's organizational leaders came together in space and time, the system of practice involved what Spillane, Diamond, Sherer, and Coldren (2005) would call a *collaborated* distribution of leadership.

6. For further discussion, see Goldstein (2007c).

7. For example, standard 6 on the California Standards for the Teaching Profession includes the dimension "balancing professional responsibilities and maintaining motivation." This dimension includes items such as demonstrating professional conduct and integrity, balancing professional responsibilities and personal needs, and maintaining a positive attitude (California Commission of Teacher Credentialing and the California Department of Education, 1997).

## Chapter 10

1. The NEA-affiliated California Teachers Association (CTA) originally opposed the tier 2 assessment gate for teachers to earn a professional clear credential, ultimately added to the SB 2042 program standards and supported by the AFT-affiliated California Federation of Teachers (CFT). The CTA also opposed a tier 3 assessment for teachers to serve in roles as mentors (such as PAR coach), supported by the CFT, which remained off the table.

2. This reduction was part of a broader reduction in state funding for professional development programs that resulted from an increasingly constrained state fiscal situation. Four of the five main state-funded professional development programs were reduced from $222 million in 2000–2001 to roughly $62 million in 2003–2004 (Esch et al., 2005).

3. In contrast to their clear authority in the evaluations of new teachers, consulting teachers in Toledo do not engage in the summative evaluation of intervention cases.

4. Examples include the Masters in Teacher Leadership at San Jose State University and the Scaffolded Apprenticeship Model (SAM) at Baruch College, City University of New York.

## Chapter 11

1. As explained already, this study did not examine the assessment documentation itself, but instead relied on the perception of the quality of the assessments by those involved.

# References

Abbott, A. (1988). *The system of professions: An essay on the division of expert labor.* Chicago: The University of Chicago Press.

Achinstein, B. (2002). *Community, diversity, and conflict among schoolteachers: The ties that blind.* New York: Teachers College Press.

Achinstein, B., & Athanases, S. Z. (Eds.). (2006). *Mentors in the making: Developing new leaders for new teachers.* New York: Teachers College Press.

Anderson, G. (2009). *Advocacy leadership: Toward a post-reform agenda in education.* New York: Routledge.

Baier, V. E., March, J. G., & Saetren, H. (1988). Implementation and ambiguity. In J. G. March (Ed.), *Decisions and organizations* (pp. 150–164). New York: Basil Blackwell Inc.

Baratz-Snowden, J. (2009). *Fixing tenure: A proposal for assuring teacher effectiveness and due process.* Washington, DC: Center for American Progress.

Bascia, N. (1994). *Unions in teachers' professional lives: Social, intellectual, and practical concerns.* New York: Teachers College Press.

Bascia, N. (1997a). Invisible leadership: Teachers' union activity in schools. *Alberta Journal of Educational Research, 43*(2/3), 69–85.

Bascia, N. (1997b). Teacher unions and teacher professionalism in the U.S.: Reconsidering a familiar dichotomy. In B. J. Biddle, T. L. Good, & I. F. Goodson (Eds.), *The international handbook of teachers and teaching* (pp. 437–458). The Netherlands: Kluwer Academic Publishers.

Bascia, N. (1998). Teacher unions and educational reform. In A. Hargreaves, A. Lieberman, M. Fullan, & D. Hopkins (Eds.), *The international handbook of educational change* (pp. 895–915). The Netherlands: Kluwer Academic Publishers.

Benveniste, G. (1987). *Professionalizing the organization: Reducing bureaucracy to enhance effectiveness.* San Francisco: Jossey-Bass.

Bidwell, C. (1965). The school as a formal organization. In J. G. March (Ed.), *Handbook of organizations* (pp. 972–1022). Chicago: Rand McNally.

Bird, T. (1986). *The mentors' dilemma.* San Francisco: Far West Laboratory for Educational Research and Development.

Bloom, G., & Goldstein, J. (Eds.). (2000). *The peer assistance and review reader.* Santa Cruz, CA: New Teacher Center, University of California, Santa Cruz.

Boyd, D., Grossman, P., Lankford, H., Loeb, S., & Wykoff, J. (2006). How changes in entry requirements alter the teacher workforce and affect student achievement. *Education Finance and Policy, 1*(2), 176–216.

Bridges, E. M. (1986). *The incompetent teacher: The challenge and the response.* Philadelphia: The Falmer Press.

Bridges, E. M. (1992). *The incompetent teacher: Managerial responses.* Washington, DC: The Falmer Press.

California Commission on Teacher Credentialing and the California Department of Education. (1997). *California standards for the teaching profession: A description of professional practice for California teachers.* Sacramento, CA: Author.

Callahan, R. E. (1962). *Education and the cult of efficiency.* Chicago: University of Chicago Press.

Carver, C. L. (2002). *Principals' supporting role in new teacher induction.* Unpublished doctoral dissertation, Michigan State University.

Coburn, C. E. (2001). Collective sensemaking about reading: How teachers mediate reading policy in their professional communities. *Educational Evaluation and Policy Analysis, 23*(2), 145–170.

Cochran-Smith, M., & Lytle, S. L. (1996). Communities for teacher research: Fringe or forefront? In M. W. McLaughlin & I. Oberman (Eds.), *Teacher learning: New policies, new practices* (pp. 92–112). New York: Teachers College Press.

Cochran-Smith, M., & Lytle, S. L. (1999). Relationships of knowledge and practice: Teacher learning in communities. *Review of Research in Education, 24,* 249–305.

Cogan, M. (1973). *Clinical supervision.* Boston: Houghton Mifflin.

Copland, M. A. (2001). The myth of the superprincipal. *Phi Delta Kappan, 82*(7), 528–533.

Costa, A. L., & Garmston, R. J. (1994). *Cognitive coaching: A foundation for renaissance schools.* Norwood, MA: Christopher Gordon Publishers.

Costa, A. L., & Garmston, R. J. (2000). Peer assistance and review: Potentials and pitfalls. In G. Bloom & J. Goldstein (Eds.), *The peer assistance and review reader* (pp. 63–79). Santa Cruz, CA: New Teacher Center, University of California at Santa Cruz.

Costa, A. L., Garmston, R. J., & Lambert, L. (1998). Evaluation of teaching: The cognitive development view. In S. Stanley & W. J. Popham (Eds.), *Teacher evaluation: Six prescriptions for success* (pp. 145–172). Alexandria, VA: Association for Supervision and Curriculum Development.

Cuban, L. (1988). *The managerial imperative and the practice of leadership in schools.* Albany: State University of New York Press.

Cuban, L. (1990). A fundamental puzzle of school reform. In A. Lieberman (Ed.), *Schools as collaborative cultures.* New York: Falmer Press.

Danielson, C. (1996). *Enhancing professional practice: A framework for teaching.* Alexandria, VA: Association for Supervision and Curriculum Development.

Danielson, C., & McGreal, T. L. (2000). *Teacher evaluation to enhance professional practice.* Alexandria, VA: Association for Supervision and Curriculum Development.

Darling-Hammond, L. (1984). The Toledo (Ohio) public school intern and intervention programs. In A. E. Wise, L. Darling-Hammond, M. W. McLaughlin, & H. T. Bernstein (Eds.), *Case studies for teacher evaluation: A study of effective practices* (pp. 119–166). Santa Monica, CA: RAND.

Darling-Hammond, L. (1990). Teacher professionalism: Why and how? In A. Lieberman (Ed.), *Schools as collaborative cultures: Creating the future now* (pp. 25–50). Bristol, PA: The Falmer Press.

Darling-Hammond, L. (1997a). *Doing what matters most: Investing in quality teaching.* New York: National Commission on Teaching and America's Future.

Darling-Hammond, L. (1997b). *The right to learn: A blueprint for creating schools that work.* San Francisco: Jossey-Bass.

Darling-Hammond, L. (1998). Teachers and teaching: Testing hypotheses from a national commission report. *Educational Researcher, 27*(1), 5–15.

Darling-Hammond, L. (2004). Standards, accountability, and school reform. *Teachers College Record, 106*(6), 1047–1085.

Darling-Hammond, L., Bullmaster, M. L., & Cobb, V. L. (1995). Rethinking teacher leadership through professional development schools. *The Elementary School Journal, 96*(1), 87–106.

Darling-Hammond, L., & McLaughlin, M. W. (1995). Policies that support professional development in an era of reform. *Phi Delta Kappan, 76,* 597–604.

Darling-Hammond, L., & Sykes, G. (Eds.). (1999). *Teaching as the learning profession: Handbook of policy and practice.* San Francisco: Jossey-Bass.

Darling-Hammond, L., Wise, A. E., & Klein, S. P. (1995). *A license to teach: Building a profession for 21st-century schools.* San Francisco: Westview Press.

Darling-Hammond, L., & Youngs, P. (2002). Defining "highly qualified teachers": What does "scientifically-based research" actually tell us? *Educational Researcher, 31*(9), 13–25.

DeBray, E. H. (2006). *Politics, ideology, & education: Federal policy during the Clinton and Bush administrations.* New York: Teachers College Press.

DiMaggio, P. J., & Powell, W. W. (1983). The iron cage revisited: Institutional isomorphism and collective rationality in organizational fields. In W. W. Powell & P. J. DiMaggio (Eds.), *The new institutionalism in organizational analysis* (pp. 63–82). Chicago: The University of Chicago Press.

Dornbusch, S. M., & Scott, W. R. (1975). *Evaluation and the exercise of authority.* San Francisco: Jossey-Bass.

Elmore, R. (2003). *Doing the right thing, knowing the right thing to do: The problem of failing schools and performance-based accountability.* Cambridge, MA: Harvard Graduate School of Education and Consortium for Policy Research in Education.

Elmore, R. (2006, November 11). *Education leadership as the practice of improvement.* Paper presented at the Annual Meeting of the University Council for Educational Administration, San Antonio, TX.

Engeström, Y. (1996). Developmental studies of work as a testbench of activity theory: The case of primary care medical practice. In S. Chaiklin & J. Lave (Eds.), *Understanding practice: Perspectives on activity and context.* Cambridge: Cambridge University Press.

Englund, T. (1996). Are professional teachers a good thing? In I. F. Goodson & A. Hargreaves (Eds.), *Teachers' professional lives* (pp. 75–87). Washington, DC: Falmer Press.

Esch, C. E., Chang-Ross, C. M., Guha, R., Humphrey, D. C., Shields, P. M., Tiffany-Morales, J. D., Wechsler, M. E., and Woodworth, K. R. (2005). *The status of the teaching profession 2005.* Santa Cruz, CA: The Center for the Future of Teaching and Learning.

Etzioni, A. (1969). *The semi-professions and their organization: Teachers, nurses, social workers.* New York: The Free Press.

Feiman-Nemser, S. (1998). Teachers as teacher educators. *European Journal of Teacher Education, 21*(1), 63–74.

Feiman-Nemser, S. (2000, January). How mentor teachers combine support and assessment: Perspectives from research to practice. In *Keeping the dream alive: An excellent teacher for every child*. Symposium conducted by the Santa Cruz New Teacher Center, Monterey, CA.

Feiman-Nemser, S. (2001, April). *Embracing contraries: Assistance and assessment in beginning teacher induction*. Paper presented at the Annual Meeting of the American Educational Research Association, Seattle, WA.

Feiman-Nemser, S., & Floden, R. E. (1986). The cultures of teaching. In M. C. Wittrock (Ed.), *Handbook of research on teaching* (3rd ed.). New York: Macmillan Publishing Company.

Feiman-Nemser, S., & Parker, M. (1993). Mentoring in context: A comparison of two U.S. programs for beginning teachers. *International Journal of Educational Research, 19*(8), 699–718.

Fideler, E. F., & Haselkorn, D. (1999). *Learning the ropes: Urban teacher induction programs and practices in the United States*. Belmont, MA: Recruiting New Teachers, Inc.

Finn Jr., C. E., & Ravitch, D. (1995). *Education reform, 1994–1995: A report from the education excellence network to its education policy committee and the American people*. Indianapolis, IN: Hudson Institute.

Firestone, W. A., & Bader, B. D. (1991). Professionalism or bureaucracy? Redesigning teaching. *Educational Evaluation and Policy Analysis, 13*, 67–86.

Firestone, W. A., & Bader, B. D. (1992). *Redesigning teaching: Professionalism or bureaucracy?* Albany: State University of New York Press.

Freidson, E. (1986). *Professional powers: A study of the institutionalization of formal knowledge*. Chicago: The University of Chicago Press.

Freidson, E. (1994). *Professionalism reborn: Theory, prophecy, and policy*. Chicago: The University of Chicago Press.

Gallagher, J. J., Lanier, P., & Kerchner, C. T. (1993). Toledo and Poway: Practicing peer review. In C. T. Kerchner & J. E. Koppich (Eds.), *A union of professionals: Labor relations and educational reform* (pp. 158–176). New York: Teachers College Press.

Goe, L. (2007). *The link between teacher quality and student outcomes: A research synthesis*. Washington, DC: National Comprehensive Center for Teacher Quality.

Gold, Y. (1996). Beginning teacher support: Attrition, mentoring, and induction. In J. Sikula, T. J. Buttery, & E. Guyton (Eds.), *The handbook of research on teacher education* (2nd ed.). New York: Macmillan.

Goldstein, J. (2003). *Teachers at the professional threshold: Distributing leadership responsibility for teacher evaluation*. Unpublished doctoral dissertation, Stanford University, Stanford, California.

Goldstein, J. (2004). Making sense of distributed leadership: The case of peer assistance and review. *Educational Evaluation & Policy Analysis, 26*(2), 173–197. [Reprinted with apology, originally *25*(4), 397–421, Special issue on Educational Leadership.]

Goldstein, J. (2007a). Easy to dance to: Solving the problems of teacher evaluation with peer assistance and review. *American Journal of Education, 113*(May): 479–508.

Goldstein, J. (2007b). Debunking the fear of peer review: Combining supervision and evaluation and living to tell about it. *Journal of Personnel Evaluation in Education, 18*(4): 235–252.

Goldstein, J. (2007c). Distributed accountability: How district leaders create structures to ensure teacher quality. *Journal of School Leadership, 17*(4), 504–536. [Special issue on Distributed Leadership.]

Goldstein, J. (2008). Taking the lead: With peer assistance and review, the teaching profession can be in teachers' hands. *American Educator, 32*(3): 4–11, 36–38.

Goldstein, J. (2009a). Designing transparent teacher evaluation: The role of oversight panels for professional accountability. *Teachers College Record, 11*(4).

Goldstein, J. (2009b). Union bashing won't reform our schools (and neither will job protectionism). *Education Week,* March 10.

Goldstein, J., & Noguera, P. (2006). A thoughtful approach to teacher evaluation. *Educational Leadership, 63*(6), 31–37.

Gravani, M. (2007). Unveiling professional learning: Shifting from the delivery of courses to an understanding of the processes. *Teaching and Teacher Education, 23,* 688–704.

Grant, G., & Murray, C. E. (1999). *Teaching in America: The slow revolution.* Cambridge, MA: Harvard University Press.

Gronn, P. (2002). Distributed leadership as a unit of analysis. *Leadership Quarterly, 13*(4), 423–451.

Grubb, W. N., & Flessa, J. J. (2006). A job too big for one: Multiple principals and other nontraditional approaches to school leadership. *Educational Administration Quarterly, 42*(4), 518–550.

Haberman, M. (1993). Predicting the success of urban teachers (the Milwaukee trials). *Action in Teacher Education, 15*(3), 1–5.

Halverson, R. R. (2003). Systems of practice: How leaders use artifacts to create professional community in schools. *Education Policy Analysis Archives, 11*(37).

Halverson, R. R., & Zoltners, J. (2001). *Distribution across artifacts: How designed artifacts illustrate school leadership practice.* Paper presented at the Annual Meeting of the American Educational Research Association, Seattle, WA.

Hanushek, E. A., Kain, J. F., & Rivkin, S. G. (2005). Teachers, schools, and academic achievement. *Econometrica, 73*(2), 417–458.

Hanushek, E. A., & Pace, R. R. (1995). Who chooses to teach (and why)? *Economics of Education Review, 14*(2), 101–117.

Hawley, W. D., & Valli, L. (1999). The essentials of effective professional development: A new consensus. In L. Darling-Hammond & G. Sykes (Eds.), *Teaching as the learning profession: Handbook of policy and practice* (pp. 127–150). San Francisco: Jossey-Bass.

Hazi, H. (1994). The teacher evaluation–supervision dilemma: A case of entanglements and irreconcilable differences. *Journal of Curriculum and Supervision, 9*(4), 195–216.

Heller, M. F., & Firestone, W. A. (1995). Who's in charge here? Sources of leadership for change in eight schools. *The elementary school journal, 96*(1), 65–86.

Hess, F. M., & Kelly, A. P. (2006). Scapegoat, albatross, or what? The status quo in teacher collective bargaining. In J. Hannaway & A. J. Rotherham (Eds.), *Collective bargaining in education: Negotiating change in today's schools* (pp. 53–87). Cambridge, MA: Harvard Education Press.

Hewitt, D. (2000). The Cincinnati plan. In G. Bloom and J. Goldstein (Eds.), *The peer assistance and review reader* (pp. 115–121). Santa Cruz, CA: New Teacher Center, Univerity of California, Santa Cruz.

Hill, P. T. (2006). The costs of collective bargaining agreements and related district policies. In J. Hannaway & A. J. Rotherham (Eds.), *Collective bargaining in education:*

*Negotiating change in today's schools* (pp. 89–109). Cambridge, MA: Harvard Education Press.

Holland, P. & Garman, N. (2001). Toward a resolution of the crisis of legitimacy in the field of supervision. *Journal of Curriculum and Supervision, 16*(2), 95–111.

Huling-Austin, L. (1990). Teacher induction programs and internships. In W. R. Houston, M. Haberman, & J. Sikula (Eds.), *Handbook of research on teacher education* (pp. 535–548). New York: Macmillan.

Hunter, M. (1988). Effecting a reconciliation between supervision and evaluation—A reply to Popham. *Journal of Personnel Evaluation in Education, 1,* 275–279.

Ingersoll, R. M. (2003). *Who controls teachers' work? Power and accountability in America's schools.* Cambridge, MA: Harvard University Press.

Ingersoll, R. M. (2004). Four myths about America's teacher quality problem. In M. Smylie & D. Miretzky (Eds.), *Developing the teacher workforce: 103rd Yearbook of the National Society for the Study of Education* (pp. 1–33). Chicago: University of Chicago Press.

Iorio, J. E. (1987). The relevance of *Yeshiva* to public education. *Journal of Law and Education, 16,* 95–103.

Iwanicki, E. F. (1998). Evaluation in supervision. In G. R. Firth & E. F. Pajak (Eds.), *Handbook of research on school supervision.* New York: Macmillan.

Johnson, S. M. (1984). *Teacher unions in schools.* Philadelphia: Temple University Press.

Johnson, S. M., & The Project on the Next Generation of Teachers. (2004). *Finders and keepers: Helping new teachers survive and thrive in our schools.* San Francisco: Jossey-Bass.

Kaboolian, L., & Sutherland, P. (2005). Evaluation of Toledo Public School District Peer Assistance and Review Plan. Unpublished report, Harvard University, John F. Kennedy School of Government, Cambridge, MA.

Kahlenberg, R. (2006). The history of collective bargaining among teachers. In J. Hannaway & A. J. Rotherham (Eds.), *Collective bargaining in education: Negotiating change in today's schools* (pp. 7–25). Cambridge, MA: Harvard Education Press.

Kelly, P. P. (1998). *Teacher unionism and professionalism: An institutional analysis of peer review programs and the competing criteria for legitimacy.* Unpublished doctoral dissertation, Michigan State University.

Kerchner, C. T., & Caufman, K. D. (1995). Lurching toward professionalism: The saga of teacher unionism. *The Elementary School Journal, 96*(1), 107–122.

Kerchner, C. T., & Koppich, J. E. (1993). *A union of professionals: Labor relations and education reform.* New York: Teachers College Press.

Kerchner, C. T., Koppich, J. E., & Weeres, J. G. (1997). *United mind workers: Unions and teaching in the knowledge society.* San Francisco: Jossey-Bass.

Kerchner, C. T., & Mitchell, D. E. (1988). *The changing idea of a teachers' union.* New York: Falmer Press.

Koppich, J. E. (1998). *Spotlighting teacher quality: A review of teacher evaluation.* Unpublished manuscript.

Koppich, J. E. (2006). The as-yet unfulfilled promise of reform bargaining: Forging a better match between the labor relations system we have and the education system we want. In J. Hannaway & A. J. Rotherham (Eds.), *Collective bargaining in education: Negotiating change in today's schools* (pp. 203–227). Cambridge, MA: Harvard Education Press.

Koppich, J. E., & Kerchner, C. T. (1999). *Developing careers, building a profession: The Rochester Career In Teaching plan.* Unpublished manuscript.

Koretz, D. (2008). A measured approach: Value-added models are a promising improvement, but no one measure can evaluate teacher performance. *American Educator, 32*(3), 18–27, 39.

Lambert, L. (2002). Toward a deepened theory of constructivist leadership. In L. Lambert, D. Walker, D. P. Zimmerman, J. E. Cooper, M. D. Lambert, M. E. Gardner, & M. Szabo (Eds.), *The constructivist leader* (2nd ed.) (pp. 34–62). New York: Teachers College Press.

Lankford, H., Loeb, S., & Wyckoff, J. (2002). Teacher sorting and the plight of urban schools: A descriptive analysis. *Educational Evaluation and Policy Analysis, 24*(1), 37–62.

Lawrence, D. (1987). The relevance of *Yeshiva* to public education: A union perspective. *Journal of Law and Education, 16,* 113–117.

Lawrence, D. (2000). California's opportunity. In G. Bloom & J. Goldstein (Eds.), *The peer assistance and review reader* (pp. 50–62). Santa Cruz, CA: New Teacher Center, Univerity of California, Santa Cruz.

Leithwood, K., & Jantzi, D. (2000). The effect of different sources of leadership on student engagement in school. In K. A. Riley & K. S. Louis (Eds.), *Leadership for change and school reform: International perspectives* (pp. 50–66). New York: Routledge/Falmer.

Leithwood, K., & Mascall, B. (2008). Collective leadership effects on student achievement. *Educational Administration Quarterly, 44*(4), 529–561.

Lieberman, A. (Ed.). (1988). *Building a professional culture in schools.* New York: Teachers College Press.

Lieberman, A., & McLaughlin, M. W. (1996). Networks for educational change: Powerful and problematic. In M. W. McLaughlin & I. Oberman (Eds.), *Teacher learning: New policies, new practices* (pp. 63–72). New York: Teachers College Press.

Lieberman, A., & Miller, L. (Eds.). (1991). *Staff development for education in the '90s: New demands, new realities, new perspectives.* New York: Teachers College Press.

Lieberman, A., & Miller, L. (1999). *Teachers—transforming their world and their work.* New York: Teachers College Press.

Lieberman, A., & Miller, L. (2004). *Teacher leadership.* San Francisco: Jossey-Bass.

Lieberman, M. (1994). *Teacher unions: Is the end near? How to end the teacher union veto over state education policy.* Providence: Rhode Island University.

Little, J. W. (1982). Norms of collegiality and experimentation: Workplace conditions of school success. *American Educational Research Journal, 19*(3), 325–340.

Little, J. W. (1988). Assessing the prospects for teacher leadership. In A. Lieberman (Ed.), *Building a professional culture in schools* (pp. 78–106). New York: Teachers College Press.

Little, J. W. (1990). The mentor phenomenon and the social organization of teaching. *Review of Research in Education, 16,* 297–351.

Little, J. W. (1993). Teachers' professional development in a climate of educational reform. *Educational Evaluation and Policy Analysis, 15*(2).

Little, J. W. (1995). Contested ground: The basis of teacher leadership in two restructuring high schools. *Elementary School Journal, 96*(1), 47–63.

Little, J. W. (2003). Inside teacher community: Representations of classroom practice. *Teachers College Record, 105*(6), 913–945.

Lortie, D. (1975). *Schoolteacher*. Chicago: The University of Chicago Press.

Loup, K. S., Garland, J. S., Ellett, C. D., & Rugutt, J. K. (1996). Ten years later: Findings from a replication of a study of teacher evaluation practices in our 100 largest districts. *Journal of Personnel Evaluation in Education, 10,* 203–226.

Mangin, M. M., & Stoelinga, S. R. (2008). *Effective teacher leadership: Using research to inform and reform*. New York: Teachers College Press.

March, J. G. (1988). *Decisions and organizations*. New York: Basil Blackwell Inc.

March, J. G. (1994). *A primer on decision making: How decisions happen*. New York: The Free Press.

Margolies, G. H. (1987). The relevance of *Yeshiva* to public education: A management perspective. *Journal of Law and Education, 16,* 105–111.

Marshall, K. (2008). The big rocks: Priority management for principals. *Principal Leadership,* March, 16–22.

McDonnell, L. M., & Pascal, A. (1988). *Teacher unions and educational reform*. Santa Monica, CA: RAND.

McGreal, T. L. (1997). Can a supervisor be a coach? Yes. In J. Glanz & R. F. Neville (Eds.), *Educational supervision: Perspectives, issues, and controversies* (pp. 92–99). Norwood, MA: Christopher-Gordon Publishers, Inc.

Meyer, J. W., & Rowan, B. (1977). Institutional organizations: Formal structure as myth and ceremony. In W. W. Powell & P. J. DiMaggio (Eds.), *The new institutionalism in organizational analysis* (pp. 41–62). Chicago: The University of Chicago Press.

Miles, K. H., & Darling-Hammond, L. (1998). Rethinking the allocation of teaching resources: Some lessons from high-performing schools. *Educational Evaluation and Policy Analysis, 20*(1), 9–29.

Miles, M. B., & Huberman, A. M. (1994). *Qualitative data analysis*. Thousand Oaks, CA: Sage Publications.

Miller, L. (1988). Unlikely beginnings: The district office as a starting point for developing a professional culture for teaching. In A. Lieberman (Ed.), *Building a professional culture in schools* (pp. 167–184). New York: Teachers College Press.

Moir, E. (1999, November). Presentation at the annual meeting of the Teacher Union Reform Network, California Satellite, Santa Cruz, CA.

Murphy, J., & Seashore Louis, K. (1999). *Handbook of research on educational administration* (2nd ed.). San Francisco: Jossey-Bass.

Murray, C. E. (1998). Teacher peer review: Possibility or pipedream? *Contemporary Education, 69*(4), 202–204.

Murray, C. E. (1999). Rochester teachers struggle to take charge of their practice. In B. Peterson & M. Charney (Eds.), *Transforming teacher unions* (pp. 46–49). Milwaukee: Rethinking Schools.

National Board for Professional Teaching Standards. (1994). *What teachers should know and be able to do*. Washington, DC: Author.

National Association of Secondary School Principals. (2004). *Breaking ranks II: Strategies for leading high school reform*. Reston, VA: Author.

National Commission on Teaching & America's Future. (1996). *What matters most: Teaching for America's future*. New York: Author.

National Commission on Teaching & America's Future. (2003). *No dream denied: A pledge to America's children*. Washington, D.C.: Author.

*National Labor Relations Board v. Yeshiva University*, 444 U.S. 672 (1980).

Neild, R. C., Useem, E., & Farley, E. (2005). The quest for quality: Recruiting and retaining teachers in Philadelphia. Philadelphia, PA: Research for Action.

New Teacher Project. (2007). *Hiring, assignment, and transfer in Chicago public schools.* New York: Author.

Newmann, F. M., & Associates. (1996). *Authentic achievement: Restructuring schools for intellectual quality.* San Francisco: Jossey-Bass.

Nolan, J. F. (1997). Can a supervisor be a coach? No. In J. Glanz & R. F. Neville (Eds.), Educational supervision: Perspectives, issues, and controversies (pp. 100–112). Norwood, MA: Christopher-Gordon Publishers, Inc.

Odell, S. (1987). Teacher induction: Rationale and issues. In D. M. Brooks (Ed.), *Teacher induction: A new beginning* (pp. 69–80). Reston, VA: Association of Teacher Educators.

Ogawa, R. T., & Bossert, S. T. (1995). Leadership as an organizational quality. *Educational Administration Quarterly, 31*(2), 224–243.

Painter, S. R. (2000). Principals' perceptions of barriers to teacher dismissal. *Journal of Personnel Evaluation in Education, 14,* 253–264.

Payne, C. (2008). *So much reform, so little change: The persistence of failure in urban schools.* Cambridge, MA: Harvard Education Press.

Peske, H. G., & Haycock, K. (2006). *Teaching inequality: How poor and minority students are shortchanged on teacher quality.* Washington, DC: The Education Trust.

Peterson, K. D. (1995). *Teacher evaluation: A comprehensive guide to new directions and practices.* Thousand Oaks, CA: Corwin Press.

Popham, W. J. (1988). The dysfunctional marriage of formative and summative teacher evaluation. *Journal of Personnel Evaluation in Education, 1,* 269–273.

Qazilbash, E. K., Johnson, S. M., Fiarman, S. E., Munger, M. S., & Papay, J. P. (2009, April). *Peer assistance and review: A cross-site study of labor-management collaboration required for program success.* Paper presented at the annual meeting of the American Educational Research Association, San Diego, CA.

Reeves, D. B. (2003). *Assessing educational leaders: Evaluating performance for improved individual and organizational results.* Thousand Oaks, CA: Corwin Press.

Resta, V., Huling, L., White, S., & Matschek, D. (1997). The teacher fellows program: A year to grow. *Journal of Staff Development, 18*(1), 42–45.

Rodgers, C. R. (2002). Seeing student learning: Teacher change and the role of reflection. *Harvard Educational Review, 72*(2), 230–253.

Rosenholtz, S. J. (1989). *Teachers' workplace.* New York: Longman.

Rowan, B. (1990). Commitment and control: Alternative strategies for the organizational design of schools. *Review of Research in Education, 16,* 353–389.

Roza, M., & Hill, P. T. (2004). How within-district spending inequities help some schools to fail. In D. Ravitch (Ed.), *Brookings papers on education policy 2004.* Washington, DC: Brookings Institution Press.

Schön, D. A. (1983). *The reflective practitioner: How professionals think in action.* New York: Basic Books.

Scott, W. R. (1995). *Institutions and organizations.* Thousand Oaks, CA: Sage Publications.

Scott, W. R. (1998). *Organizations: Rational, natural, and open systems.* Upper Saddle River, NJ: Prentice-Hall.

Seashore Louis, K. (2002). Changing the culture of schools: Professional community, organizational learning and trust. *Journal of School Leadership, 16*(5).

Sebring, P. B., Hallman, S., & Smylie, M. (2003, April). *When distributed leadership is called back.* A paper presented at the annual meeting of the American Educational Research Association, Chicago, IL.

Shanker, A. (1985, April). *The making of a profession.* Edited remarks before the Representative Assembly of the New York State United Teachers. Niagara Falls, NY. Retrieved from Walter P. Reuther Library, AFT President's Office: Shanker, Box 64, file 64.1.

Shields, P. M., Esch, C. E., Humphrey, D. C., Young, V. M., Gaston, M., & Hunt, H. (1999). *The status of the teaching profession: Research findings and policy recommendations.* Santa Cruz, CA: The Center for the Future of Teaching and Learning.

Showers, B. (1985). Teachers coaching teachers. *Educational Leadership, 42*(7), 43–48.

Shulman, L. (1986). Those who understand: Knowledge growth in teaching. *Educational Researcher, 15*(2), 4–14.

Smith, T. M., & Ingersoll, R. M. (2004). What are the effects of induction and mentoring on beginning teacher turnover? *American Educational Research Journal, 41*(3), 681–714.

Smylie, M. (1997). Research on teacher leadership: Assessing the state of the art. In B. J. Biddle, T. L. Good, & I. F. Goodson (Eds.), *International handbook of teachers and teaching* (pp. 521–592). Boston: Kluwer Academic Publishers.

Smylie, M. A., & Brownlee-Conyers, J. (1992). Teacher leaders and their principals: Exploring the development of new working relationships. *Educational Administration Quarterly, 28*, 150–184.

Smylie, M. A., Conley, S., & Marks, H. M. (2002). Exploring new approaches to teacher leadership for school improvement. In J. Murphy (Ed.), *The educational leadership challenge: Redefining leadership for the 21st century* (*101st yearbook of the National Society for the Study of Education, Part I*) (pp. 162–188). Chicago: NSSE.

Smylie, M. A., & Denny, J. W. (1990). Teacher leadership: Tensions and ambiguities in organizational perspective. *Educational Administration Quarterly, 26*(3), 235–259.

Spillane, J. P. (2006). *Distributed leadership.* San Francisco: Jossey-Bass.

Spillane, J. P., & Diamond, J. B. (2007). A distributed perspective *on* and *in* practice. In J. P. Spillane & J. B. Diamond (Eds.), *Distributed leadership in practice.* New York: Teachers College Press.

Spillane, J. P., Diamond, J. B., Sherer, J. Z., & Coldren, A. F. (2005). Distributing leadership. In M. J. Coles & G. Southworth (Eds.), *Developing leadership: Creating the schools of tomorrow.* New York: Open University Press.

Spillane, J. P., Hallett, T., & Diamond, J. B. (2003). Forms of capital and the construction of leadership: Instructional leadership in urban elementary schools. *Sociology of Education, 76*(1), 1–17.

Spillane, J. P., Halverson, R., & Diamond, J. B. (2001). Investigating school leadership practice: A distributed perspective. *Educational Researcher, 30*(3), 23–28.

Spillane, J. P., Halverson, R. & Diamond, J. B. (2004). Towards a theory of school leadership practice: Implications of a distributed perspective. *Journal of Curriculum Studies, 36*(1), 3–34.

Spillane, J. P., Reiser, B., & Reimer, T. (2002). Policy implementation and cognition: Reframing and refocusing implementation research. *Review of Educational Research Quarterly, 72*(3), 387–431.

Stanulis, R. N. & Russell, D. (2000). "Jumping in": Trust and communication in mentoring student teachers. *Teaching and Teacher Education, 16*, 65–80.

Stiggins, R. J., Arter, J. A., Chappuis, J., & Chappuis, S. (2006). *Classroom assessment for student learning.* Princeton, NJ: ETS.

Stroble, E., & Cooper, J. M. (1988). Mentor teachers: Coaches or referees? *Theory into Practice, 27*(3), 231–236.

Strong, M. (2004). *Induction, mentoring, and teacher retention: A summary of the research.* Santa Cruz, CA: The New Teacher Center.

Stronge, J. H. (1995). Balancing individual and institutional goals in educational personnel evaluation: A conceptual framework. *Studies in Educational Evaluation, 21*, 131–151.

Supovitz, J. A. (2006). *The case for district-based reform.* Cambridge, MA: Harvard Education Press.

Sykes, G. (1987). Reckoning with the spectre. *Educational Researcher, 16*(6), 19–21.

Toch, T., & Rothman, R. (2008, January). *Rush to judgment: Teacher evaluation in public education.* Washington, DC: Education Sector.

Tucker, P. D. (1997). Lake Wobegon: Where all teachers are competent (Or, have we come to terms with the problem of incompetent teachers?). *Journal of Personnel Evaluation in Education, 11*, 103–126.

Tyack, D. B. (1974). *The one best system.* Cambridge, MA: Harvard University Press.

Tyack, D. B., & Cuban, L. (1995). *Tinkering toward Utopia.* Cambridge, MA: Harvard University Press.

Urbanski, A. (1999, November). Presentation at the annual meeting of the Teacher Union Reform Network, Santa Cruz, CA.

Van Maanen, J., & Barley, S. R. (1984). Occupational communities: Culture and control in organizations. *Research in Organizational Behavior, 6*, 287–365.

Villaraigosa, A., Strom-Martin, V., & Alquist, E. K. (1999). California Assembly Bill 1X. Introduced January 19. Amended in assembly February 12 and 18.

Wasley, P. A. (1991). The practical work of teacher leaders: Assumptions, attitudes, and acrophobia. In A. Lieberman & L. Miller (Eds.), *Staff development for education in the '90s: New demands, new realities, new perspectives* (pp. 158–183). New York: Teachers College Press.

Wasley, P. A. (2001). *Embracing contraries: Assistance and assessment in beginning teacher induction.* Presentation at the annual meeting of the American Educational Research Association, Seattle, WA.

Wayne, A. J., & Youngs, P. (2003). Teacher characteristics and student achievement gains: A review. *Review of Educational Research, 73*(1), 89–122.

Weber, M. (1968). *Economy and society: An interpretive sociology* (G. Roth & C. Wittich, Eds.; E. Fischoff et al., Trans.) New York: Bedminster Press. (Original work published 1924)

Webster-Wright, A. (2009). Reframing professional development through understanding authentic professional learning. *Review of Educational Research, 79*(2), 702–739.

Weick, K. E. (1995). *Sensemaking in organizations.* Thousand Oaks, CA: Sage Publications.

Weick, K., & McDaniel, J. R. R. (1989). How professional organizations work: Implications for school organization & management. In T. J. Sergiovanni & J. H. Moore (Eds.), *Schooling for tomorrow: Directing reforms to issues that count* (pp. 330–355). Boston: Allyn and Bacon.

Weisberg, D., Sexton, S., Mulhern, J., & Keeling, D. (2009). *The widget effect: Our national failure to acknowledge and act on differences in teacher effectiveness.* New York: The New Teacher Project.

Wenger, E. (1998). *Communities of practice: Learning, meaning, and identity.* Cambridge, UK: Cambridge University Press.

Wise, A. E., Darling-Hammond, L., McLaughlin, M. W., & Bernstein, H. T. (1984). *Teacher evaluation: A study of effective practices.* Santa Monica, CA: RAND.

Yin, R. K. (2003). *Case study research: Design and methods* (3rd ed.). Thousand Oaks, CA: Sage Publications.

York-Barr, J., & Duke, K. (2004). What do we know about teacher leadership? Findings from two decades of scholarship. *Review of Educational Research, 74*(3), 255–316.

Youngs, P. (2003, April). *Responding to changes in state teacher policy: How principal leadership shapes mentors' practices.* A paper presented at the annual meeting of the American Educational Research Association, Chicago, IL.

# Index

# About the Author

Jennifer Goldstein is motivated by the urgent need to improve the quality of teachers and teaching in schools serving low-income children and children of color in the United States. While her interest in education policy was born as an undergraduate at the University of California, Berkeley, her specific interest in teaching quality as an equity and civil rights issue was solidified as an elementary school teacher in Compton, California. She taught fourth grade in Compton for 3 years through Teach for America, and later taught in a Newcomer Academy in Campbell, California, before completing her Ph.D. in Administration and Policy Analysis at the Stanford University School of Education.

Jennifer's areas of specialization are education policy and leadership, in particular teacher professionalization and teacher workforce quality. She focuses on ways in which district leaders may strategically employ human resource policies in order to develop the local teacher workforce, and ways in which teachers themselves can advance teaching as a profession. These two interests come together in the policy of peer review. She has published numerous articles on the subject, including pieces in *Educational Evaluation and Policy Analysis, American Journal of Education, Teachers College Record, American Educator,* and *Educational Leadership.*

Jennifer is an associate professor in the Baruch College School of Public Affairs of the City University of New York, where she serves New York City teachers seeking the credentials to become school and district administrators. In addition to courses in her areas of specialization, she teaches courses on the leadership of urban schools utilizing problem-based learning pedagogy and inquiry teams.